NEW COMMUNICATION TECHNOLOGIES
AND THE PUBLIC INTEREST

NEW COMMUNICATION TECHNOLOGIES AND THE PUBLIC INTEREST
Comparative Perspectives on Policy and Research

edited by
Marjorie Ferguson

SAGE Communications in Society Series
Series editor: Jeremy Tunstall
SAGE Publications · London · Beverly Hills · New Delhi

SAGE Publications Ltd
28 Banner Street
London EC1Y 8QE

SAGE Publications Inc
275 South Beverly Drive
Beverly Hills, California 90212

SAGE Publications India Pvt Ltd
C-236 Defence Colony
New Delhi 110 024

British Library Cataloguing in Publication Data

New communication technologies and the public
    interest: comparative perspectives on policy and
    research. — (Sage communications in society series)
    1. Communication — Social aspects
    I. Ferguson, Marjorie
    302.2   HM258

ISBN 0-8039-9727-2
ISBN 0-8039-9728-0 (pbk)

Library of Congress Catalog Card Number 85-061798

Printed in Great Britain by J.W. Arrowsmith, Bristol

First printing

Contents

Acknowledgements

This book is the outcome of two workshops which explored the academic and policy issues of 'New Communications Technologies and the Public Interest'. The workshops were sponsored by the Economic and Social Research Council (ESRC) and held at the University of Bristol and the London School of Economics in June 1984. Thanks are expressed to the Council for its support and to its Secretary, Dr Cyril Smith, for his encouragement.

A general vote of thanks should also be paid to the distinguished group of participants — academics, researchers and policy makers from a range of disciplines, institutions and countries — who attended the workshops. A selection of the papers arising from those workshops is printed here. Regrettably, considerations of space do not permit publication of all, but to those who have contributed to this volume my particular thanks for their cooperation in meeting deadlines and editorial points.

Finally, I want to express my personal thanks and appreciation to Linda Smith for all her research assistance and organizational help and to Bridget Atkinson for her patience and skill in word-processing the manuscript.

Marjorie Ferguson
London School of Economics
May 1985

Preface

This book explores a broad spectrum of policy and research issues arising from technological innovation in telecommunication and broadcasting systems and examines their application to information and entertainment services at the domestic, national and global levels. It focuses on the transformational logic which these developments contain and the ways in which they may, or may not, set off deep waves of social, economic, political and cultural change.

Scholarly attention has focused on the 'new media' of cable, video and satellites because of the growing pervasiveness and invasiveness of these technologies within the divergent economies and cultures of the more affluent societies and because of the emergence of a global media system characterized by internationalized production and consumption at both the carriage and content levels. It did not take long for this enlarged vision to embrace a considerably wider horizon of economic, political and legal issues than that previously prompted by the 'old media' of press, radio and television.

These issues included policy-relevant questions about political priorities, about the public expenditure related to high-technology development and concerns about its contribution to 'the public good'. This led in turn to more specific questions about how or whether the public interest was being served. For example, was equity of access to communication channels being maintained, was privacy being invaded by electronic surveillance, and how were such questions being dealt with at the levels of institutional change and policy response?

The chapters of this book provide a sequence of comparative approaches to the examination of such questions. They cover a range of disciplines, including economics, law, sociology and political science, and use different levels of theoretical and empirical analysis. These comparative dimensions are extended further by case studies of the policy responses of different societies to aspects of innovation in communications media in Europe, Canada, the United States and Japan.

One common concern of these comparative approaches to the transformational potential of these new technologies is their explicit focus on whether or not they will serve the general public interest or only the particular interests of those who stand to gain from the material or cultural production that they stimulate. Some flavour of the comparative perspectives that are applied to this theme is given below.

Which theoretical insights and explanatory models can communications scholars and other social scientists explore and develop most usefully to aid our understanding of the wider social, economic and cultural consequences of the new communications media? In Part I 'Theoretical Perspectives', Denis McQuail explores the question 'Is media theory adequate to the challenge of new communications technologies?' Having identified social values such as freedom, equality and order in relation to existing theories such as 'media-centred' or 'society-centred', he points to the two principal areas for theory application: media research and policy issues, and the interaction between them. McQuail also identifies areas which will require new analytical frameworks: conditions of differentiation created by the new media that will require a more sophisticated analysis of power; or how the questions raised by audiences able to choose according to individual needs and tastes will require the development of a theory of choice-making under varying conditions.

Ian Miles and Jonathan Gershuny offer a critique of the post-industrial and service society theses and suggest an alternative explanatory model of their own in 'The social economics of information technology'. They suggest that the key question surrounding the introduction and re-shaping of informatics is that these processes need be viewed not as a 'cure' for the existing socio-technical system but rather as compatible with a new one, and with social and economic innovation. For example, the development of new interactive services and of a new telecommunications infrastructure can create opportunities for new working environments and for the passage of people in and out of the labour market through reduction in the working week, earlier retirement or the re-alignment of work between the sexes.

Discussing the economics of the information revolution Stan Metcalfe recognizes that the acceptance and adoption of new technologies in societies where facilities for creating, communicating and storing information already exist will depend on their cost advantage and the provision of a superior service. However, several factors will make it difficult to assess their impact; for example, uncertainty relating to demand and acceptance and the problems associated with displacement and compensation in employment as the technologies are diffused. Metcalfe uses the development of cable television in the UK to illustrate the kinds of issues affecting all information technologies.

In Part II, 'Industrial, Cultural and Social Strategies', Marjorie Ferguson explores the climate of neo-technological determinism which pervades the industrial and cultural strategies of industrialized societies. She uses the case of Britain to illustrate the highly relative record of innovation and application in this field which it provides, and compares its progress with the world leaders, the United States and Japan. Turning to the social consequences of these industrial and cultural strategies raises questions about which social groups will have access to the new technologies and who will be the new generation of 'haves' and 'have nots' in this promised era of 'electronic abundance'. Peter Golding and Graham Murdock examine questions of unequal access and take-up of the new technologies within the context of a reduction in public sector provision of information and leisure facilities and widening inequality in disposable incomes and argue that disadvantaged groups will be forced into a position of increased inequality if ability to pay becomes the sole criterion for the utilization of services.

In Part III, 'Issues of Regulation and Privacy', the advent of new technology unhampered by regulation is explored for its possible effect on the public service tradition of broadcasting which in turn may affect cultural values and political awareness, discussion and balance. The United States demonstrates the impact of deregulation on telecommunications and broadcasting policy at the national level. Muriel and Joel Cantor show how the politics of telecommunications and the relevant power positions of the protagonists in the United States continue to influence policy outcomes to their benefit as they have in the past.

The global expansion of telecommunications services and data bases around the world has also brought with it a host of regulatory and 'privacy' problems. The absorption of personal and corporate data banks into national and transnational telecommunications networks poses serious problems for ensuring individual and organization 'privacy'. James Michael shows how legal precedents comprise a maze of contradictions rather than provide a set of guidelines to the politics of information law emerging in the fields of data protection and privacy. He also examines how the regulatory structure of European broadcasting is and is not adapting to the potential challenge of cable and satellite.

In Part IV, 'Comparative Policy Perspectives' are explored. The experience of Europe, for example, exemplifies the responses of several societies acting individually or (occasionally) collectively across a range of cultures, as well as within a variety of telecommunications and broadcasting systems. Denis McQuail presents his overview of the main issues underlying policy debates in Europe and explains the variety of policy response in terms of the media traditions in any one country, its political climate and the balance of power of the interests involved in policy formulation. The structure of telecommunications and broadcasting within the member states of the European Community are discussed by Nicole Dewandre in relation to the effects of increased international competition and the tension between the public and private sectors with respect to deregulation. She suggests an analytical framework for their further exploration.

The experiences of Canada also can teach Europeans about the viability of cultural sovereignty when satellite footprints span continental as well as national boundaries. Richard Collins discusses the experience of communications sovereignty in Canada and the policy measures used to promote Canadian media production and counter US-transmitted programming — issues which have not been encountered in Britain or Europe until just recently. The final comparative perspective is provided by Jill Hartley who discusses the implications of technological diversity for local community and domestic life in relation to experimental communities set up by the Japanese government. Testing the social impact of new communication technology, the Japanese government provides the telecommunications infrastructure while leaving the provision of new media services to the private sector — evidence of policy concern to encourage experimentation on the development of software for new media applications as a deliberate attempt to shift the emphasis away from hardware alone.

As these chapters show, the comparative and complementary social science perspectives of these authors both individually and collectively provide useful insights into the broader issues of the public interest which follow in the wake of continuing innovation in communication systems and services. These insights are crucial not only to the formulation of more policy-relevant research questions, but also to the exploration of the unintended as well as intended consequences of technological change.

Marjorie Ferguson

I
THEORETICAL PERSPECTIVES

1

Is media theory adequate to the challenge of new communications technologies?

Denis McQuail

The 'old' media – of cinema, radio, recorded music and (even older) the newspaper and periodical – began life without benefit of much that is recognizable as theory, whether social or social scientific. The least old of the currently established media – broadcast television – was, through war-induced delay, established more consciously than its predecessors with an eye or ear to social and political considerations and with some awareness of potential consequences for society. Social scientific theory has been accumulated and worked out during the last 35 years or so to an extent that it may not unreasonably be characterized as the old, or established, theory for old media, even if these are still, for the most part, the only media we have. The new media will, in any case, have an extensive inheritance when they reach maturity and the question is whether they will have much value or be too linked to the older realities to serve for the emerging future.

To pose a question about adequacy is to presume some utility and relevance and also some criteria for assessment. There are two main potential areas of application for theory – one is research on communication and the other is policy making for the new media. Thus, what is being asked is, first, whether the existing body of theory helps give direction to relevant research and, second, whether it helps in locating problems for (social) policy in relation to new media. For either purpose, the requirements from theory are not so different. It should validly capture the reality of the applications, implications and consequences of new media. It should provide terms or concepts for describing this reality. It should help explain what is happening. It should have some predictive power – pointing at least to relevant possibilities of media development and effect. For policy application, the main emphasis should be on problem identification and the evaluation of alternative courses of action. For research what is needed from theory is, first of all, concepts, and secondly, hypotheses. Media theory is essentially an informed consciousness of what is happening when systems of public communication change. The title adopted for this chapter seems to presume that a fundamental change is at hand. One of the subsidiary functions of theory will be to help to decide whether this is so or not, aside from the more obvious changes in 'hardware' and behaviour.

Basic social values

Media, or mass communication, theory has itself deep roots in earlier, more fundamental, thought about society and, like all social theory, it has strong normative elements. Before examining what is specifically 'media-related' theory, it is worth identifying the most relevant basic social values which have influenced both the media themselves and thinking about mass communication.

The first is *freedom*, which has helped to legitimate the expansion and diversification of all kinds of media activity and has been the basis for opposition to paternalist, authoritarian and manipulative uses of media or to interference by state or church in communication. More specifically, freedom has meant ease of access to channels, resistance to monopoly or censorship, maximum freedom of expression consistent with safeguarding the rights of others and the ultimate security of the state. The second main relevant value is that of *equality*, which favours a fair distribution of the cultural and informational goods which communication offers, including access both as sender and receiver to the means of communication. In the 'first communications revolution', this value was invoked in favour of near-equal distribution of reception possibilities and a representative approach to access as senders for different groups and interests. The relative strength of the equality norm has helped to justify some interference with market forces and a degree of control inconsistent with complete freedom to send and receive. The third value of the classic trio is less easy to render by a single English word or to recognize as a direct influence on media arrangements. It is the value of 'togetherness' – favouring community, solidarity, cooperation, integration, against isolation, fragmentation, individuation, 'privatization'. It is likely to be invoked in defence of established patterns of life and culture, of the specificity of language and belief. It translates also into support for national, regional and local media forms and may also, less widely, be expressed in those forms of media which correspond to other bases of solidarity, such as class, religion or political allegiance. Related to this value (although sometimes viewed more as simply the reverse of freedom) is the value placed on *order*, in the sense of morality, tradition and continuity, as opposed to unregulated change and deviance from established standards.

These remarks may seem a diversion from the announced subject, but by naming these values and then considering the difficulty which one would have in adding to them, one already has a provisional answer to part of the question posed in the title. These will be necessary elements in any social theory relevant to new media and it is hard to imagine any significant additions, subtractions or alternatives.

Dimensions of media theory
What follows is an attempt to summarize conscious efforts to make sense of and predict the course of historical processes which have occurred and are occurring, as the means of communication have developed, especially in the 'first age' of mass communication, which extends from the start of this century to the present time. The theory discussed is not value-free, but it is more than a statement of preferences and has some claim to offer an objective account of mass media experience. The available 'old theory' can most economically be summarized in terms of three main dimensions or oppositions which, between them, map out the space occupied by different versions of the communication–society relationship and the likely social implications of developments and applications of communication technology. These dimensions can be related to each other and used to differentiate and compare possible positions in respect of the new media.

(i) Media or society as first mover?
The question indicates a choice between a 'media-centred' and a 'society-centred' view of the relationship. The former stresses the means of communication as a force for change, either through technology or the typical content carried. The latter emphasizes the dependence of both on other forces in society, especially those of politics and money. From this second point of view, the forms of mass media are an outcome of historical change − a reflection and consequence of political liberalization and industrialization and a response to demands for servicing from other social institutions. The media-centred view, which has found its advocates in the work of the 'Toronto school' (Innis, 1951, and McLuhan, 1962) and its best example in the case of the printing press, allots an independent causal role to the dominant communication technology of the epoch in question. If we deal with the immediate past and forget the niceties of inter-media differences, which really interested McLuhan, the dominant form underlying the first communications revolution has

been one of large-scale distribution from central sources to many widely scattered individuals. There are strong and weak versions of media-centred theory and there are also possibilities for attributing causal influence to some media in some cases for some social institutions, without having to reject a view of media dependency 'in the last resort'.

A distinction between technology and content also allows some scope for negotiation between one or other global alternative. For instance, the 'cultivation' theories of Gerbner et al. (1980) seem to involve the view that 'dominant message systems' (i.e. content) owe more to the working of certain institutional forces in society than to the intrinsic properties of television as a medium − hence reconciling a 'sociological' with a 'communicative' perspective. The 'society-centred' view is also open to differentiation, since the forces of 'society' can either be formulated as matters of class, culture and social structure broadly and collectively conceived, or as individual differences of interest, motive, or social location which account for selective use of, and response to, communication and subordinate media to the needs of personal and micro-social life. The media are seen as dependent, in much more specific ways, but the same broad conclusion − that people and society are users rather than used − is reached.

The distinction between media and society goes with other relevant theoretical lines of division, which can really only be named: between base and superstructure explanations of social change; between more idealistic and more materialistic approaches; between an emphasis on communication as expression or consummation or a view of it as a means of transmission or an instrument for achieving some end. This last distinction also helps to differentiate 'culturalist' traditions of study from sociological ones, each with its characteristic aims and methods of enquiry. It directs attention also to a major issue which has to be faced in dealing with new media possibilities − that of weighing cultural against material consequences. In general, media-centred theory is more supportive of a view of powerful mass media, the power lying either in the consistency and repetition of messages reaching many people or in the inevitablility of adaptation by social institutions to the opportunities and pressures of communication forms, with consequences for the messages carried and the relations between senders and receivers.

(ii) 'Dominance' versus 'pluralism'
The second main dimension of theory is less easy to describe apart from its normative and ideological elements, separating as it does those who view media as an instrument of dominance in a class-

divided society from those who accept the premise of pluralism – that in free societies media have developed so as to reflect and express a wide and representative range of views and interests. The objective aspect of this dimension lies in the different assessment of the actual condition of most media systems – they are more or less pluralistic according to measures which can be applied. Less open to objective assessment is the cause, nature and further tendency of trends towards 'dominance'. The normative component is readily apparent – most who subscribe to theories of dominant media are also critical of media for this reason, although not always espousing pluralistic alternatives. Most of those who see the media as pluralistic value them for being so and may also value the liberal society which, in most cases, provides the guarantee for pluralism. While pluralist theorists oppose trends towards media dominance, they do not always identify economic concentration, for instance, as inevitably inconsistent with a pluralistic media reality.

There are too many different views of society and pieces of theory underlying the simple opposition under discussion to be dealt with adequately, but it is relevant to the present purpose to mention some of the main sources of the 'dominance' attributed to the media. One is the location of ownership and control in a given class with other kinds of power. Another is the fact of economic concentration and integration and of semi-monopolies of public control in some cases. A third is the industrial basis of mass communication, with its associated mass production and dissemination, leading to homogeneity of content and monopolizing of attention. A fourth is the market economy in which media operate which tends to exclude or discourage minority or deviant products in a consistent way, thus helping to keep the system stable and unified. A fifth source is the prestige and status which the media tend to acquire and which rubs off on those with access to mass media.

Thus, the posited dominance has several sources – conscious efforts to use power in class interests, technological factors reducing diversity, economic arrangements favouring uniformity and the management of demand, social forces which ensure that some social power and influence go with access to mass media. The belief in the reality of media pluralism rests mainly on confidence that supply will be determined by demand and if this is allowed free expression by individuals and interest groups, pluralism will be ensured, given the capacity of media systems to increase and diversify. In addition, pluralistic theory tends to resist the view that the efforts of a single dominant class consciously seeking to use media for class ends provides the key to understanding the working of the media we now have.

(iii) Centrifugal versus centripetal effects of media
The third relevant dimension, which is closely related to the value of
'togetherness', distinguishes the view that mass communication
contributes to change, fragmentation, diversity and mobility from the
alternative view that it is a force for unity, stability, integration and
homogeneity. In turn, this reflects the larger sociological dilemma of
reconciling change with the maintenance of order. The picture is
further complicated by differences in the relative value placed on
order and change respectively and we can identify both a 'positive'
and a 'negative' version at each pole of the dimension. The positive
version of a centrifugal effect stresses modernization and individual
freedom, while the negative version points to isolation, privatization,
alienation and vulnerability to manipulation. The positive version of
the centripetal effect stresses the potential for integrating and
unifying, the negative version indicates centralized control, repression
or manipulation. In one way or another, each of these four sub-
versions of media effect derive from some key aspect of 'old' media –
centralized production and dissemination to scattered individuals,
high attractiveness and ubiquity, tendencies to homogeneity of
content and unity of control.

There is an obvious relationship between this dimension and the
previously summarized ideas of dominance and pluralism. For
simplicity, this correspondence can be expressed by locating along
with 'dominance' the two negative versions mentioned – media as
promoting either isolation or centralized represive control – and with
'pluralism' the two positive versions – media as promoting freedom,
choice and 'healthy' (because self-chosen) forms of social cohesion on
the basis of group, place, politics or religion. The assimilation of these
two dimensions helps to provide a fuller account of two opposed
versions of media tendency – towards uniformity and repressive
control or towards pluralism and voluntarism. The result of this
discussion can be summarized by plotting the two main dimensions
against each other, as in Figure 1.1. It is worth pointing out that the
'technology' variant of media-centred theory indicated in this figure
corresponds with the 'structural' variant of society-centred theory (at
the other end of the horizontal line), since both are in some sense
'materialist' notions and new technology is often an example, or a
consequence, of structural change. So too does the 'content' aspect of
media relate to the 'individualist' variant of society-centred theory,
since, if content does have its own effects, it has them first of all on
individuals and, in addition, individuals relate more directly or
consciously to content than to technology.

FIGURE 1.1
Main dimensions of media theory

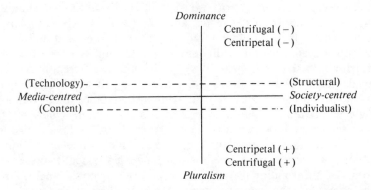

If this account of dimensions of media theory is reasonably complete and correct, it should be possible to locate in the space of Figure 1.1 most of the interpretations of, and attitudes to, the working of 'old' media, with some guidance from the values summarized at the outset. The most important amongst such ideas have already been noted in arriving at the dimensions and need not be repeated. However, it may be worth pointing out the following general guides to location. The more pessimistic views about media tend to belong to the upper quadrants, the more optimistic to the lower. Hence, questions of control belong above, and of freedom, below. Concerns about content and culture belong on the left-hand side, and about social structure, on the right. Correspondingly, questions of supply belong on the left and those about demand on the right. In the top left belong fears about cultural harm from dominant media, in the top right fears of political repression. In the bottom right belong functional theories about the positive contribution of media to social life at the level of group and community. In the lower left belong theories of individual need satisfaction through media content and its consumption or use.

The second communication revolution

So much has been said or written about the significance of new media that it would be tedious to repeat it, especially as so much is speculation. Nevertheless, an answer to the question posed in the title of this chapter needs some statement of what the challenge of new media is usually taken to involve. Some of the changes which are either expected or possible can be summarized in a few key terms, which are often held to differentiate the future of new media from the past (or present) of the old, especially: abundance of production and supply; freedom of choice; interactivity; narrowcasting; loss of central control; decentralization; search and consultation. The new media seem, especially, to offer the potential of a shift in the balance of power, away from the sender and towards the receiver, making much more content of all kinds more accessible to users and choosers, without dependence on mediating and controlling systems of mass distribution. There is also likely to be much differentiation of available information services and a blurring of the institutional boundaries between 'mass' and individual communication as well as between private and public spheres of communication. One way of representing and comparing the key features of 'old' and 'new' media flow has been suggested by the work of two students of telecommunications, Bordewijk and van Kaam, who have tried to identify the main forms of 'information traffic'. For them, drawing on the analogy of the computer, the two main features of communication flows are storage of information on the one hand and access to, or use of, information on the other. They locate the key variables which differentiate information systems (not simply human communication) firstly in terms of the centrality or otherwise of the store of information and, secondly, the centrality or otherwise of control over access − in effect over choice of subject matter to be consulted or received and over the time at which this takes place. Their scheme, given below as Figure 1.2, assumes a set of participants arranged in the pattern of a wheel around a central hub. Communication flows (traffic) can take place between any set of participants at the rim or between the centre and any one or more of the participants at the rim. By considering each participant (including the centre) as having a store of information which is drawn on (accessed), or added to, in communication, a fuller picture of possible communication patterns can be arrived at.

By cross-tabulating 'information store' against 'control over choice of time and subject', in terms of whether each is 'central' or 'individual', a set of four categories of communication traffic is arrived at, as in Figure 1.2. The difference between a central and individual information store, while deriving from that between a large data bank and a single person, is also analogous with the difference between a mass media organization and a single audience member or that between a library and a reader. It can also correspond with the difference between 'information-rich' individuals or groups and those which are 'information-poor'. The difference between central and individual control of access to information, while it can be taken literally, also corresponds to that between constraint and freedom and low and high communication potential.

FIGURE 1.2
Four patterns of information traffic

	Information store	
	Central	*Individual*
Control of time and choice of subject: *Central*	Allocution	Registration
Control of time and choice of subject: *Individual*	Consultation	Conversation

Key:

Allocution The simultaneous transmission of a centrally constituted 'offer' of information intended for immediate attention, according to a centrally determined time scheme.

Conversation An exchange between individuals of information already available to them, according to a mutually convenient time scheme.

Consultation The selective consultation by individual participants of a central store of information at times determined by each individual.

Registration The collection in a central store of information available to, or about, individual participants, according to a centrally determined choice of subject and time.

Source: Adapted from Bordewijk and van Kaam (1982).

For the most part, the entry labelled 'allocution' (derived from a Latin word meaning direct address from a leader to followers) stands for the typical 'old media' forms of communication − from a central source to many separated receivers and at times and on subjects determined by the sender. This is especially apposite for national broadcasting. The consultation pattern is also long established as a mode of communication (e.g. libraries) and newspapers can be considered as consultation as well as allocution media. The conversation pattern is currently represented, in media terms, mainly by telephone and postal services and the 'registration' pattern (of which more below) is hardly known as yet in public communication, although it is a long established element in many organizations for record-keeping, control and surveillance. In brief, the potential of new media is to increase the possibilities for consultation (telematics, multi-channel cable and video) and for conversation (via interactive cable, radio and linked computers) and for registration (central recording by computer of all uses of information media connected to a system). The general pattern which can be predicted from the potential of new media is of a shift away from the top left cell of Figure 1.2 and a redistribution of communication 'traffic' to the other three cells. This seems to indicate a general increase in individual freedom to gain information and a reduction in the dominance of centralized sources.

This seems to offer some qualitative guidance in handling those features mentioned above as characteristic of new media, especially in relation to control, narrowcasting and interaction. On the first of these, it suggests that individuals will acquire more control over what and when they receive and consult. Even so, what is available for consultation in central stores can still be centrally determined and much will depend on how diverse the central stores are in content and management. Further, it is possible to interpret the 'registration' pattern, as many have done, as significantly increasing the potential for central control through surveillance of information and information-related activities, which may often be politically sensitive. Lastly, it is possible for individual information stores to develop, so that much more extensive 'conversation' patterns could reduce dependence on central information stores, with diminished chances for surveillance. On the question of 'narrowcasting', besides multiplication of allocutive channels (via multi-channel cable and many satellites), the main implication of the scheme presented is that, by expressing demand through acts of consultation, users will stimulate specialist kinds of supply. In respect of interaction, two main developments open up – a wider range of conversational possibilities with other individuals and various kinds of interactive consultation with collective agencies, for the supply of goods and services. One further use of the scheme in Figure 1.2 is to note that the top row entries (allocution and registration) are associated with a need for regulation and the bottom row (consultation and conversation) with absence of regulation. The left-hand column indicates issues of property rights in information and the right-hand column identifies issues of privacy.

Assessment of media theory
The issues suggested by consideration of the media theory dimensions discussed above can serve as an agenda for the assessment and can be named as follows. The central question, we should recall, is whether the old theory alerts us to the problems of new media and provides us with relevant concepts, ideas and organizing principles. The issues are:

1. The degree of control which society has or can have over media development and the extent to which media independently shape societal developments.
2. The allocation of power over media between social actors and interests and the use of media in the exercise of power.
3. The contribution of communication to change and order in society and culture.
4. The pattern of social relationships as mediated by communications media.

On the question of the balance of control as between media and society, the values and dimensions named above do seem to identify the main problems and offer concepts and a framework for anticipating or evaluating alternative lines of development. In particular, we are alerted to aspects of the new media which seem to restrict the control which society can exercise: the increased flow across national frontiers; the very fact of abundance; the momentum behind technological change which can force the hands of policy makers; the fact that the expanding types of communication traffic and relationship, especially 'conversation' and 'consultation', are neither as easy nor as legitimate to control as 'allocution'. The case for media-centred theory in its technological variant is strengthened by the little experience already available, since the future is already being defined by governments and influential parties as an information society, with new information technology as driving force and its accumulation as a primary goal.

The main issue of power as formulated in old media theory is still very relevant to the emerging new media situation, although changes in the way in which informational power operates call for theoretical revision. The implications for power are fairly apparent: the power or competitive position of some actors will be strengthened by having more access to useful information than is available to others; it is quite likely that new media will widen overall differentials of knowledge between social groups, because of the unequal distribution of competence in using the new information tools and the relative decline in allocutive channels, which have until now tended to be distributive and equalizing in tendency. These remarks apply mainly to information for instrumental application in decision-making or opinion-forming (but also in the production and managing of exchange or control relationships). It is less clear what to expect in respect of the ideological function of information, which has been well performed by allocutive media in the past, according to current theory. It would seem, at first sight, that if 'allocution' declines, so will the possibility for hegemonic control of mass consciousness weaken. Much depends on the nature of the increased diversity made possible and on precisely where power over content and distribution will come to be concentrated. Media theory concerning power has mainly developed in relation to public opinion and the public sphere of politics and new media pose a broad challenge to both.

Change and order issues are unlikely to be very different in the new media situation, although we are promised more rapid change as a result of more information and threatened with some instability brought about by: greater freedom to choose from abundant messages; less uniformity of the audience or public; less consistency or predictability of behaviour by the audience. The new communication situation seems to suggest greater individuation and functional specification of audiences (user groups), greater disparities and lower degrees of collective consciousness. There are ideas for handling these matters in existing theory, but the latter is not very sensitive in the sense of helping to distinguish between the variety of conditions of knowledge differentiation which can be expected. Existing theory is also rather simple-minded in its implicit valuations: mainly against over-control and in favour of freedom; against isolation or anomie and for solidarity and integration. These terms seem rather more easy to apply to older, allocutive media situations than to the more complex pattern of offer and reception which characterizes new media. The issue of relationships belongs here as well, since in 'old theory' it goes mainly with ideas of solidarity and integration. According to the scheme presented in Figure 1.2, new media seem to have quite profound implications for patterns of relationships, promoting more symmetry, less dependence on central sources, more response and interaction, yet also threatening loss of visibility and openness, of stability and durability of ties between senders and receivers and therefore having a potential for weakening the moral ties between individuals and their societies, of the kind sustained by voluntary social institutions.

In the summary evaluation of the version of 'old media theory' presented above, it seems that most implications of new media and of the alternative futures being opened up are not 'off the map' of current thinking. We can provisionally identify what seem the most relevant questions, even if the working out of values and propositions for application to the new situation has yet to be done. Since these new situations are still more heralded than here, this is not a very negative judgement. The main attitudes to new media are also possible to account for according to the scheme presented. The horizontal dimension (in Figure 1.1) still differentiates a belief in the capacity of new media to change society from a belief in the primacy of societal arrangements and of individuals in determining the shape of any communications revolution and thus of any attendant change in society. For the most part, appropriate values and preferences go with these alternative assumptions, in a predictable way. The vertical dimension still separates those who see the new media as strengthening the hand of political and economic elites from those whose pluralistic assumptions and values make them optimistic about the future in an information society, which they generally welcome. On the crucial question of whether the changes in prospect really do constitute a revolution, theory still offers alternative positions.

Media theory and public policy for new media
One strand in the evaluation promised at the outset relates to media policy: does existing theory offer guidance in choices which have to be made now or in the near future? The question is much too large to deal with adequately, but it can be opened up for attention by summarizing what appear at the moment to be the main dilemmas of policy. These are given in Figure 1.3, on the assumption that there is a more or less agreed version of the potential of new media.

FIGURE 1.3
Dilemmas of media policy

New media potential

First choice	Discourage	Encourage
Second choice	Public	Private
Third choice	Monopoly	Diversity
Fourth choice	Content regulation	Technical regulation

The choices are arranged so that there is a fair amount of consistency between the items in each column, although each choice has a certain independence from the others and a 'right-hand' choice at one option, for instance the encouragement of new media, does not preclude the option of public institutional means for achieving this. There is however some tension between the options listed on the left and those on the right and, for the most part, one would not expect them to be associated with each other. It is a feature of the current political reality, in Europe at least, that the climate of decision-making favours industrial and economy policy, which gives more weight to the set of right-hand options, which happen generally to be those of the political right. The alternative, 'cultural policy', which has tended to dominate media policy in the past in Europe, is mainly associated with caution over, if not actual discouragement of, rapid new media growth and generally goes with the options on the left-hand side in Figure 1.3.

Not surprisingly, there are links between these choices and media theory. To begin with, 'cultural policy' has tended to go with a position in the upper left quadrant of Figure 1.1 − a combination of awareness of media power and sensitivity to the content of what is made available. Industrial policy, as usually formulated, belongs more to the lower right cell − going with a belief in pluralism and the individual and a confidence in societal mechanisms as levers of change (the structural variant, with its link to technology). Encouragement of new media rests on a belief in pluralism, positive views of change, individualistic theories of media and society and probably a techno-logical version of media-centred theory. Discouragement generally goes with dominance theory, societal pessimism and (possibly) the content version of media-centred theory. The option of private (financially and institutionally) frameworks for development is more consistent with pluralism than with dominance theory and the latter would favour public control in the wider general interest and so as to limit the commercial exploitation of media by large monopolistic corporations. The diversity−monopoly choice may not seem like a very real dilemma, but there is often a practical issue of retaining or weakening existing public monopolies or quasi-monopolies and there is a real concern that commercial development can strengthen the monopoly control of private business over sectors of the media. Attitudes and preferences in these matters are distributed in fairly obvious ways along the vertical dimension of Figure 1.1. On the fourth choice, aside from the direction given by cultural policy (towards the regulation of content) or by industrial policy (technical regulation only), the differences are to be accounted for in terms of varying positions on the horizontal dimension. The more media-centred one's theory, the more attention one gives to control of content, and the more society-centred, the greater is one's inclination to attend only to technical regulation.

This discussion suggests that theory is still adequate for describing and classifying policy positions and probably also for justifying them. This does not, however, say a great deal and it is relevant to point out that so far the most significant choices which have been faced in the context of the development of new media have mainly been decisions about old media. In a sense, therefore, the true issues of new media have not yet really entered into the policy-making debate, except as issues of property, area of competence (as between private and public sector) or as matters of moral standards.

Gaps and deficiencies
Some inadequacies of theory have already been suggested. They derive, in the main, from concentration on the allocutive mode of

communication which has been and remains the dominant form. This shows, first of all, in the analysis of power. Current theory seems to offer a very unnuanced view – a choice between monolithic media in the hands of a class or state or a neutral arena in which power struggles are played out between more or less equal competitors. The first view attributes great powers of persuasion, mobilization and 'cultivation' to the media over a passive and dependent audience, the second offers a power vacuum in which individuals choose freely and resist unwanted influence. The new media are likely to be less monolithic, but they are still likely to be relevant for the exercise of power, as sources and carriers of information of potential value for instrumental uses and rational calculation. Direct persuasion and mobilization of a large mass following is both less easy and less possible in a very differentiated society. Not everything will change, but media theory has not been sufficiently sensitive in the past in its handling of matters to do with power and this lack of sensitivity is likely to be an increasing liability, if not made good.

Secondly, there are deficiencies in matters to do with media systems and organizations. The main problems likely to emerge fall under two headings, one to do with relations to society and the other concerning relations between media and their own audiences. On the first it can be argued that existing media, growing up relatively slowly in relation to society, have acquired adequate institutionalized arrangements for handling many rights and responsibilities. Some of these belong to the sphere of professional self-regulation, as in matters of information quality, moral and cultural standards, respect (or not) for privacy, editorial responsibility. Others concern matters of the media system as a whole, for instance diversity, representativeness, access, equal availability, obligation to carry channels, service to other institutions or to society in general. With the rapid emergence of new media, there is a risk of some deprofessionalization and destabilizing of institutional control. The rapid growth of new media, often fragmentary and functionally specific in what they do, is quite likely to undermine, or at least challenge, a whole network of norms, understandings, arrangements and interdependencies which are rooted in social theory and are taken for granted as part of the media scene. They also happen to be somewhat taken for granted by media theory and the study of media will not be made easier by the lack of a well-developed framework of ideas in this area of social theory.

On the second matter – concerning relations between media and public – 'old theory' does provide a framework in which to place the notion of solidary and moral relations between a communication source and its own public, even if the emphasis has tended to be somewhat negative. Thus, there is more theorizing about the absence of this kind of relationship than about its positive character — pointing, for instance, to manipulation from above or calculative choice-making from below. While this emphasis is not so mistaken in the case of much mass communication, there do still exist possibilities for moral ties to form and endure between mass media and their publics and the media still play a not unimportant part in the public sphere of social life and in democratic politics, as platform, critic, watchdog and mobilizer. While new media promise more interaction and smallness of scale, they may also entail a new kind and degree of social atomization and an impoverishment of the arena of public life, even an increase in the degree of depoliticization, which has already been remarked upon as a feature of the television age. It is unclear what the future holds in store for the audience which is neither a target mass, nor a set of freely choosing individuals, but a public in the classic sense of a dispersed but self-aware set of persons with similar interests and aims. New interactive media benefit such communities of interest, but there are also counter-forces towards fragmentation. The area of intra-organizational communication based on expert knowledge will extend, on the one hand, and, on the other, the network of more or less private, individual or intra-group contacts is also likely to grow. This is not necessarily bad, but it does not seem fully accounted for by theory, which is mainly based on the notion of large-scale communication of rather similar content to many people. It is not really a task for theory to imagine futures or to moralize about them, but it is a task of theory to identify questions of this kind and provide tools for handling them.

In respect of the audience, existing theory offers two main alternative conceptualizations – either as object for assault and capture or as a set of individuals choosing actively according to needs and circumstances. Until more is known of how new media will develop it is hard to judge the adequacy of one or the other version. There may actually be more of the 'old' allocutive media traffic, by way of broadcast satellites and seeking to increase total audiences. There may also be more selectivity as a result of more supply and more flexibility in control and access for users. Where existing theory may be deficient is in its dependence on, or derivation from, a view of audiences as selectively reacting to a flow or stream of material, rather than choosing consciously according to individual needs and tastes. The difference is one of degree of activity since the latter, the pattern encouraged by the new media, presupposes a goal-directed and less habit-determined set of behaviours. In the future, audiences are also less likely to be aggregates open to characterization in terms of a set of choices of content. Some development of theory of choice-making under varying conditions is likely to be needed. These brief remarks about gaps and deficiencies can also serve as a source for a research agenda.

References

Bordewijk, J.L. and B. van Kaam (1982) *Allocutie*. Baarn, Netherlands: Bosch and Keuning, n.v.

Gerbner, G., L. Gross, M. Morgan and N. Signorielli (1980) 'The Mainstreaming of America', *Journal of Communication*, 30: 10–27.

Innis, H. (1951) *The Bias of Communication*. Toronto: University of Toronto Press.

McLuhan, M. (1962) *The Gutenberg Galaxy*. Toronto: University of Toronto Press.

2

The social economics of information technology

Ian Miles and Jonathan Gershuny[1]

'Information society': a second coming of post-industrial society?

From post-industrial society to the information economy

According to a widely accepted view of economic development, the economy can best be seen as consisting of three main sectors: agriculture and other primary production, industries such as construction and (especially) manufacturing, and a tertiary or 'residual' sector producing services. Economic development is then viewed as a progressive shift in the focus of activity, first from the primary to the secondary sector, and then from the secondary to the tertiary.

Post-war developments seem at first sight to demonstrate the usefulness of this view. Agricultural employment declined rapidly with the introduction of mechanized, fertilizer-intensive and factory-farming methods. And service employment grew more rapidly than manufacturing, so that by the 1960s economists were talking of the 'service economy': more than 50 percent of all workers were employed in the service sector in the 1970s for the European Economic Community (EEC) as a whole. If we include workers from white-collar and other service-type jobs in the primary and secondary sectors, the dominance of such 'non-production' work is overwhelming.

The idea of a march of workers from primary through secondary to tertiary employment was taken to mean that there was little reason to be alarmed by the prospect of automation in manufacturing industry. The service industries would soak up surplus employment, it seemed — although close inspection of the data would have revealed that rather little of the growth in tertiary employment represented a migration of employees from the secondary sector into these industries of the future.

The implications of this process for social development more generally were elaborated in terms of certain assumptions about changes in social values. The progression through the economic sectors was attributed to shifts in consumer demand resulting from affluence and social equality. As people's basic needs were satisfied, the role of foodstuffs in their expenditure declined relative to that of manufactures (Engels' Law). And as they became satiated with material abundance, their desires for intangibles such as health and education grew in prominence. This hierarchy of values explains the march through the three economic sectors, and in turn has other social consequences that justified an intellectual shift from service *economy* to post-industrial *society*. 'Post-industrialism' became a dominant diagnosis of the present, and prognosis for the future, of the Western world.[2]

Social and economic developments were seen to be mutually reinforcing. As people's attitudes shifted away from a concern with the bare necessities of life, there would be a growth in demand for political participation, for care of the environment and for weaker members of society. These concerns, rather than the traditional issues of management of the economy, entered the political agenda in the late 1960s and early 1970s – what Inglehart called the 'silent revolution'. Furthermore, with the growth of white-collar and knowledge-intensive work, increasing power would be vested in scientific and technical workers, in people whose work depends upon their intellectual or interpersonal abilities, rather than in the owners of capital or other traditional bearers of power. Emerging as a dominant force in post-industrial society is a *new service class* of 'knowledge workers', with the values, skills and resources appropriate for the new agenda of political and economic development.

Thus there would be a shift toward greater social planning, and a subordination of business interests to values of meritocracy and welfare. The existence of some stresses and strains was conceded – such as the conflict between libertarian and personal-growth values and those of preserving high culture and maintaining media standards – but the general expectation was that of an end of ideology. Disagreement over social goals would be reduced to a minimum (especially as East–West conflict subsided with the convergence of both blocs towards post-industrial societies); that over the means to achieve the goals would be transformed into a technical debate in which tools such as technology assessment, social indicators and computer simulation would allow for the fine-tuning of social progress....

Despite the traumas of the last decade, the term 'post-industrial society' remains remarkably respectable. Admittedly it tends to be used as a hand-waving description – but, as we shall argue, many of the underlying assumptions of post-industrialism are still commonly reproduced, and enter into the currently fashionable concept: the 'information society'.

The information society literature has moved on in some respects from the post-industrialists. Concern over job loss and de-skilling has become prominent with the industrial application of microelectronics, so the literature is more marked by disagreement over positive and negative consequences of technological and organizational changes than was the case for the post-industrialists. One recent study lists debates over whether informatics leads to: decentralization or increased centralized decision-making, upgrading or de-skilling of work, increased computer literacy or alienation from everyday technology, economic dualism or a more participatory economy, and intensified or debilitated interpersonal relationships. Most authors see one pole to be the logical consequence of current tendencies, rather as post-industrialists saw their future to be a logical consequence of social evolution: but in the economic climate of the 1980s the information society commentators add the imperative for countries to compete to make use of new processes and to produce new products to gain comparative advantages in international trade. Information society (perhaps with concomitant future shock and unemployment) or economic failure (with even more stress and unemployment): this is the implicit choice. But there remain a number of fundamental points where agreement between the 'post-industrial' and the 'information' society schools is strong.

The march through the sectors underpins much information society literature. However, some influential writers have proposed updating the three-sector model. Recognizing that the model loses much of its usefulness when an extremely diverse set of tertiary industries rise to the prominence which they now occupy, these authors suggest adding a fourth sector – the information sector. They similarly describe information occupations – all formal employment that is largely concerned with the production, processing or distribution of information, or with the installation, operation and maintenance of associated physical, electronic and mechanical infrastructure – which have formed an increasing proportion of the labour force (more than a third of all employment in the UK and North America by the 1980s).

Information society, then, rests upon the expansion of economic activities concerned with information flows. This expansion is attributed the centrality that was earlier accorded to the services. New technologies may check the growth of employment in information occupations by enabling increases in labour productivity; but they will also dramatically reduce the costs of information, leading to a considerable growth in demand for existing information services and informatics products, and the development of a host of new ones. Information services are seen as particularly important emerging areas of public demand (manipulated by media moguls according to some critical accounts). Industries too are seen as being forced to become more information-intensive owing to the changing nature of products and markets, and because of the drive for increased productivity. (For example, it is argued that rapid shifts in product design – corresponding to innovation or fashion – require production technologies that can be readily geared to different volumes of production and designs, as in computer-aided design–computer-aided manufacture (CADCAM).)

The debate over the relative rates of job replacement and job generation in information activities, relating closely to public and media concerns about unemployment, has helped raise the concept of information society to greater prominence than that achieved by post-industrial society. But other concerns have also surfaced: fears about the erosion of public service broadcasting (and the standards it has promoted) by cable and satellite services, and fears of surveillance and other forms of insidious social control, in particular. While this means that there is more critical thought about the prospects afforded by informatics, the shared core of assumptions here is suspiciously like that used by the post-industrialists. Is there any essential difference between the information workers, and the older new class of knowledge workers? What is it about information that makes it sufficiently desirable to form a base for a future general expansion? What will consumers be doing with all the information produced by the expanding army of information workers? The literature is rather short on answers to these workers.

Beneath the trends
Let us look a little more closely at the factors that underpin the growth of the service economy. The tertiary sector includes very diverse types of economic activity, which, as they have grown to be major areas of employment, appear increasingly incongruous when lumped together. More detailed classifications give a rather different picture of the rise of the service economy.[3]

For one thing, not all tertiary activities have been growing. In the UK, employment in personal services has declined since the last war. Employment in transport and distribution has been declining since the 1960s. In contrast, employment has increased in social services and also in producer services – that is, services sold to firms. Thus the growth in service sector employment in part reflects political choices and changes in industrial structure rather than changes in private demand for services. But has not private demand for services increased – and does this not reflect a shift away from materialist values?

Demand for services has increased with increasing affluence – but so has demand for goods. There is little evidence for services *per se* having a greater income elasticity than goods. There has been a shift in household expenditure along Engels' Law-like lines, away from basic purchases such as food and shelter and towards education, entertainment, etc. But within these latter categories, there has been a shift in private expenditure *away from services and towards goods*. Thus more money is spent on cars, televisions and washing machines, less on rail, theatre and laundry services. This would mean, other things being equal (which they are not), that service employment would decline relative to that in manufacturing – with the creation of some new service employment, for example in garages, TV studios and domestic equipment repairs. These service the use of manufactured goods by consumers producing their own final services (the shift to domestic production that Toffler suggests in his neologism of 'prosumers'), rather than supplying final services. Just as the producer services are supplying intermediate services to industries, we have here intermediate consumer services. Thus a portion of service sector growth derives from these two types of intermediate service, which appear to be contributing largely to the manufacture and operation of goods.

But service sector employment has grown mainly under the impetus of two other factors. First, increases in labour productivity have been lower in most services than in most other economic sectors. (This is why we suggested above that not all other things were equal.) Similar rates of demand increase across sectors will mean shifts in relative employment to those with lower rates of productivity growth. Second, collectively-provided services have been responsible for a very large share of the growth in tertiary employment. Again, as far as can be established given the problematic accounting methods available here, low productivity growth is involved in the rapid expansion of employment in these sectors.

The view of the service economy provided by this analysis is radically different to that of the post-industrialists. Rather than there being an inherent bias in favour of the purchasing of services with increasing affluence, the growth of services reflects rather complex political and economic trade-offs made by the state, firms and households. In several countries the growth of many skilled occupational categories in the first few post-war decades had much to do with the aerospace industry and the Cold War; and the expansion of social services can be related to the strength of socialist and social-democratic movements in different Western countries. Firms have participated in an increasing division of labour and found it expedient to purchase many of the services that might otherwise have been provided in-house: this choice, shaped by technological change, fiscal policy and employment protection legislation and unionization, has led to the development of new intermediate producer service industries. And while consumers have been more concerned with sophisticated luxury expenditure, the choice about how to make that expenditure has increasingly been weighted toward goods rather than services. This reflects a variety of factors shaping the relative cost and convenience of different modes of provision of final services, and hardly bears out the idea of a growth of post-material attitudes; indeed, the groups most prepared to endorse Inglehart's 'post-bourgeois' values have the highest aspirations for material affluence.

The future of the service economy, then, cannot be as rosy as post-industrialists imagined. The march through the sectors is less a disciplined advance than a scattering of the tribes. There are at least four distinct elements in the service sector (the intermediate producer and consumer service, and the marketed and non-marketed final service, subsectors). Low productivity growth in tertiary sectors may lead to increased limits on public expenditure and increased shifting of consumers to goods rather than services. Or, if the use of new technologies does permit more innovation in tertiary industries, service employment may be restricted through job displacement: unless, that is, new service products can find mass markets.

What does this imply about accounts of information society, which follow the post-industrialists in projecting a march through the sectors, but provide little substantial analysis of the growth of what are quite heterogeneous varieties of activity? Lumping together a variety of 'new' activities under a common heading is a gesture of recognition to the problem, not a step toward solving it. If the tertiary sector is internally diverse, the 'information sector' is equally so. The range of occupations covered under the heading of information workers includes research scientists, typists, broadcasters, telephone operators and television repairers. It can be useful to group together all these jobs as belonging to one industry: the ones we have chosen could all be associated with television, and one could relate their patterns of development together as part of a systems analysis of the industry. But when we consider that there are a host of industries in which these categories of occupation are found, the notion of information occupations begins to look more like a handy slogan ('vanguard of the information age') than a concept of any real explanatory relevance. The Organization for Economic Cooperation and Development (OECD) does list such a range of 'information occupations', and distinguishes between primary information industries (whose purpose is the production of information as a final commodity or benefit), and secondary information industries (which provide information as an input to the production of material commodities); but it fails to reveal the diverse prospects for growth within these categories.

A better understanding of the rise of information-related activities, and the potential transformations that may be associated with the introduction of informatics, really requires an analysis of large-scale processes of social change. But in the first instance, we can take the distinction between information work concerned with production, processing, distribution and infrastructure as a helpful guide to the sorts of activity that might take place in any location. In addition to this we would distinguish between activities that are intermediate inputs to producers, intermediate inputs to consumers, and final inputs to consumers, and between those that are marketed and non-marketed. Within these different types of activities there are information flows, and different applications for informatics. 'Information work' has different meanings within these different sectors. The development of these activities is closely interrelated: by considering the costs and benefits to the different actors involved we may gain some idea of the likely course of social change in the future, the possibilities for use of new technology, and the conflicts and broader consequences that might result.

Long-run processes of social change

The end of the post-war boom
Can our account of the growth of the tertiary sector account for the drastic way in which the predictions of post-industrial theory were undermined by the changes of the 1970s and 1980s?

To a large extent, the end of the post-war boom reflects the erosion of the various structures that formed the post-war political settlement – and the basis for the pattern of growth described above, and the view of the post-industrial future it fostered. The growth of welfare states and the application of Keynesian counter-cyclical measures was part of the post-war political settlement within the West. These arrangements helped regulate demand and provide markets for a wide range of other products, including those central to the boom, and facilitated a large growth in service sector activities. The breakdown of the post-war settlement was related to internal problems of these arrangements as well as to international travails. A view of long-run social change is required to grasp this process.

With the world economic crisis has come renewed interest in the 'long waves of economic life', and researchers have focused on the technical paradigms in manufacturing industry that characterize each of these waves. They argue that long downswings are associated with industries maturing and their technological systems becoming subject to cost-cutting, rationalizing innovation. The upswings are in contrast associated with new products and processes, with new industries and technological systems. Innovations in 'heartland technologies' permit the development of diverse new products and processes, and the development of infrastructure makes possible the diffusion and widespread application of these new technologies. But these researchers have paid little attention to social innovations: changes that people make in their ways of life so as to take advantage of the opportunities offered by new technologies — and to cope with the changed social relationships that are thus created. Whether or not they are 'cycles' with a definite periodicity, long waves should be interpreted in terms of the growth, maturity and stagnation of socio-technical systems, of which technical paradigms form just one, albeit important, part.[4]

The post-war boom involved considerable change in technologies — and in ways of life. The key industrial sectors — consumer durables and automobiles — relied on new methods of mass production and industrial organization (which meant, among other things, the 'tertiarization' of secondary industries), and sold their products to newly affluent populations. Infrastructures — mains electricity, telecommunications and modern road systems — made possible the widespread application of these products, changing their cost and convenience relative to other modes of service provision. New ways of life were developed in which the automobile and telephone, washing machine and television played an important role, and often involving shifts away from the purchase of final services to self-service provision of transport, domestic services, entertainment, etc. And collective provision of social services expanded, reflecting changes in the family, the workforce, and in social aspirations.

Women's employment (and part-time working) grew, with the expansion of the services and the greater division of labour, and domestic technology was used to reduce 'their' housework load. While some de-skilling of work was the norm for many traditional occupations and within whole industrial sectors, there was also considerable growth of white-collar posts of various kinds, and the expansion of the services — especially, as noted, non-marketed and producer services — meant the creation of large numbers of professional and semi-professional posts. Employees belonging to these groups became bearers of 'post-bourgeois values', and a major social basis for many of the new social movements of the 1970s and 1980s.

But the growth of state expenditure of the post-war boom fuelled inflationary tendencies. The expansion of employment in the services meant an increasing proportion of national income going to the relatively lagging sectors of the economy − and the new public sector unionism placed obstacles in the way of attempts to keep wages at low levels here. The market was showing signs of maturity and stagnation by the end of the 1960s. No radically new products were emerging, worldwide overproduction was becoming apparent in several sectors − if not actually saturating, markets were no longer as elastic as they had been. Government policies in the UK and many other countries were directed towards shoring up mature and traditional industries rather than stimulating innovation; and these industries were rationalizing rather than developing substantially new products. The post-war boom petered out, with constraints being placed upon public expenditure, with the downturns of business cycles creating increasing unemployment − a general exhaustion of a pattern of growth involving a particular set of products, processes, infrastructure and ways of life. The destabilization of the international economy, and the appearance of a baby boom generation (born in the upswing) on the labour market, set the scene for a long period of economic trauma.

The transformation that we are undergoing, then, involves more than just technical change − although new technologies would form part of any return to long-term growth, if a future growth wave is to resemble past experience. Informatics are clearly central, if for no other reason than that they offer to reduce the bottlenecks in information flow created during the post-war boom. But changes in institutions, infrastructures and ways of life are also required for the opportunities they present to be seized. The design of products and infrastructures has considerable relevance to the ways of life that may evolve, the values and practices that are integral to a new sociotechnical system. But the question is not really about the *impact* of informatics on ways of life, values and culture, but the way in which societies reproduce and adapt themselves, using and reshaping technologies in the process.

An informatics upswing?
Informatics provides heartland technologies for process innovations: CADCAM, rapid information transfer and retrieval, new paradigms of industrial organization. It provides new products: home computers, control devices for household equipment, new telecommunications facilities. It involves new infrastructures: cable and satellite systems. But innovations in people's ways of life would be both precondition and consequence of the widespread adoption of informatics.

The potential uses of new technology extend well beyond the proliferation of video games and television channels, which do not exactly sound like the recipe for renewed economic growth. A new telecommunications infrastructure could permit the development of new services, and the transformation of many existing ones. Changes in entertainment are obvious enough. Distribution and transport could be transformed through teleshopping, improved travel booking and scheduling, telebanking, telework. Education could move more to Open University-type formats, with public information utilities for informal and community education and training. In medicine, in addition to remote diagnosis and monitoring services for chronic disorders, preventative advice and improvement of community care could involve informatics. Even domestic services might be the focus of innovation: pensioners' safety, household security and energy use can be monitored, payments and purchasing could be substantially automated, and so on.

Cable TV and home computers may be dominant at present, but this does not mean that the other innovations are unlikely. Indeed, the advent of improved telecommunications infrastructure is a prerequisite for most of the services outlined above to be effective. The development of an infrastructure for entertainment purposes may precede its use for a much broader range of interactive services – although this may well depend crucially upon appropriate design of the systems.[5]

There are many different ways in which informatics could be developed within our society, with correspondingly varied implications for economic expansion and the details of ways of life. To reduce the rate of diffusion of new technologies in industry would be likely to lead to continued stagnation. To concentrate on improving industrial efficiency by process innovation could lead to considerable improvements in delivery of many existing products – although in practice this seems likely simply to mean labour-saving and cost-cutting change in non-marketed services, and an overall reduction in employment. A combination of product and process innovation, of infrastructural and way-of-life changes is also possible: while this may not be able to restore full employment as understood in the post-war boom, we can outline areas where formal employment might begin to expand.

On the one hand, we can expect to see some jobs created in the manufacture of informatics equipment and the installation of the infrastructure, although neither may be as demanding of labour as some optimists hope. We might see some loss of work in final services, although this *could* be offset by improvements in service quality: for example, increased efficiency of travel services, and the associated tasks of booking and scheduling, might go some way toward reversing the trend away from public transport. Political choices are very important here: again, it is not the potential of the technology, but the application of that potential that is the key issue.

As for intermediate services, contradictory trends would operate in the case of producer services (increased labour productivity through the use of informatics, but also increased need for information services of various kinds), but there may be considerable growth of intermediate consumer services. Consumer uses of informatics like those discussed above often require extensive backup services including, as well as maintenance and related functions, various sorts of information brokerage. And the intermediate consumer services would involve people in the production of software, which we understand to mean more than the material that is purchased (or pirated) to run on computers, to cover information encoded on media for use in informatics hardware more generally. Software production involves the embodiment of applied human skills in information-storage devices for use in the production of services, then; it spans recorded entertainment and expert systems, the writing of video games and that of Teletext pages. This means seeing actors in a television studio as producing software (the TV broadcast or video) as an intermediate consumer service, to be used by consumers in their application of their manufactures (TV sets); in contrast the actor on the public stage is providing a final entertainment service (with the aid of a built infrastructure rather than a telecommunications one). (The self-same actor may provide both sorts of service at once, just as one production process in industry may yield two different products simultaneously, or yield one product which can be used both as a capital good and as a consumer item.)

This pattern of introduction and reshaping of informatics might be compatible with social and economic innovation in general, with the establishment of a new sociotechnical system rather than the recuperation of the existing one. The diffusion of domestic equipment and infrastructure might be led by demands for entertainment and further education. But existing services might be transformed: and there could be the emergence of new information and advice services, and the growth of interactive informal use of telematics (to establish like-minded or like-needful groups for car-sharing, pressure groups, romantic liaisons, consumer advice, bartering of child-care or do-it-yourself (DIY) work, personal advice, the sponsorship of performances and cultural events. . .). Some shift away from formal provision of final services to self-service provision might be expected to continue, even to accelerate. The key questions of political choice here relate to the future of collective services: will informatics be used to substitute for existing provisions, or to expand and augment them?

Social choice and information societies
We have suggested that distinctive periods of growth and stagnation in

the world economy are related to the 'life cycle' of vigour and exhaustion of particular sociotechnical systems, of specific constellations of process and product technology, infrastructure, social organization and ways of life. These constitute different ways of representing and satisfying consumer demands through the political economy. The choice between the different available *modes of provision* of final service functions – i.e. between, on the one hand, purchases of final services, or, on the other, communal- or self-servicing (cars versus public transport, laundry versus washing machine, traditional performance versus information-technology-mediated entertainment etc.) – has become as important as the shifting of priorities from one of these functions to another.

Informatics may well help underpin a wave of innovation, but it has not arrived like the fifth cavalry at the whim of a benevolent scriptwriter. Its emergence is built upon the achievements of the last long upswing, and is a response of technicians and engineers to their perception of the developing problems in that growth paradigm. (This is one of the reasons why our view of informatics is liable to be blinkered, to be framed too much in terms of incremental solutions to pressing problems, such as the costs of clerical work.) A leap in the dark is inevitable in any major process of technological change. Can we avoid stumbling into some of the obstacles which are more likely to be encountered by less innovative strategies? What implications for social organization and political choice are raised by our analysis?

Employment and industrial organization

It is evident that employment in primary and secondary production is likely to continue its decline. In addition, employment in many of the 'information occupations' of the traditional services is likely to be reduced by the application of informatics, even though some compensation for this labour-saving might be brought about by increased demand due to reduced prices related to innovation in the services. More significantly, informatics could also be used to bring about quality improvements in services – reduced waiting time and delay, more personalized services, resources freed from routine business to deal with priority cases. This might stem or reverse the trend from services to goods in some areas, and also defuse opposition to expenditure on social services (where anger about cuts is attenuated by the perception that costs have risen much more than output). Some producer services may continue to expand, and new consumer services, especially information services and other intermediate consumer services, may undergo rapid growth.

These developments are unlikely to restore the total amount of formal work to a level sufficient to restore full employment as it has been known. Two extreme consequences would be the development of a highly dualistic economy, with regional and class differences sharpened between those with employment, those in insecure work, and the permanently unemployed; and the redistribution of work through reduced lifetime working hours and the expansion of life-long education, community activities, etc. Informatics could be used to support either kind of development – arguments that it inevitably fosters either one, or can magically restore the previous sociotechnical system to its full vigour, should be discounted. The new technology might increase the strains of a dualistic economy: for example, accentuating awareness of the extremes of poverty and wealth that coexist. On the other hand, new security systems, new types of pass and credit card, surveillance and psy-ops methods could be used to bolster up an increasingly repressive social order. Or 'bread and circuses' could be the order of the day: wall-to-wall video games and computer nasties.

Despite ominous portents, there are prospects for more positive changes – not least in the public discussion over information society. One of the problems, however, is the relative paucity of analysis of the interrelations of social and technical innovation. Trade unionists have been pressing for substantial reductions in the working week, and have begun to pay attention to the design of technologies as well as to their introduction into the workplace. But the sorts of innovation required for a new sociotechnical system are more wide-ranging. The point of our analysis is not that anything can happen, but that it is necessary to establish linkages between different sorts of change around which shared interests could be mobilized.

For example, reduced working lifetimes have social implications that could bring together diverse social interests. Women might see this as an element in a strategy to reconstruct the sexual division of labour, since men typically blame their evasion of child-care, etc. upon the requirements of full-time breadwinning. Recurrent training may be necessitated by a rapid pace of technological change, so sectors of management could support changes in this direction, which educationalists would doubtless welcome. Many leisure industries would benefit from a more equitable distribution of leisure time. Education and entertainment – and various forms of meaningful leisure – also offer possibilities for innovative applications of informatics to the delivery of final and intermediate services.

What of the quality, rather than the quantity, of employment? The post-war boom involved the de-skilling of many traditional production activities, with a growth of middle-skill jobs in secondary and tertiary sectors alike. Informatics offers the prospect of subjecting service occupations to a similar 'capital-deepening' and division of labour. The tertiarization of the secondary sector is likely to be complemented by a secondarization of the tertiary sector. Despite some increase in scientific and technical skills, many existing semiprofessional jobs could be substantially de-skilled, leading to polarization of the labour force within industries. (This has obvious implications for the prospects for reduced lifetime working hours and retraining discussed above.) Again, this is not an inevitable consequence of the potential of the technology, nor is it necessarily the preferred management strategy. In manufacturing industry, lessons are being learned from Japanese methods of production, where the Taylor/Ford types of assembly-line division of labour are modified so as to give workers more responsibility for a coherent set of tasks (with the eminently non-altruistic goal of reducing costs incurred in bottlenecks and stockpiles). The automation of tasks only means a de-skilling of jobs if the range of tasks covered by a job remains fixed: in this instance conventional demarcation systems may run counter to improving the quality of working life.

There is considerable opportunity for different actors to intervene in the resolution of these contradictory tendencies. Outcomes are liable to be quite different in firms of different sizes and based in different sectors. Legislation over working conditions and training processes may make a difference, as will the organizational culture of firms from different national bases. But on balance, we would expect that the relative autonomy enjoyed by many service workers will be somewhat decreased, with informatics used to introduce more monitoring of operations into areas of activity where control and accountancy has to date remained more formal than substantial.

Another issue of industrial organization concerns the spatial and managerial dimensions of economic restructuring. Informatics can support a wide variety of different combinations of centralized and decentralized information processing and decision-making. The strategy of larger corporations, at least, seems to involve increased centralized monitoring and control of the overall performance of more specialized subunits or branches, with these given more responsibility for their own data processing and specialized decision-making. There may be considerable reduction of the middle ranges of the managerial pyramid, with the functions that are now typically performed by these levels in the head office being partly shifted upward and partly distributed among branches. This would reinforce the occupational trends discussed above.[6]

Households and lifestyles

Post-industrialists' theories that mass communications would bring about a massification of society, with increased commonality of opinions and practices across different social groups, have proved inaccurate to date. The social developments of the post-war boom supported heterogeneity, although this can be a mutually rewarding 'cultural pluralism' or a destructive 'social fragmentation': recent trends have displayed elements of both processes. Narrowcasting and interactive services might permit these processes to continue apace. The privatization of individual households might be accompanied by a greater segregation of social groups distinguished in lifestyle terms. But the choice of lifestyle, and the access to diverse views and practices, could also be widened.

Lifestyles remain overwhelmingly structured by class and stage in the family/employment life cycle. Thus the evolution of the employment situation − in terms of greater dualism or a decreased emphasis on formal employment in everyday life − would be an important determinant of the evolution and diversity of household consumption patterns. A dualistic labour market may mean a dualistic market more generally: for example, shops, products and discount rates that cater for owners of 'intelligent' credit cards, increased differentiation between luxury and basic goods. Working life is also extremely relevant to the development of lifestyles: and a culturally active society would be more likely to develop were informatics used to upgrade working conditions and skills and reduce weekly hours of employment.

Informatics could be used by an active citizenry to engage in more varied leisure and cultural activities, and to take part in and create new forms of social participation. Indeed, using the technology in this way − by making interactive services available to individuals and communities − might render increased leisure more attractive for many working people. We would see household consumption shifting from services to goods, with people applying informal labour to help produce many of their own final services. In some cases this 'production' would imply little more creativity than that involved in selecting a videotape; but the potential would be there for access to more educational opportunities, more networking of people with common interests, more use of recreational facilities and development of specialist services.

Social welfare

The shift toward self-servicing may be expected to continue within areas that are largely catered for by social services. Many services are likely to remain a matter of collective organization, and the main issues may surround 'community care' versus central provision. Informatics could be used to improve community facilities – monitoring the circumstances of pensioners, relating the need for services to provisions at a local level, supplying access to expert systems for paraprofessionals in health and welfare (along the lines of the computerized benefit claim systems used by some Citizens' Advice Bureaux).

The trend toward community care is deeply ambiguous. It combines genuine recognition of the problems of impersonal, bureaucratized service organizations – oriented toward cure rather than prevention, labelling and institutionalizing their clients, allowing them little autonomy and creating dependency – with cynical efforts to reduce costs and to shift the burden of care onto charities and families. And in the background in Britain is the pressure towards the privatization of (profitable) areas of social service. This tendency toward a two-tier structure of welfare services is found sufficiently threatening by most employees in public services to reduce their interest in innovation: it is difficult constructively to criticize what one is desperately struggling to defend. By and large, privatization means allowing the relatively privileged to jump queues and segregate themselves from other social strata. But valuable experiments in care for the elderly, education, and self-help are taking place outside of the public services (though often with their financial support). Furthermore, alongside institutional moves in the direction of community care are attempts to develop alternative services along the lines of free schools and self-help health groups. (Social innovators could learn a great deal from the experience of different countries in these respects: for example, the extremely original educational experiments of the Folk High Schools in Denmark.) It would be possible to direct informatics toward advancing and promoting their methods.

These strategies will interact with the ongoing shift toward self-service provision. Self-servicing in areas of health and education (and social and political organization) is bound to grow with the cheapening of informatics. Public and voluntary services, then, need to capitalize on these developments. This might mean pressing for community access to informatics facilties (so that these do not remain the preserve of the more affluent or better educated), and designing appropriate intermediate services. It might involve improving the scope and quality of both routine and non-routine service delivery, as part of a wider strategy of rebuilding social services to cater for the needs of late industrial society. Just as new technologies, by offering possibilities for product and process change, simultaneously threaten employment in private services and offer possibilities for demand expansion through reduced costs or new facilities, so may public services face a choice of whether merely to rationalize existing practices, and thus save costs, or to develop new services, and perhaps gain wider public support for their efforts.

Critical issues for information society
We have contrasted a strategy of social innovation with other possible information societies: societies based on protectionism and greater social dualism. But the leap in the dark that we have tried to illuminate is by no means assured of a comfortable landing. Any process of technical change unevenly benefits people at different locations in a structure of social inequality. People may differ in their financial or cognitive abilities to make use of the technology, or to assess how its use by others will impinge upon them. Some inequalities could be amplified. Therefore the reduction of major inequalities should be explicitly incorporated as a goal in the design of information society. Otherwise, poorer communities are liable to receive poorer services, women are likely to be accorded greater burdens of caring, etc. the key issues include:

— the *distribution* of informatics resources. Infrastructural provision is of considerable importance in *regional* development and in the rise and decline of *urban* areas. Given the potential of informatics for making training and information services available, the provision of facilities for *social groups* disadvantaged by restructuring is of considerable importance. This may involve policies of positive discrimination, and adaptation of different media (or their 'programmes') to different social groups.
— the *design* of informatics. How far do the technologies permit interactivity rather than just expand the transmission of information in hierarchical structures? This raises questions for the design of infrastructure: whether the nodes of the cable systems can communicate with each other, rather than act as mere passive receivers of broadcast information as in a root-and-branch system; whether the systems have sufficient channel capacity to carry two-way video signals, and so on. The state and the market are unlikely to promote – or even formulate – the whole range of social innovations here. It will be necessary for a wide range of interest groups to evaluate technical alternatives and affect the process of technical change. Given that choices with long-term consequences are already under way, it is important that debate and analysis of these alternatives be promoted more widely.

Given the eventual importance of these issues for the future quality of life, the *public debate* on these issues is muted to the point of inaudibility. The questions posed above, together with those about the implications for privacy and the possibilities of public surveillance and control, all need to be asked *before* the systems are developed and installed. Firms and telecommunications authorities, in this country and elsewhere, are busily designing and building: where is the debate?

Notes

1. The authors are currently funded by the Joseph Rowntree Memorial Trust, to which we express our gratitude. Rather than provide numerous notes, we cite below only the main texts relevant to our arguments.

2. The main theoretical contribution on post-industrial society is Bell (1974); see also Kahn et al. (1976). Provably the best critique of the political assumptions of post-industrialism is Kleinberg (1973). The 'silent revolution' in values is the theme of Inglehart (1977). An early statement of our views concerning the social and psychological approaches of this school is Miles (1975); see also Miles (1980). The information society dichotomies we outline are drawn from Colombo and Lanzavecchia (1982); for similar perspectives see a related collection, Barry et al. (1982). The most influential proponent of an information sector is Porat (1977).

3. Our discussion follows Gershuny and Miles (1983). See also Gershuny (1983) and Gershuny and Miles (1985). The term 'prosumer' is introduced in Toffler (1981), one of the better popular books attempting to explicate information society. The OECD text is an output of its series 'Information Computer Communications Policy' (1981).

4. The most interesting study of long waves is Freeman, Clark and Soete (1982). For the relation between automation and the economic crisis, see Kaplinsky (1984). See also various papers (especially those by Freeman and Coombes) in Martstrand (1984).

5. For a wide-ranging account of potential uses of cable systems, see the CNET/INA volume (1983); also relevant are the collections on information society referred to in note 2, and the popular discussions of Grossbrenner (1983) and Nilles (1982).

6. Our thinking here has been enriched by the work of Carlota Perez Perez: in particular by discussions around her papers in *Futures* (1983) and *World Development* (1985).

References

Barry, U., L. Bannon and O. Holst (eds) (1982) *Information Technology: Impact on the Way of Life.* Dublin: Tycooly.

Bell, D. (1974) *The Coming of Post-Industrial Society.* New York: Basic Books.

CNET/INA (1983) *Images pour le Cable.* Paris: La Documentation Française. (Centre National d'Etude des Télécommunications/Institut National de la Communication Audiovisuelle).

Colombo, J. and G. Lanzavecchia (1982) 'The Transition to an Information Society', in N. Bjorn-Andersen, M. Earl, O. Holst and E. Mumford (eds), *Information Society: For Richer, For Poorer.* Amsterdam: North Holland.

Freeman, C., J. Clark and L. Soete (1982) *Unemployment and Technical Innovation.* London: Frances Pinter.

Gershuny, J. (1983) *Social Innovation and the Division of Labour.* London: Oxford University Press.

Gershuny, J. and I. Miles (1983a) *The New Service Economy.* London: Frances Pinter.

Gershuny, J. and I. Miles (1983b) 'Towards a New Social Economics', in B. Roberts,

R. Finnegan and D. Gallie (eds), *New Approaches to Economic Life.* Manchester: Manchester University Press. (Published in 1985.)

Grossbrenner, A. (1983) *Personal Computer Communications.* New York: St Martin's Press.

Inglehart, R. (1977) *The Silent Revolution.* Princeton: N.J., Princeton University Press.

Kahn, H., W. Brown and L. Martell (1976) *The Next 200 Years.* New York: Morrow.

Kaplinksy, R. (1984) *Automation.* London: Longman.

Kleinberg, B. (1973) *American Society in the Post-Industrial Age.* Columbus, Ohio: Charles E. Merril.

Martstrand, P. (ed.) (1984) *New Technology and the Future of Work and Skills.* London: Frances Pinter.

Miles, I. (1975) *The Poverty of Predication.* Farnborough, Hants: Saxon House.

Miles, I. (1980) 'Effacing the Political Future', *Futures,* (12) 6: 436–52.

Nilles, J.M. (1982) *Exploring the World of the Personal Computer.* Englewood Cliffs, N.J.: Prentice-Hall.

OECD (1981) *Information Activities, Electronics and Telecommunications Technologies.* Vol. 1. Paris: Organization for Economic Cooperation and Development.

Perez Perez, C. (1983) 'Structural Change and Assimilation of New Technologies in the Economic and Social Systems', *Futures,* October: 357–74.

Perez Perez, C. (1985 forthcoming) 'Microelectronics, Long Waves and World Structural Change', *World Development.*

Porat, M. (1977) *The Information Economy.* Office of Technology Special Publication, US Department of Commerce; Washington, D.C.: Government Printing Office.

Toffler, A. (1981) *The Third Wave.* London: Pan.

3

Information and some economics of the information revolution

Stan Metcalfe

In this chapter it is proposed to discuss some general issues relating to the activities of producing and communicating information, and to consider briefly the development of cable television in the UK as an example of the market-led development of a new information technology. In the course of this discussion I wish to highlight three considerations. First, that the significance of a technology is to be judged in terms of its degree of economic and social application and that this depends upon the services which the new technology provides relative to those provided by existing technologies. It is dimensions of economic and social performance which are crucial, not simply the dimensions of technological performance, and there is no necessarily simple relationship between the two dimensions. Secondly, while the creation of any new technological opportunity may provide an impulse to economic activity, the working through of this impulse is a gradual competitive process in which new activities displace existing activities. During this competitive process both new and existing technologies are often improved and mutually adapted to the new situation. In understanding these mechanisms a historical perspective appears of particular value. Thirdly, in taking a broad perspective upon information technology it is important to distinguish implications for the internal operation of organizations from implications for market relations between the producers and consumers of information services. Not only will the boundary between internal organization and market be affected by new information technologies, the very idea of a market in information services is subject to difficulties in that information is not a conventional economic commodity. For this reason we conclude with some discussion of cable television, since this activity involves the market provision of new information services in the form of entertainment. In identifying cable television with the provision of information services we are explicitly recognizing the links between media activities and information activities in general.

Information and economic progress

Among the many stylized facts of modern economic growth, none is more instructive than the one which identifies advances in knowledge as the mainspring of economic growth and development. Economic historians together with historians of science and technology have identified a sequence of developments in materials and energy technologies which, in the period since 1750, radically transformed the economic and social organization of the world. However, at least since the publication in 1776 of Adam Smith's *Wealth of Nations* (1945), if not before, students of society have also recognized that man's command over nature depends not only upon an intellectual mastery of science and technology but equally upon a capacity to organize the social process of production. Central to Smith's insight was the concept of the division of labour as a principle of economic and social organization: this principle to be interpreted not simply in broad occupational terms — the butcher, the baker and the candlestick maker — but in terms of the specialization of task within occupations for which the famous pin factory provided the perfect exemplar.

Now the force of the division of labour is to raise human productivity but to do so at a cost which reflects two organizational problems posed by specialization. The solution to these problems requires the continual creation and communication of information, that is, the division of labour created the information society. The first problem is that of organization or teamwork narrowly defined, the coordination of many specialized tasks within an institution such as a firm, a hospital, or a bureaucracy of any kind. Here the information problem is to see that each individual knows what to do, to marshall the appropriate inputs and to ensure that they are carried out in the right sequence in the most economical way. To achieve this objective the organization must collect, manipulate, store and disseminate information within its field of coordination. These activities require resource inputs and naturally they also benefit from the division of labour. As the scale and range of operations of the organization increase so do its information requirements and, frequently, effective growth will require organizational innovations which change the internal information gathering, processing and disseminating systems.[1]

The second information problem relates to the effective coordination of the activities of different organizations and of individuals operating outside organizations. The classic statement of this problem is posed by coordination within a market economy, in which the individual plans of many consumers and producers are reconciled by the price mechanism such that there is a mutual consistency of planned actions to buy and sell. The market mechanism is a fundamental social institution and its operation depends upon the availability of two types of information: about conditional intentions to buy and sell, and about the identity of buyers and sellers. In practice this information is gathered and processed directly by firms or indirectly by the specialized middlemen and traders which make up the wholesale and retail trades. In a developing world of ever-changing demand structures and technologies these information problems are certainly non-trivial.

In short, because of its dependence upon the division of labour modern society requires for its development a complex information system which creates information, communicates information between agents at a point in time, and permits the storage of information so that it can be transmitted over time.

Information activities

In all but the simplest societies, where the only form of communication is verbal, the set of institutions which perform the information gathering, communicating and storing activities is inevitably complex. This complexity arises to a great extent because of the complexity and variety of forms in which information is required for the effective operation and development of modern society. To speak of an information revolution *simpliciter* courts the danger of missing important distinctions between different categories of information, and the different conditions in which they are produced and applied. It must be recognized first that the cognitive capacity of individual brains is limited, so it is not efficient to require that everyone knows about everything. Indeed a central problem in organization theory is precisely to create a division of task, and thus of access to knowledge, which prevents individual information overload. The extent to which different categories of information are disseminated is thus a matter of prime importance. Some knowledge should be widely disseminated, for example, that in the UK one drives to the left, while, at the other extreme, a piece of information may only need to be communicated between two individuals. A second axis of complexity is provided by the fact that some knowledge is codified while other knowledge is tacit and exists only in individual minds. Methods of access to the two types of information are vastly different. However, for our purposes, the most relevant distinctions relate to the uses to which knowledge and information can be directed. At this point we can no longer escape a more precise definition of information. Following Machlup we shall define information as the flow of knowledge between different individuals, that is as the transmission of a state of knowing.

From this perspective information activities are concerned with changing states of knowing, they are 'effectively designed to create, alter or confirm in a human mind – one's own or anyone else's – a meaningful appreciation, awareness, cognizance or consciousness of whatever it might be' (Machlup, 1980: 186). Creation of knowledge, storage of knowledge and transmission of knowledge are the functions involved in all information activities. In terms of the outcomes resulting from changing states of knowledge we can identify three broad classes of information activity: providing final consumer services; providing services of a capital nature when the change in states of knowledge is relevant for future production of conventional goods and services or further knowledge; and providing intermediate services used as inputs in the current production process. Live theatre, scientific research and weather reports for farmers provide illustrative examples of each type of activity.[2] Clearly different information activities require different institutions and mechanisms for their production and dissemination. Furthermore, the effects of advances in information technology are certain to be very different in their impacts upon these different kinds of activity, and this is central to any understanding of the information revolution.

It is a characteristic of a developing society that its requirements for all these kinds of information increase with the level of development. The growing scale of production, rising standard of living and extending division of labour increase the demand for knowledge while, on the supply side, the stock of knowledge has its own internal dynamic – a tendency to exponential growth as knowledge cumulatively builds upon knowledge.[3] Quite remarkably, the measured stock of knowledge tends to grow at rates well in excess of recorded economic growth (cf. Kendrick, 1976). Moreover, stocks of knowledge have expanded at rates in excess of the growth of labour productivity in the creation, dissemination and storage of information: hence the well documented tendency for the proportion of the population engaged in the information sector to rise over time.[4] The productivity gap between agricultural, manufacturing and information activities is all the more remarkable given the long history of technological innovation in the information sector. Indeed while the advances associated with the convergence of computing and telecommunications are of profound importance, they also represent an important element of historical continuity in the growing productivity of information activities.

Previous information revolutions
This is not the place to engage in a detailed exegisis of information technology past or present,[5] but it is worthwhile drawing attention to

the long historical sequence of developments in information technology. In simple societies the technology of communication is dominated by direct personal contact and the only means for storing knowledge lie within folklore and the society's culture. It is obvious that the information demands of a society based upon the division of labour are incompatible with such primitive information technology, and in historical terms one can identify a sequence of important innovations which greatly facilitated the creation of knowledge, its communication and storage. These innovations overcame the tyranny of time and distance and permitted the extension of the division of labour to its modern degree.

The first and most obvious improvements in information technology came with the great transport revolutions, associated with shipping, railways, the automobile and aircraft. By lowering the costs of transporting individuals, they greatly reduced the real costs of communication and encouraged greater interpersonal transmission of information. Moreover, the greater freedom to travel had profound effects on man's knowledge of the physical environment, stimulating advances in the knowledge base which continue today in the exploration of the hostile environments of the seabed and space. The second major strand of technical development relates to printing, paper, the book and its derivatives from about 1450 onwards. Again the effects were profound. By embodying information in a durable, easily transportable form, information could now move independently from the movement of people and at negligible real cost. Thus the book, the newspaper and the letter capitalized upon the innovations in physical transportation. Perhaps, more significantly, the book permitted the storage of information and its transmission over time, so that each generation could build upon the codified knowledge of its predecessors without the risk of continually reinventing the wheel. Indeed, without the book and the vitally important institution of the library the development of society as we know it would have been impossible. The book permitted societies for the first time to create and house a collective memory.[6]

More recently, a quite different strand has emerged — that of tele-communications innovations, associated with the telegraph, the telephone and finally radio and television. Neither movement of people nor codified knowledge are now necessary for communication, which can proceed independently from conventional transport technology and may ultimately be freed from the technologies of printing and paper.

It is within this context that one should view the modern developments in computer and communications technology. The environment in which these technologies will develop is the environment of existing information societies, in which there are established technologies and institutions for creating, communicating and storing information. The acceptance of the new technologies will depend upon their performance relative to existing technologies and this will vary with the precise information activity and its economic and social context. Only if they generate cost advantages or superior information services will the new technologies be adopted. The profundity of these effects follows not from the radically new directions of technological change but rather from the centrality of information activities to modern societies.

The impacts of new technology

To assess the impact of new information technologies it is important to distinguish the two kinds of information problem that we have associated with the division of labour. Information activities internal to organizations will be affected, as will those which require the production and exchange of information services. Indeed one important consequence is likely to be a change in the boundary between those activities internal to the organization and those involving exchange with other organizations. For example, the economies of scale associated with computer technology make it efficient for some information activities currently carried out individually by organizations to be contracted out to specialist providers of these information services on a market basis. While we shall expand on the market economies of information activity below, we now turn to the question of the impact of the new technologies.

A first principle to be guided by is that the economic effects of new technologies build up gradually in a process of competition with and displacement of existing technologies. That the effects are gradual and not immediate relates to a number of issues. The uncertainty surrounding both the uses to which the new technology may be put and its relative advantages slow the growth of demand, as do the perceptions of consumers, workers and managers formed with respect to established technology. The more radical is a new technology, the greater will be the constraints of uncertainty and convention upon its use. Furthermore the relative advantages associated with the new information technology depend on the organizational environment in which it is to be placed. To optimize the use of the technology will often require changes in organizational structure and work patterns which impose additional costs of change over and above the direct capital costs of the new technology.[7] On the supply side it takes time to build up capacity to supply relevant equipment and infrastructure, time to train a labour force, and time to build up expertise in supplying information services based on the new technology.

One way of viewing this process of absorption is to compare the problem of competition between technologies with the ecological problem of competition between populations for a given environment. The new technology has a niche and the rate of diffusion into this niche is determined by the factors outlined above. However, one should not imagine that a technology's niche is invariant over time. In particular, important technologies are rarely if ever fully developed at their time of initial market introduction. Rather they implicitly present an agenda for development, an agenda to be explored progressively in directions which frequently depend upon experience gained in the use of that technology. Such induced improvements in the technology continually redefine and expand its equilibrium niche. Matters are further complicated when we recognize that the success of any one technology may depend upon development in a cluster of complementary technologies such that the application of one component depends crucially upon the state of technology in other elements of the cluster. The pressures and inducements to advance technology then become interdependent as successive bottlenecks and imbalances in performance suggest fruitful paths of development. The advances in telecommunications illustrate this point well. Enhanced powers of manipulation of data have created a potential for communicating data beyond the capacity of analogue telephony systems, and this imbalance has been removed by the development of high-capacity communications networks based upon satellite, cable and digital transmission technologies.

It is hardly surprising that one cannot foresee with any accuracy the impact of new communications technologies. The very process of their application will further advance these technologies and suggest functions that are only tenuously perceived, if at all, by today's observers. Indeed this is one reason why the effects of technology upon employment often appear so drastic. It is apparent that labour will be displaced from identifiable existing activities and, although it is usually possible to identify some compensation from employment in the construction of a communications infrastructure and associated hardware, it is extremely difficult to foresee the longer-run compensation which arises only gradually as the technologies are diffused and new activities are generated. The history of technical change is one in which, in overall terms, compensation outweighed displacement while at the same time having major effects on the occupational structure of the labour force, as new skills are defined and old skills become obsolete. For this reason, our knowledge of the qualitative impact of new information technologies would be substantially enhanced by historical studies of the development and application of previous technological revolutions in the handling and communication of information (cf. de Sola Pool, 1983).

The market economics of information activities

Because the impact of new communications technologies will depend to a considerable degree upon the supply of and demand for information services – creation, communication and storage – we turn now to some peculiar aspects of information as a marketable commodity.

As with all activities in a market economy, the crucial question is how rewards are linked to productive efforts, which inevitably involves questions as to the definition of property rights and their ultimate sanction in law. Information activities create and handle intellectual property and we can begin by identifying some serious impediments to the efficiency of a market economy in linking the demand for and supply of information activities.

First we note the sharp distinction between the efforts involved to create new knowledge and the efforts involved to communicate that knowledge subsequently to enquiring individuals. The creation of any new knowledge, irrespective of the degree of imagination employed, involves a once for all outlay of time and effort which does not need to be repeated, and is quite independent of the extent to which that knowledge is subsequently put to use. A greater demand spreads the fixed costs of creation over a greater information output, creates increasing returns to application and generates a natural tendency towards a monopoly of the information-creating activities in question. In the market for data bases, for example, this raises serious regulatory issues which involve not only questions of competition and monopoly in the economic sense but also questions monopoly control over access to information. Similar issues surround the economics of communications networks which also fall into the category of natural monopoly.

The second aspect of knowledge creation relates to the inherent uncertainty in the links between efforts and outcomes and between outcomes and market demand. All knowledge creation is a risky process, and this is one reason why major investments in knowledge creation, for example, scientific research, are publicly funded. On the buyer's side there is equally a problem of risk, in that the nature of information cannot be entirely known before it is purchased, for if it were, the seller would have divulged the information in question and sacrificed the property rights without extracting payment. It is largely for this reason that questions of seller reputation and buyer goodwill play such an important part in the markets for information activities.

Each of the above issues relates to the difficulty of establishing property rights in knowledge and thus strikes to the core of the problem of linking rewards to effort. Uncertainty as to outcomes and their valuations diminishes the incentive to engage in information-creating activity, while the fact that knowledge is more costly to create than to communicate or imitate means those who do not generate the knowledge may still capture a share of the rewards from application. The patent and copyright systems are imperfect ways of coping with this difficulty, and the consequence of these imperfections is to reduce the returns to creativity and create a premium upon secrecy, neither of which are conducive to efficiency in the exploitation and creation of information.

The most important peculiarity of knowledge, from an economic point of view, lies in its nature as a public good. With knowledge there is non-rivalry in use, for any individual's awareness of an item of information in no way restricts the potential ability of any other individual to acquire that information. This creates problems in identifying the market demand for particular classes of knowledge and in excluding individuals from access to that knowledge on a basis of willingness to pay – the conventional way of repaying production labour. Within the technology of information activities, solutions to the public-goods problem have proceeded along two clear routes. The first, where the information is produced in non-durable form, is to limit physical access to the information in question. This is the method basic to the economics of the performing arts, whereby the theatre, concert hall and sports arena create a barrier which can only be surmounted by payment of the appropriate fee. In that way rivalry in access to information is re-established and a revenue base generated to support artistic creativity. The second route has proceeded to embody information in durable objects which are themselves private goods. The book, the record and, more recently, video are the classic examples of this phenomenon and they provide a revenue base from which the creators of the appropriate knowledge can be rewarded for their efforts. Even so, they are not perfect solutions. Copyright can be evaded, piracy is a recurring problem in video and record markets and, most obvious of all, the library is precisely an institution which could not operate without the public-good nature of knowledge.

While the technologies of the book and the record partially solve the public-goods problem, other mass communications technologies actively exploit the publicness dimension. Here the public-good nature of information is explicit and with it the difficulty in excluding individuals from off-air reception on the basis of their willingness to pay. There is no unambiguous way of assessing market demand for such public goods or of relating demand for service to the willingness to supply service. The consequence is that broadcasting services have to be financed either from taxation or from advertising revenue, that is, independently from the direct consumption of entertainment information.

While the above problems apply in various degrees to all entertainment services it is instructive to turn to the provision of entertainment services via cable television to illustrate in more concrete terms some aspects of the new information technologies.

Cable television in the UK[8]

A convenient but misleading focus for much public debate about information technology has been provided by the UK government's plans to foster the development of broad-band cable television. Here the declared aim is to promote cable television as one means to a greater end, namely 'To develop and exploit the most modern telecommunications infrastructure to meet the needs of commerce and industry while simultaneously meeting the social and domestic needs of all parts of the country' (Home Office, 1983). Cable television has been presented as a telecommunications revolution but as with many revolutions it can claim a long history. A cable television industry has existed in the UK since the advent of broadcasting, developing as a relay system to serve areas with poor off-air reception. Indeed in 1981 some 14 per cent of UK TV households were connected to cable systems. However, these traditional cable systems faced severe problems of commercial decline. Limited by the 1949 Wireless Telegraphy Act to relay activities only, their natural market was eclipsed by the development of the off-air broadcasting network which currently provides high-quality reception to all but 1 per cent of the UK population. Moreover, capacity of cable companies to conduct experiments in community and subscription television under the provisions of the 1969 Post Office Act were limited by the obsolete 'twisted-pair' cable technology which restricted the service to generally four and at most six channels of television.

The developments in modern cable technology render such systems obsolete, for they provide the technological opportunity to bring into households upwards of thirty TV channels, together with interactive services. The emerging technological opportunities coincided with a change to a government eager to promote the case for the entrepreneurial development of new technology. The change in climate was indeed remarkable, for as late as 1977 Lord Annan's Committee of Enquiry had argued firmly against the private development of cable TV in the UK (Home Office, 1977). Yet within five years this negative response had been replaced by an atmosphere of euphoria with modern cable systems promoted as a vehicle for bringing households into the age of information technology. First, the report of the Information Technology Advisory Panel (1982), followed by Lord Hunt's Committee of Enquiry (Home Office, 1982) and finally the White Paper of April 1983 (Home Office, 1983) defined a new climate for cable systems while the first eleven franchises were allocated in January 1984. The essential principles of cable development as laid down in the White Paper were as follows.

On cable technology: entrepreneurs may install any viable technology subject to its meeting specific minimum performance standards and providing the capacity for two-way interactive services.

On the franchising and licensing process: this is to be controlled by a statutory Cable Authority (established in 1984) which organizes and oversees the franchise bidding process and allocates licences to install cables and monopoly franchises to provide cable services.

On programme services: franchise holders must carry all existing British Broadcasting Corporation (BBC) and local Independent Broadcasting Authority (IBA) transmissions but otherwise have a free hand apart from questions of public taste and decency.

For our purposes it is best to begin by distancing ourselves from the claims and counter-claims about the viability of cable systems and by identifying a number of reasons why the study of cable TV is of interest. Firstly, cable TV systems illustrate the changing boundaries which exist between traditional entertainment media and other information activities and their unification within electronic information technology. While the initial stages of cable development will be based on the provision of entertainment services, it is generally foreseen that cable systems will provide in the longer run a wide range of intermediate information services to households, including home shopping and banking, electronic mail, and access to data bases of a conventional or expert kind. In providing these services cable systems will be enmeshed in all the difficult problems of establishing markets for information, for the infrastructure and hardware of cable systems is only a means to an end, viz., the supply of information services which households are willing to buy.

A second reason for an interest in cable systems is that they exemplify the nature of competition at the early stages of the development of new technologies. There are competing design configurations for cable systems depending upon network design and the choice of optical fibre or co-axial transmission, and cable technology as a whole is in competition with other information technologies. On the one hand there is the telephone network which, if upgraded to a full digital system, would provide formidable competition as a means of access to data bases and other intermediate services. On the other hand there are developments in satellite technology which introduce direct broadcasting by satellite (DBS) as a potential competitor for cable systems in the market for broadcasting services. The uncertainties about respective market niches are further enhanced when it is realized that all of these technologies have considerable potential for future development, and will draw upon further advances in optical and electronic signal processing.

The third aspect of the development of cable TV lies in its prospects for generating economic activity; in the creation of a communications infrastructure and appropriate hardware, in the operation and maintenance of systems, and in the creation of entertainment and information services. Clear prospects for job creation can be foreseen but their extent and timing will depend crucially upon the economics of cable systems. Finally, there are important issues for public policy in the promotion and regulation of new technological activities in the information sector. The current UK government has promoted a policy of incremental, market-led development of cable systems, with finance from the private sector and decisions as to service and technology in the hands of cable entrepreneurs. However, public policy cannot leave cable without any regulating provision, in part because cable franchises are natural monopolies, and also because of the influence of broadcasting media on public opinion and the perceived need to satisfy minimum standards of public taste and decency. In this respect the UK policy stance is very different from that of France and Germany, where there is substantial public-sector funding of cable development and a commitment, in France in particular, to the creation of advanced technology systems based upon fibre optics.

The fundamental economic issues with respect to cable television relate to the public-good nature of existing broadcasting activities, the monopoly nature of cable franchises, and the time phasing of costs and revenues in cable networks. It is the chief characteristic of cable transmission that it provides a means for excluding individuals from reception and for charging for broadcast entertainment services in proportion to the volume of services consumed. In this way a market is created and cable entrepreneurs will be able to levy differential charges according to the strength of demand, and to relate their programme and investment strategies to these market signals.

For the prospective cable entrepreneur the important question becomes that of the willingness of consumers to pay for access to an expanded range of entertainment services, given that the service must include existing public broadcasts from the BBC and IBA as part of the overall programme package. Willingness to pay will naturally depend on the quality of programmes as well as their variety, and so the response of the programme-making industry to the opportunities provided by cable will be a principal determinant of the success of cable systems as providers of entertainment services. Here again we see the significance of the service as distinct from the communications hardware in determining the success of new information technology systems. Not surprisingly, little is yet known about the demand for cable services and how it varies across socio-economic groups or with the allocation of leisure time. Swindon Cable is the only one of the initial franchises to have commenced operation, with a thirteen-channel service, charging an annual fee of £165 together with a monthly charge of £8 for the basic programme package and an extra £7 for premium programmes.

On the supply side there is the problem of natural monopoly which arises from the dominant position of the indivisible and fixed costs of infrastructure and programming in the supply of cable services. It is simply cheaper to provide a service from a single cable system rather than from two or more cable systems. It is largely for this reason that the government is allocating monopoly franchises to cable systems but this naturally raises a number of regulatory problems which are likely to be shared by all information service activities. Any monopoly implies distortions to the market process and these could turn a franchise into a 'licence to print money' if conditions were right.

Clearly, the scale of market demand and the rate at which cable penetrates a franchise are important factors determining franchise profitability and one can foresee a willingness to cable densely populated urban areas but a complete lack of interest in rural and small-town cable systems. It is obvious that the market for franchises does not cohere with the government's declared objective of developing a national broad-band network on the back of cable television. It is almost certain that the government will need to exert a firm guiding hand in the design of cable franchise boundaries. A degree of regulation has already been applied with the policy of a competition for a cable franchise, and with licences issued for a duration of no more than twenty years. Whether this competitive process will be effective in limiting abuse of monopoly power remains to be seen.

The economics of cable are also greatly influenced by the fact that a substantial part of the fixed costs of operation, the overwhelming component of the cost structure, have to be incurred prior to commencing service irrespective of the scale of demand. Consequently all cable systems will have a negative cash flow in the initial years; indeed it may take a decade to break even and longer before the present value of profits exceeds the compounded value of initial losses.[9]

In the light of these considerations a slow development of cable is not difficult to predict. The profitability of a franchise is sensitive to programming costs, the rate of market penetration and the rate of interest. Uncertainty about demand, and high real rates of interest have certainly contributed to the problems faced by many franchises. More fundamentally, the prospect of a rapid rate of technical improvement in cable systems together with the delay in the development of demand are powerful reasons for delaying the investment in cable. Paradoxically the anticipation of future technological and market development can result in a slowing down in the actual pace of development of a new-technology-based activity (cf. Metcalfe et al., 1983). Supply-side constraints are also important both with respect to the availability of UK-produced equipment and with respect to programme material. So we find a familiar situation of interdependence between the development of the components of complex new-technology-based activities. If no component can take the lead in stimulating development then the application of the innovations may be severely curtailed. In this respect the government's unwillingness to recognize the difficulties faced by cable entrepreneurs is certainly not consistent with a desire to establish a national broad-band network.

In summary, we see within the emerging cable television industry a number of the general issues which will affect the development of all information technologies in the new communications era. The uncertain nature of demand, the problem of rewarding the creators of information services and the tendency toward natural monopoly will be of general significance and will pose major regulatory issues for any government. The success of any new information activity will depend upon its competitive edge over rival, existing activities and cable systems will not be exempt from this rule. In this the quality of the information service will be the final arbiter and this will depend on a complex of economic and social considerations relating to the demand for and supply of information as well as upon the technical questions associated with the information infrastructure. As always the application of new technology is a question far too important to confine to matters of technology alone.

Notes

1. As brilliantly explored in Chandler (1977).

2. The difference between knowledge as intermediate input and knowledge as capital input rests on the different rates of obsolescence of the knowledge concerned. Yesterday's weather report is of no present or future value to the farmer but yesterday's discovery of a new grain variety may be of permanent value.

3. On the relation between the demand for communications services and the level of economic development, see Saunders and Warford (1983). The exponential growth of scientific knowledge was first identified by de Solla Price (1963).

4. Cf. Bell (1979). According to the figures there quoted, the proportion of the US civilian labour force employed in the information sector has risen from 12.8 per cent in 1900 to 46 per cent in 1970.

5. A recently published dictionary (Longley and Shain, 1982), contains four hundred pages with roughly eighteen items per page.

6. In this category of technology should also be placed film technology since it too provided durable forms for pictorial information.

7. Cf. Discussion of the 'Xerox effect' in Macdonald and Mandeville (1983).

8. A more extensive discussion of the questions touched upon below can be found in Evans et al. (1983), Gibbons et al. (1984) and Metcalfe et al. (1985).

9. Hence the concern over the withdrawal of 100 per cent initial-year investment allowances in the 1985 Budget. The effect of this change should not be overestimated given the other problems faced by cable entrepreneurs.

References

Bell, D. (1979) 'The Social Framework of the Information Society', in M.L. Dertouzos and J. Moses (eds), *The Computer Age: A Twenty-Year View*. Cambridge, Mass.: Massachusetts Institute of Technology.

Chandler, E. (1977) *The Visible Hand*. Harvard, Mass.: Harvard University Press.

Evans, J., J. Hartley, J. Simnett and J.S. Metcalfe (1983) *The Development of Cable Networks in the UK*. London: Technical Change Centre.

Gibbons, M., J. Hartley, J. Evans, J. Simnett and J.S. Metcalfe (1984) 'Technology and Policy in Cable TV Development in the UK', *Telecommunications Policy*, September: 223–35.

Home Office (1977) *Report of the Committee on the Future of Broadcasting*. Cmnd 6753. London: Her Majesty's Stationery Office.

Home Office (1982) *Report of the Inquiry into Cable Expansion and Broadcasting Policy* (Hunt Report). Cmnd 8679. London: Her Majesty's Stationery Office.

Home Office (1983) *The Development of Cable Systems and Services*. Cmnd 8866. London: Her Majesty's Stationery Office.

Information Technology Advisory Panel (1982) *Cable Systems*. London: Her Majesty's Stationery Office.

Kendrick, J. (1976) *The Formation of Stocks of Total Capital*. New York: National Bureau of Economic Research.

Longley, D. and M. Shain (1982) *Dictionary of Information Technology*. London: Macmillan.

Macdonald, S. and T. Mandeville (1983) 'Information Technology and Employment Levels', in D. Lamberton, S. McDonald and T. Mandeville (eds), *The Trouble with Technology*. London, Frances Pinter.

Machlup, F. (1980) *Knowledge: Its Creation, Distribution and Economic Significance*. Vol. 1. Princeton, N.J.: Princeton University Press.

Metcalfe, J.S., J. Evans, J. Hartley, M. Gibbons and J. Simnett (1983) 'The Economic Development of Cable TV in the UK', *Metroeconomica*, 35: 235–59.

Metcalfe, J.S., J. Simnett, J. Hartley, J. Evans and M. Gibbons (1985, forthcoming) 'The Economic and Technological Development of Cable TV Policy Making in an Era of Rapid Technological Change', *Transactions of the Manchester Statistical Society*.

Saunders, R.J. and G. Warford (1983) *Telecommunications and Economic Development*. Baltimore, Md.: Johns Hopkins University Press.

Smith, Adam (1945) *The Wealth of Nations*. Chapter 1. London: G. Bell and Sons (first published 1776).

de Sola Pool, I. (1983) *Forecasting the Telephone*. New York: Ablex.

de Solla Price, D.J. (1963) *Little Science, Big Science*. New York: Columbia University Press.

II
INDUSTRIAL, CULTURAL AND
SOCIAL STRATEGIES

4

The challenge of neo-technological determinism for communication systems, industry and culture

Marjorie Ferguson

The examination of a society's communications system reveals that it concerns more than decisions about spectrum allocation, digital transmission and switching, fibre optics, cable systems, deregulated telecommunications or geo-stationary orbit positions. Such decisions represent more than technical, market or organizational decisions about *means*. They are also political decisions about *ends*, and the particular social objectives − industrial, cultural or military − which communications systems contain and mediate.

The public policies which mould communications systems are also social policies − by design or by default. The social nature of decisions (or indecisions) about the ownership, regulation and accountability of information networks and entertainment services is evident in that they have intended or unintended consequences for individuals and groups as well as for the telecommunications or entertainment industries. A government's actions or inactions concerning its investment in or control over the communications system are no less social in their implications than are those which concern the distribution of income and wealth or the provision of health and education services.

The relevant choices are ones which involve familiar social issues: the maintenance of a plurality (or monopoly) of views, the openness or equity of access to them, the confidentiality of personal, state or corporate information, and the balance between public service and private profit in telecommunications or broadcasting. All point to the increasing social significance of communications systems over the past decade and the ways in which they are both cause and conse-quence of the convergence and integration of old and new information and entertainment technologies.

This chapter focuses on the two strands in these developments, the industrial and cultural strategies employed by governments of industrialized societies to achieve specific social policy ends through their communications systems. These are discussed firstly in relation to 'neo-technological determinism', that is the extent to which policy choices are technologically driven rather than socially derived. This technological imperative as a factor in the development and application of new communication services is examined also in its power for redefinition – its potential to alter not only the communications infrastructure but also previously understood categories of meaning and experience. For example, what is still meant by information and which categories of it belong in the public or private domains? Specific issues and examples of industrial and cultural strategies are then discussed before exploring the British case and the presumptive evidence it supplies about the intended and unintended consequences of neo-technologically-determined policies.

Neo-technological redefinition

The extent to which technologies are a 'deterministic' factor in industrial and cultural strategies is both an empirical and a comparative question. It is also a theoretical one. Who acts in which ways in whose interest to what effect are familiar questions to communication researchers and public policy scholars alike. The rapid expansion of communications modes and information processing capacities over the past decade points to their potential consequences. These concern their capacity to be of 'benefit' or 'detriment' to differing social groups as a capacity contingent on the ways in which they are *applied*; and the structure of institutional controls over the technologies themselves (Melody, 1973: 165).

To an extent the impact of their present and future application has been both over-amplified and under-estimated. Competing parables of progress and prosperity or of doom and disadvantage present the two faces of neo-technological determinism whereby these new technologies are (almost) entirely good, or (almost) entirely bad. What is common to both advocates and critics alike is the belief that telecommunications-assisted commerce and trade, and computer-assisted learning, design, manufacture and leisure could transform social life. Less evident a priori is the extent to which these technologies will remain the *means* by which such transformations are intentionally or unintentionally affected, or will themselves become transformed into *ends*.

This climate of change and uncertainty fosters several dynamic processes of redefinition. One such concerns the distinction between the public and the private spheres and the ways in which different societies already are using technologies to define and redefine the boundaries between the individual and the state and the social and the personal. Such processes of redefinition of what is public and what is private are also processes of interaction which extend beyond the individual to the state and influence relations between the two. This blurring of boundaries and conflation of categories extends beyond the social and political to challenge past certainties and shared meanings. The electronic means exist to redefine what we now understand by information, entertainment, communication, access, regulation, service, profit; or what we have hitherto experienced as education, training, work, leisure – or as government policy itself. The technologies themselves form part of this redefinition process. They, too, shape and are shaped by the universes which they are designed to serve (as one small episode illustrates – the initially negative consumer response to teletex and videotext subsequently led to a revision of their graphics and services).

When we explore the extent to which technology can determine industrial or cultural strategies we find that, historically, governments have used both to effect their social policy objectives. The introduction of extensive national railway systems in the nineteenth century, for example, served for many the economic goal of industrialization and the political goal of nationalism by fostering the transport of ideas as well as passengers and goods. The rapid development of mass circulation popular newspapers in Britain in the late nineteenth century attests to this. Similarly the historical development of telecommunications from the telegraph to telematics shows how a policy to further national defence can spur the development of more widely used communications systems (see, for example, Schiller, 1982).

This close relationship between departments of defence research and development (R&D), technological innovation and commercial application continues as a major role for the military in fostering and funding telecommunications research. This is illustrated by specific technologies which were first developed for military use, such as pulse code modulation (PCM) transmission, microwave and satellite communications, and packet switching. As noted by the Organization for Economic Cooperation and Development (OECD), 'increased government interest in telecommunications reflects the growing national security and defence importance of telecommunications and electronics generally . . . (they) will become increasingly important in terms of output and, more disputedly, of employment' (OECD, 1983: 111). Further evidence for this consortium of interest seems assured with research funding for the futuristic 'Star Wars' defence programme being developed in the United States, costed at $3.7 billion for 1986 (*Times*, 1985a).

Thus, just as public expenditure on military research represents a social policy grounded in defence strategies directed at protection against future threats to national security, so decisions about the industrial strategies of communication systems also involve social policy choices in terms of who will be included or excluded from their intended beneficial or unintended detrimental consequences.

Industrial strategies and technological priorities
Within national or global communications systems the arena of public policy where neo-technological determinism is most evident is that of industrial strategy. This refers to the extent to which technological imperatives take precedence over, or are conflated with, other social policy choices in the search for market leadership or a more competitive manufacturing and trading position in the global communications system.

The scramble to participate, to find both manufacturing and distribution 'niches' in the new technological world order, is a major feature of economic policy and industrial strategy amongst most developed nations around the world. It attests to the power of neo-technological determinism to shape such responses. Where does the impetus come from for this order of priority or this scale of potential transformation and social change? A society's record of invention and innovation relates to its underlying cultural assumptions as well as to its scientific and technological infrastructure, to its education, training, research and patent systems or its existing technology base. The cultural assumptions¬ and social policy choices which cumulatively produce this infrastructure are manifest in those areas of public expenditure which nourish R&D, for example tax and tariff policy, investment grants, or industrial restructuring.

Although public policy for industry has a long history in terms of episodes of protectionism, taxation, or public procurement, the emergence of 'innovation policy' as a part of government is a new development. It represents 'a fusion of science and technology policy and industrial policy' (Rothwell and Zegveld, 1981: 1). The innovation policies relevant to communications are those intended to stimulate competitiveness with new technology hardware and software. The differing responses of governments to this challenge are primarily directed towards structural changes within the economy. The winding down of 'sunset', and the gearing up of 'sunrise' industries are no longer purely domestic policies with consequences for national communication systems. They are 'part of domestic adjustment to international trade' and employ specific mechanisms such as the fostering of inward capital investment and bilateral trade agreements, or the provision of grants, loans or R&D finance, or by the control of technology imports and exports through quotas, tariffs or licensing (Hills, 1984: 17).

These strategies which are promoted as innovative or expansive are more often reactive and defensive, representing as they do the responses of differing governments to the trading dominance of two nations – the United States and Japan. The comparative approach provides insights into the expansion of state (and industry) control, and the emergence of telecommunications as the global routes for competitive commerce and trade. In this context no country's communication system, innovation policy or industrial strategy should be analysed in isolation. Rather, cross-national analysis must be used to show us the relative status of aspirant traders, as well as world leaders. For example, it enables us to see 'the United States not as above or different from other nations, but as subject to the same inexorable forces of the growing intrusion of the state in all sectors and global economic competition' (Milward and Francisco, 1983: 290).

This charge is relevant to American industrial strategies aimed at maintaining its world leadership in computing and telecommunications, and to the alternative explanations offered by sceptics of the benign or beneficial nature of neo-technologically determined policies in general. Is the 'communications revolution' a coordinated attempt on the part of transnational corporations to push governments in the direction of 'public policy for private profit', as various writers assert? The case against any such collusion of the public and private spheres is argued by Schiller (1982):[1]

> It has not therefore, been some inert and mute new technology called telematics that has carried us over the threshold of an information age. The reality is that business users demanding advanced telematics services have mustered policy makers' support effectually, so as to enhance their private control over not merely information technology – but our economy and society as a whole (p. 105).

One reason for the worldwide leadership of the United States in information technology has been its strong national R&D tradition funded by the military. Together, industrial output in telecommunications, and government and industrial investment and sales in computers, contributed to a $6.9 billion balance of trade surplus in 1981 in computers and business machines alone (Office of Technology Assessment, 1983: 72). With structural shifts in industry and increased international competitiveness the full extent of government investment in specific technologies can only be approximate, particularly as no figures are divulged by the Department of Defense. However an estimate of federal funding, given in Table 4.1, shows that the total amount spent by just six civilian departments rose from $825.5 million in 1980 to $1561.6 million in 1983[2] – ample evidence of

TABLE 4.1

Estimated federal funding of specific technologies by major R&D agencies[a]
for fiscal years 1980 and 1983 (in millions of current dollars)

	1980	1983
Computer science	113.7	149.4
Material science	196.9	232.2
Engineering robotics	283.0	599.7
Bioengineering	231.9	580.3
Total	825.5	1561.6

Source: Congressional Budget Office (1984): extracted from Table 9, p. 67.

[a]Figures for the following agencies are included: National Institute of Health, National Science Foundation, National Bureau of Standards, National Aeronautics and Space Administration, Department of Agriculture, Department of Energy. The Department of Defense is not included.

the relative scale of investment required of countries who aspire to trading partner status with the United States.

For its promoters in government and industry, the relationship between technological innovation and economic development is logical, positive and inevitable, and here Japan provides a singular example of how innovation policy can be applied to the fields of consumer, telecommunications and computer technologies. It has supported innovative policy as its industrial strategy to staggering effect. The early policy measures it took in the 1970s to promote the information industry included financial assistance for hardware and software research and development; loans to software companies and information processing service firms; restrictions on foreign investments and import regulations prior to 1976 when Japan's computer industry was not yet self-supporting; tariff policies to protect industry; and the incorporation of academic theories and patent information into a data bank system to assist research and development (OECD, 1981).[3] Using such means, Japan easily moved into the first league of telecommunications manufacturing nations, with its annual technological exports of computer hardware, software and consumer electronics running at ¥184.9 billion in 1983 (Statistics Bureau, Prime Minister's Office, 1983), second only to the United States.

What of those nations less well placed industrially, culturally or socially to adopt the Japanese approach? The inability to achieve competitive or self-sufficient status is a problem for countries such as those of Europe where smaller scientific–technological infra-structures cannot sustain infant high-technology industries, nor compete with American ones stimulated by huge defence and space programmes. Smaller countries, especially of the Second and Third

Worlds, cannot match such rates of public investment; moreover, whatever the scale of innovation subsidies used to stimulate initial development, marketing of the product must be worldwide to assure survival. This dimension of the international division of labour provokes still further questions about the pecking order of world trade and technological transformation. Have the competitive possibilities attributed to innovation policy and technologically driven industrial strategies already taken on the status of lost or non-existent opportunities? 'Has the bus already left the station' for the majority of would-be manufacturers of robotics, fibre optics or digital switches amongst the smaller industrial nations when the dominant innovator and producer nations are the USA and Japan?

At this stage of their application, the comparative study of communications systems provides insights rather than answers to such questions. It shows the extent to which the global communications system increasingly reflects not the assumptions of single societies but the assumptions of an exclusive club. It is a club with excessively high entry fees, exceedingly few members and exceptionally large benefits. The few nations and transnational companies who belong to it will, on current evidence, continue to dominate the supply of telecomunications, data processing and entertainment goods and services to great profit. The trading record of one American transnational corporation, International Business Machines (IBM), provides an example of this. In 1983, IBM achieved gross income from worldwide sales of $23.3 billion for its products in the field of information handling systems, equipment and services (IBM, 1983) – a scale of trading dominance which contrasts sharply with the net deficit position of the majority of countries who are its customers. This 'internationalization' of industry – and by 'international' is meant the continued dominance of American and Japanese hardware and software producers – also raises questions about the 'internationalization' of cultural products and the national strategies which are emerging in response to perceived threats of cultural invasion or dilution.

Cultural strategies and technological outcomes
The question 'whose culture is it anyway?' summarizes many of the issues raised by neo-technological determinism in the context of the coming of cable and satellite services to national communications systems. The social policy objectives of cultural strategies here refer to the responses (and non-responses) of government to new modes of creating, distributing and consuming information and entertainment. Such public policies for 'culture' reflect several meanings: culture as a vehicle of national hegemony; culture as high culture with subsidies

for the arts; or culture as popular culture, manufactured and distributed by the mass media.

These strands of meaning and of cultural debate and provision are relevant to the tensions between consumer and national sovereignty over content control and to the competing claims of public service or private profit broadcasters over audience control. Who is, and who should be, sovereign over what is offered and what is consumed? Should the individual, the market, or the nation-state be the ultimate arbiter of cultural production and consumption? Or should the cultural flame be guided and guarded by publicly-subsidized broadcasting (but not print) 'in the public interest'?

Examined in this light, the cultural strategies to be directed at new entertainment and information media appear to be the rebottling of old issues in new vessels. If many of the issues are familiar and only the modes of delivery differ, why then are these familiar issues raised to a new order of magnitude? The insights provided by comparative policy responses (and non-responses) suggest that it is the growing pervasiveness and potential invasiveness of the new technologies on a global level which heighten their relevance.

National or consumer sovereignty?
Television is the medium most relevant to the neo-technological climate in communication systems and its evidence of different national responses to cable-delivered or satellite-transmitted programmes invites the question 'broadcasting for whom?' The answer provided by the evidence from a variety of cultural strategies and audience responses suggests a strengthening of consumer, and a weakening of national, sovereignty. Audience preferences have emerged as more powerful in determining media consumption patterns than public policy directives which seek to develop 'electronic nationalism' or to oppose 'cultural invasion' with respect to imported programming.

The emergent pattern of internationalized popular culture was analysed early on by communications scholars, first as an aspect of American 'media imperialism' (see for example, Schiller, 1969, and Tunstall, 1977) and secondly as encompassing 'electronic colonialism' (McPhail, 1981). There is a growing body of contradictory evidence concerning the extent to which the 'Coca Cola culture for export' trend is still accelerating or has begun to decelerate within industrial and developing societies. The profusion of distribution modes and channels hungry for content are reinforcing previous patterns of diminishing costs for importers of popular culture and an inverse law of rising profits for the few world market producers – who remain primarily American. Very few television programmers from the public service, private profit or mixed economy traditions can afford to ignore economic imperatives and incentives – whatever the challenge to cultural sovereignty or programme 'standards'.

The responses of societies with varying communication priorities, constraints, systems and audiences to the threat of increased 'cultural invasion' as a consequence of cable or dish-delivered satellite broadcasting provides genuinely comparative evidence which both confirms and contests the media imperialism thesis. In terms of American film and video exports an estimated 80 per cent of films shown on European television networks are American (Riblier and Barbier, 1983). A study by Lealand (1984), however, suggests that the media imperialism thesis needs to be updated, where case studies of seven countries show that there is no uniform flow of American television programmes. In Italy, the world's second largest television market, over 50 per cent of imported material comes from the United States (p. 101). In Brazil, rather than rising, the level of imported television material has fallen by 32 per cent over the period 1973–82, a decline attributable in part to increased domestic production (p. 96).

The utilitarian arguments used to legitimize cultural and economic strategies which favour domestic rather than imported productions typically focus on the creation and maintenance of a 'national identity' or 'national culture'. Canada exemplifies these social policy objectives in its communication system. It shares its borders with the largest producer of popular entertainment (and information services) in the world, and is a country of sufficient affluence and heterogeneity to demonstrate the power of consumer, and the myth of cultural, sovereignty as one consequence of this.

Canadians have lived with the reality of cultural invasion since the earliest days of mass circulation periodicals and radio broadcasting. What began 60 years ago continues to this day, providing a record of how proximity *has* bred protectionist policies – accelerated by the coming of cable and satellite. Although these defensive policies have focussed on subsidizing domestic cultural production and setting levels for Canadian content – such as the 80 per cent target set for the public service network, the Canadian Broadcasting Corporation (CBC) (DOC, 1983) – they have failed. The technologies which place increased private choice and control in the hands of the audience negate the cultural control which is mandated by government. The majority, 76 per cent, of programmes viewed by English-speaking Canadians are 'foreign' and 'the viewing share of US stations is growing among both official language groups' (DOC, 1983: 9).

As the case of Canada suggests, it is audience responses to satellite transmissions in particular which challenge the assumptions of both public service advocates and media imperialist critics. Moreover, the same pattern of consumer sovereignty appears to be emerging in Europe. The launch of Sky Channel in 1983 introduced English-language satellite broadcasting which, by 1985, reached some three million homes in the Netherlands, Switzerland, Austria, West Germany, Norway, Finland, Sweden, Denmark, France and the UK.[4] Over two thirds of its programmes of music, film, sport and news content consist of imported material – predominantly American 'sit-coms' and films. Two aspects should be of interest to students of popular culture. Firstly, it has brought broadcast advertising to countries such as Norway which previously excluded it, and secondly, neither commercialism nor the 'foreign language' element appear to present 'cultural' annoyances or barriers to multi-cultural audiences in quest of light entertainment.

This innovation of increased consumer control over *how* and *when* home-based technologies and services – video cassette recorders (VCRs), visual display units (VDUs), cable and satellite receivers – are consumed has occurred with only a marginally increased choice of *what* is consumed. Yet, even this limited increase in audience control can confound the proscriptions of policy makers who seek to mandate electronic nationalism, or the prescriptions of public service broadcasters who seek to manipulate ('guide') public taste in accordance with an ethos which combines utilitarianism, elitism, pragmatism and self-interest.

Paradoxically, the technologies which enable the audience to become limited creators of individual entertainments proffer only a limited increase in the range of films, videos and television 'raw material'. Nor does creative control over content at the receiving end diminish the ultimate control exercised by the content gate-keepers, those who select and shape what will be produced or programmed. The creative control which the audience exercises over content is confined to choosing medium, volume and timing, and the principal instrument of control is the hand-held push-button panel. This permits 'zapping' and enables consumers to skip advertisements on video recordings or to wander around the multiple channels of a cable system. Such technologically determined consumer sovereignty has had disturbing and unintended consequences for the financial infrastructure of commercial broadcasting. When advertisers can no longer be guaranteed that large and 'captive' audiences will view their messages, how can television companies fix their 'peak' or 'prime time' rates?[5] Through interactive processes of this kind, consumers of the new technologies are creating more than their own information or entertainment worlds, they are also redefining the boundaries between the public and the private in shaping the formats of the new media.

The arrival of transnational satellite entertainment programmes (and advertisements) with their potential consequences of cultural dilution and social change is an issue which concerns consumer groups as well as national governments and public service broadcasters. For example, international consumer codes governing television advertisement content, and the regulation of interactive and information services with respect to access and legal protection as suggested strategies for an information age (NCC, 1984), might become fruitless exercises. Technology is predominant here. Satellite broadcasts reaching the home via a cable system offer the possibility of continued content regulation. Consumers buying their own dish aerials are beyond the reach of the receiving countries' regulations dealing with objective news reporting, advertising standards, questions of taste and decency or material suitable for children. In a climate of neo-technological determinism, any cultural strategy intended to govern the transnational flow of entertainment may stand charged with restricting a variety of freedoms, including the 'free flow' of advertising or 'commercial speech'.[6]

The case of the United Kingdom
When we turn to the United Kingdom (hereafter Britain) to see how one industrialized society is responding to the challenge of neo-technological determinism we find social policies with a marked bias towards the industrial rather than cultural.[7] The conflict in Britain has been both political and economic, between the competing objectives of public and private ownership – liberal 'free-market' ideology and state control in the area of industrial policy, and between the public service or private ownership of broadcasting in the cultural one.

In defence of British industry?
The innovation policies of the current government have produced a series of initiatives intended to transform British industry, re-route the education system and alert the general public as to how the future prosperity of their society lies with the development and application of new information and communication technologies. The extent to which this neo-technological impetus has stimulated a *mélange* of public policies and research expenditures, a good measure of humbug and a notable absence of positive results is a matter of public record.

Here British policy, if not modelled, has operated on American 'free market' philosophies: inward investment by multinationals and foreign technology have been welcomed and the highest proportion of funding of electronics R&D has been through the defence industry (Hills, 1984: 244). The government's early enthusiasm for competitive innovation was manifest in both words and deeds, as ready 'to adopt new technology and to devise and exploit new products and processes. We must strive to outstrip our competitors' (DTI, 1983: 4). Actions which echoed these sentiments included a Support for Innovation (SFI) programme launched in May 1982, the designation of 1982 as Information Technology year, and a national strategy for advanced research drawn up by the Alvey Committee into very-large-scale integration (VLSI), software engineering, man-machine interfaces and intelligent-knowledge-based systems (IKBS) at a cost of £350 million (Alvey Committee, 1982).[8]

The key innovation policy role rests with the Department of Trade and Industry (DTI) and is demonstrated by its expenditure on the Alvey Programme, electronics and information technology shown in Table 4.2.

TABLE 4.2
Department of Trade and Industry R&D on information technology/
telecommunications compared with total industrial R&D
(£ millions)

	1981–82	1982–83	1983–84	1984–85	1985–86	1986–87
Alvey Programme	0.1	0.0	1.5	7.0	15.4	20.4
Electronics	11.1	13.0	21.8	32.3	40.0	39.6
Information technology	12.1	27.1	27.7	39.4	38.0	36.8
Telecommunications	0.0	0.0	0.0	0.3	1.0	1.1
Total	23.3	40.1	51.0	79.0	94.4	97.9
Total industrial R&D	59.9	88.4	122.4	187.1	192.8	213.8

Source: Cabinet Office (1984): extracted from Table 17a, p. 113.

Other spending on space technology related to telecommunications, transport systems and remote sensing increased from £53.3 million (1981–82) to £66.3 million (1985–86) (Cabinet Office, 1984: Table 17a), while overall expenditure to advance technology in different economic sectors shows DTI expenditure increasing from £261 million in 1981–82 to £424 million in 1986–87 (Cabinet Office, 1984: Table 2.15). The impact of the technological imperative on government thinking is revealed by the growth of public expenditure in this field. In 1983–84 the DTI's share, as a percentage of total government-funded R&D, was 8.7 per cent, the highest of all the civil departments; however this is just *one sixth* of the Ministry of Defence share of 50.1 per cent (Cabinet Office, 1984: Table 2.2).

The neo-technological thrust which lies behind industrial (and military) expenditures such as these is also relevant to the transformation of information into a marketable commodity. The redefinition of whole areas of hitherto 'free' public information as saleable 'goods' illustrates the scale of transformation of previous definitions of and arenas for public service, private profit, or political control. The changing role of government as both cause and consequence of its own policies will become more clear when its transformation from provider to purveyor of information is established. When governments and industry consort to create conditions of scarcity which turn information into a product they do more than redefine a free or non-good into a chargeable commodity to be paid for as any other commercial good from a theatre ticket to an automobile: they transform the nature and role of government policy itself.[9]

Adopting this perspective, the Information Technology Advisory Panel (ITAP) Report urged the government to acknowledge the economic potential of the 'tradeable information sector' (ITAP, 1983) for a society in which all categories of public and private information, including entertainment and the permanent knowledge of national libraries, great museums, as well as census demographics, company, patent and copyright records would be equally marketable as commodities. Using pricing mechanisms to control access to multiple forms of public and published information is in accord with neo-technological determinist policies, whereby 'exploitation of these information sources for the UK information business should be an explicit policy objective ... government should seek links with appropriate private sector organizations to develop these new types of service' (ITAP, 1983: 43).[10]

Despite this level of activity, there is pessimism about the future. The fall in the 'information technology' budget between 1984–85 and 1986–87 shown in Table 4.2 suggests a re-ordering of priorities within Whitehall and second thoughts about the scale of commitment, and the problem of gauging effectiveness given the time lags between investments in research and development and eventual profitability (HM Treasury, 1984: 30). In Britain, such strategies also have had to contend with the unintended consequence of more effective international competition accounting for 50 per cent of the UK market which in turn chalked up a trade deficit in excess of £2 billion in 1984 (*Guardian*, 1985a). Just one transnational firm, IBM (UK), made profits alone of £200 million (*Times*, 1985b). Faced with evidence such as this the Information Technology Economic Development Committee (1984) soberly concluded that the relative economic decline of the UK could be reversed only if 'the UK exploits this new technology with enterprise and wisdom. However, if we fail to exploit it as urgently or effectively as other advanced nations we shall continue our decline to third world status' (p. 5).

In defence of British culture?

The scholar is hard-pressed to find the word 'culture' in the recent official literature on British communications policy. Examination of five policy documents related to telecommunications and broadcasting (DTI, 1982; Home Office, 1982; Home Office/DTI, 1982; Home Office/DTI, 1983; ITAP, 1983) reveals public service broadcasting as the only form of 'culture' considered if ITAP's (1983) classification of 'entertainment' as part of the 'tradeable information sector' is discounted. The Hunt Report (Home Office, 1982) found the introduction of private cable systems consistent with safeguarding public service broadcasting; while the Home Office/DTI White Paper on cable (1983) applauded the achievements of a system which has

> ...succeeded in bringing education, information and entertainment to the whole country in a manner which has been of profound social and cultural benefit ... above all it has operated to reinforce the democratic and open nature of our society (p. 39).

This appreciative stance towards the cultural status and broad educational role of public service broadcasting is one which many broadcasters share. It is echoed, for example, in the claim that 'between the universities and the broadcasting organisations there are notable affinities'.[11]

The Reithian ethos of public service broadcasting as guardian of a national culture and the broad consensus between policy-makers and practitioners has increasingly come under threat, however. The duopoly of amicable co-existence developed between a licence fee-funded BBC and an advertisement-funded IBA structure has been challenged: first, by the prospect of more cable and satellite delivered channels, and, second, by the setting up of the Peacock Committee to examine the feasibility of the BBC's home services being in part or in whole financed by advertising.[12] Any such change in the existing financial structure of public service broadcasting in Britain would accord with the definition put forward by the then Home Secretary that

> public service and private enterprise are entirely compatible in the sphere of broadcasting, as in other areas of economic activity ... (in the past) the task was to make a smooth transition from monopoly to duopoly for us it is the passage from duopoly to multiplicity (*Airwaves*, 1985)

To the extent that Britain is both a producer and exporter of television drama and a consumer and importer of feature films it both confirms and contradicts the theses of media imperialism and electronic colonialism. The restriction of a 14 per cent limit on broadcast hours of 'foreign' programming may artificially depress consumption and the lower average cost of imported material takes only 4 per cent of the BBC's annual television programme budget.

However, audience preference for domestic production is revealed when only one of the BBC's 'Top 10' series in 1984 was American produced (BBC, 1984). Similarly, with Independent Television (ITV) and Channel 4 during 1983/84, 'Transmissions of British origin or exempted from the quota regulations were well in excess of the minimum 86% requirement on both channels' (IBA, 1984).

This picture contrasts with the one presented by the audience-controlled, individually chosen market for feature films and videos. Here there is no effective competition from British-produced films to counter American dominance. In 1984, out of the 272 feature films then registered with the Department of Trade and Industry, 151 were imported from the United States and 37 were from Britain (*British Business*, 1985). This pattern underlines the absence of a coherent cultural (or industrial) strategy towards film or any cultural medium in Britain – as evinced by the proposal to remove what limited public subsidy existed for domestic film production, the Eady Levy, in the Film Bill, 1985.[13]

The extent to which 'internationally competitive technology' as both industrial and cultural strategy exceeds the technological, institutional and market means to achieve them in Britain is illustrated by the abortive attempts to introduce a cable network and satellite broadcasting. This failure points to the tenuous nature of the links between industrial and cultural strategies which derive from neo-technological determinism and depend on 'market forces' to restructure the communications infrastructure and services. Despite the framework set out in the Cable and Broadcasting Act, 1984 (HMSO, 1984) and the provisions of Sections 1 and 42 for the establishment of a Cable Authority and a Satellite Broadcasting Board, by 1985 there were only 300 households with broad-band cable services, and one satellite transmission, Sky Channel, operative in Britain.[14] This design for a 'wired nation' reflects not the assurance of a large potential audience and market but the zeal of the determinists of neo-technological policies.

In conclusion

This chapter has explored both national and international communication systems in the light of one single underlying assumption which has come to dominate their form and content, that of neo-technological determinism. It has shown how this technological imperative has shaped the industrial and cultural policies of different societies and how these in turn have consequences for communication systems.

This chapter also pointed to the powers of new systems and services to redefine not only the telecommunications and media infrastructure, but also their powers to redefine previously understood categories of meaning and experience, such as what we understand by information or where the boundaries lie between the public and private, or between work and leisure. Moreover, application of these technologies has the power to redefine the structure of control between the producer and the audience and between the individual and the state, in terms of how much of what is offered is consumed – and when; and who 'owns' public information and is therefore free to sell it (or who 'owns' private information and is therefore free to access it).

The priority given by the majority of industrial societies to economic competitiveness in this area is in marked contrast to the investment of political will and public expenditure directed at exploring its social, economic, cultural or political consequences. The ways in which new communication technologies are applied as means, and the ways they may be of benefit or detriment to differing social groups as ends, still remains remarkably and perhaps deliberately underexplored.

This points to the challenge raised by neo-technological determinism which lies with its potential to become a self-fulfilling prophecy in the hands of the few nations and transnationals who control its future development and intended outcomes. In this, the ultimate challenge of neo-technological determinism lies in the neo-teleology of what is perceived as its essential nature. There is no necessitarian logic for either social or economic advance – just as there is no preordained logic which places the technological over the social, the cultural or the political, however much it may currently dominate the economic sphere.

Notes

1. For discussion of the competing theoretical models concerned with corporatism see, for example, Grant Jordan (1981).

2. Source: the United States Congressional Budget Office Report on *Federal Support for R&D and Innovation* (April 1984) which states 'no comprehensive technology-based evaluation of the Federal R&D budget is available ... innovation is almost universally treated as a by-product of the mission oriented activities of federal agencies' (p. 66). Excluded Department of Defense estimates would have shown an R&D budget of almost twice the combined non-defence R&D budgets of the agencies shown in Table 4.1 in 1983.

3. The *1983 Annual Survey on Science and Technology Research* conducted by the Statistics Bureau of the Prime Minister's Office in Japan covers 12,300 companies, 1,200 research institutions and 1,900 universities and colleges. In 1982, research expenditure totalled ¥6,530 billion, 3.6 times the figure of ten years ago: central and local government accounted for 25.5 per cent and the private sector 74.4 per cent.

4. With Rupert Murdoch's News International Corporation as majority shareholder (71 per cent), Sky Channel's imported programming, purchased as a

'package' prior to its launch, includes such time-tested favourites as 'Charlie's Angels', 'Starsky and Hutch', 'Swiss Family Robinson' and 'The Lucy Show'.

5. The American television industry's concern about this margin for error in its $18 billion advertisement revenues has produced a range of sophisticated gadgets to track viewing habits, including two field trials of 'people meters' (*New York Times*, 1985).

6. The case for a 'free flow of advertising' covered by Article 10 of the European Convention on Human Rights which 'offers substantial protection against interferences with "commercial speech"' is well argued by Lester and Pannick (1984: 7).

7. In 1978, ministerial interest in microprocessors received a timely boost with a special showing for the Cabinet of the 'Horizon' television programme 'When The Chips Are Down' already seen by the Prime Minister, James Callaghan. For a detailed discussion of telecommunications policy since 1964 see Hills (1984: 109–219).

8. These initiatives built upon and expanded earlier innovation policy: the Microelectronics Industry Support Programme (launched in 1978 with a budget of £55 million); the Computer Aided Design, Manufacture and Test (CADMAT) Programme launched in 1982; the Fibre Optics and Optoelectronics Industries Scheme for the development of fibre optics (launched in 1981 with a budget of £25 million); and the Microelectronics Application Project (MAP) (with a budget of £55 million increased to £85 million in November 1982).

9. This point is made by Schiller (1982: 208) in his discussion of the relationship between the telematics industry and government with reference to the US Paperwork Reduction Act, 1980 (US Congress, 1980) (cf. ITAP, 1983).

10. The membership of this committee was itself a lesson in industrial strategy – only one member was not a managing director or chairman in the electronics industry.

11. Speech by Ian McIntyre, Controller of BBC, Radio 3, to the Johnian Society, Cambridge, quoted in *The Listener* (1984).

12. The Committee on Financing the BBC was announced in March 1985. Chaired by Professor Alan Peacock, its terms of reference were to assess the effects of advertising or sponsorship on the BBC, to identify a range of options for their introduction and to consider proposals for securing income from the consumer other than through the licence fee.

13. *The Guardian* (1985b) commenting editorially on 'A Mess of a Non-Policy on the Media', pointed to films as one the areas currently 'under some threat of law or taxation' in Britain.

14. For a brisk catalogue of these failed hopes, see Forester (1985).

References

Airwaves (1985) 'Thirtieth Anniversary Greetings from the Home Secretary', Winter 84/85: 5.

Alvey Committee (1982) Report: *A Programme for Advanced Technology*. London: Her Majesty's Stationery Office.

BBC (1984) Personal communication from Peter Meneer, Head of Broadcasting Research Department, December (British Broadcasting Corporation).

British Business (1985) 15 March. London: Department of Trade and Industry.

Cabinet Office (1984) *Annual Review of Government-Funded R&D 1984*. London: Her Majesty's Stationery Office.

Cable and Satellite Europe (1984) February.

Congressional Budget Office (1984) *Federal Support for R&D and Innovation*. Washington, D.C.: Government Printing Office.

DOC (1983) *Building for the Future: Towards a Distinctive CBC*. Ottawa: Minister of Supply and Services (Department of Communications).

DTI (1982) *The Future of Telecommunications in Britain*, Cmnd. 8610. London: Her Majesty's Stationery Office (Department of Trade and Industry).

DTI (1983) *Research and Development Report 1982–83*. London: Department of Trade and Industry.

Forester, T. (1985) 'The Cable that Snapped', *New Society*, 24 January.

Grant Jordan, A. (1981) 'Iron Triangles, Woolly Corporatism and Elastic Nets: Images of the Policy Process', *Journal of Public Policy*, 1 (1): 95–123.

Guardian (1985a) 'Holding Back What it Takes', 7 January.

Guardian (1985b) 'A Mess of a Non-Policy on the Media', 11 February: 12.

Hills, J.(1984) *Information Technology and Industrial Policy*, Beckenham, Kent: Croom Helm.

HMSO (1984) *Cable and Broadcasting Act*. London: Her Majesty's Stationery Office.

HM Treasury (1984) *The Government's Expenditure Plans 1984–85 to 1986–87*, Cmnd. 9143: II. London: Her Majesty's Stationery Office.

Home Office (1982) *Inquiry into Cable Expansion and Broadcasting Policy* (the Hunt Report), Cmnd. 8679. London: Her Majesty's Stationery Office.

Home Office/DTI (1982) *Direct Broadcasting by Satellite*, Cmnd. 8751. London: Her Majesty's Stationery Office (Department of Trade and Industry).

Home Office/DTI (1983) *The Development of Cable Systems and Services*, Cmnd. 8866. London: Her Majesty's Stationery Office (Department of Trade and Industry).

IBA (1984) *IBA Annual Report and Accounts 1983–84*. London: Independent Broadcasting Authority.

IBM (1983) *Annual Report 1983*. New York: International Business Machines.

Information Technology Economic Development Committee (1984) *Crisis Facing UK Information Technology*. London: National Economic Development Office.

ITAP (1983) *Making a Business of Information* London: Her Majesty's Stationery Office (Information Technology Advisory Panel).

Lealand, G. (1984) *American Television Programmes on British Screens*. London: Broadcasting Research Unit.

Lester, A. and D. Pannick (1984) *Advertising and Freedom of Expression in Europe*. London: International Chamber of Commerce.

Listener (1984) 'The Pursuit of Excellence in Broadcasting', 20–7 December.

McPhail, T.L. (1981) *Electronic Colonialism*. Beverly Hills, Calif.: Sage.

Melody, W.H. (1973) 'The Role of Advocacy in Public Policy Planning', in G. Gerbner, L.P. Gross and W.H. Melody (eds.), *Communications Technology and Social Policy*. New York: John Wiley and Sons.

Milward, H.B. and R.A. Francisco (1983) 'Subsystem Politics, and Corporatism in the United States', *Policy and Politics*, 11 (3).

NCC (1984) *The Information Society: A Strategy for Consumers*. London: National Consumer Council.

New York Times (1985) 'Who's Watching TV? It's Getting Hard to Tell', 6 January.

OECD (1981) *Information, Computer and Communications Policies for the '80s*. Paris: Organization for Economic Cooperation and Development.

OECD (1983) *Telecommunications: Pressures and Policies for Change*. Paris: Organization for Economic Cooperation and Development.

Office of Technology Assessment (1983) *Annual Report to the Congress for 1982*. Washington, D.C.: Government Printing Office.

Riblier, W. and J.P. Barbier (1983) *Nouvelles Technologies de l'Information et*

Création d'Emplois: L'Industrie Audio-Visuelle. Brussels: Forecasting and Assessment for Science and Technology.

Rothwell, R. and W. Zegveld (1981) *Industrial Innovation and Public Policy.* London: Frances Pinter.

Schiller, D. (1969) *Mass Communications and American Empire.* New York: Kelley.

Schiller, D. (1982) *Telematics and Government.* Norwood, N.J.: Ablex Publishing Corporation.

Statistics Bureau, Prime Minister's Office (1983) *Summaries of 1983 Survey Report (Preliminary) on Science and Technology Research, and Ancillary Reports on Energy and Life Science Research.* Japan: Foreign Press Centre.

Times (1985a) 'Reagan seeks to triple spending for "Star Wars"', 4 February.

Times (1985b) 'A UK Firm Beating its US Parent', 12 February.

Tunstall, J. (1977) *The Media Are American.* London: Constable.

US Congress (1980) *Paperwork Reduction Act*, Public Law 96-511. Washington, D.C.: Government Printing Office.

5

Unequal information: access and exclusion in the new communications market place

Peter Golding and Graham Murdock

Interest in the social effects of the new communication technologies often seems to derive from a sense of their total novelty. Our concern, conversely, is with continuity. We start from the proposition that the social organization and operation of communication systems can properly be understood only by analysing the structure of social inequality and the consequent differential access to key communication resources across the population (Golding and Murdock, 1978).

In earlier work we have particularly emphasized the importance of economic inequalities in limiting participation and choice. This perspective is crucial to current debates about the growth and likely impact of new communication technologies, not least as a counter-weight to an undue stress on technology. Many analyses are either overtly or implicitly deterministic — they start with the technical possibilities of new facilities and then speculate on their possible impact on social life. Our analysis is the reverse of this. We begin by identifying basic trends in economic and social arrangements, and then ask how new technologies, whether in communications or elsewhere, might connect with them.

Two questions in particular arise from this perspective. First, how are the new communications technologies being used to ease the current economic crisis, the crisis of profitability? This issue raises large questions about how the recent difficulties of the industrialized world are explained, and even larger questions about their prognosis. Clearly the role of information and communications technologies in the industrial response to recession is central, though this issue is not our primary concern in this chapter. The second question is how will developments in new communications technologies, and more generally in cultural and information services, impact on patterns of social inequality? It is towards the latter question that the rest of this chapter is addressed, using developments in the United Kingdom (hereafter Britain) to illustrate the point.

The crisis in information services
The prolonged recession is producing major changes in the structure of both production and consumption. The most apparent shift, and

71

the one which has occasioned most anxious comment recently, is the restructuring of the labour market. With a rise in the population of working age in the late 1970s and early 1980s, a rise which will continue until 1988, the decline of older manufacturing industries has created in Britain unemployment which is clearly structural and long-term, a problem which is common throughout Europe (OECD, 1984).

The problem is that while the labour force (those of working age and seeking work) has enlarged (from 24.9 million in 1971 to 26.2 million in 1983) traditional sectors of employment have been irreversibly destroyed. Employment in manufacturing fell from 7.91 million in 1971 to 5.49 million in 1984, while the growth of other sectors has failed to compensate for this decline (Department of Employment, 1984). By mid-1984 four out of ten of the unemployed had been so for a year or longer. As the *Financial Times* (1984) gloomily concluded, '. . . there is no reason to hope that unemployment will melt away in the warmth of any probable general recovery . . . The problem . . . is likely to last for a full generation.' Marginal employment, in homeworking or in part-time work, has increased in response to the reduced demand for labour, but has not prevented an overall decline in economic activity rates (though it has produced an increase in economic activity rates for women).

These trends have three consequences of relevance here. First, they have increased the numbers on low incomes or dependent on social security benefits, with a consequent increase both in poverty and in the range of household incomes. Second, they have increased the demand for cheap leisure and recreation facilities. Third, they have reinforced the tendency to what, *pace* Raymond Williams (1983), we would describe as immobile privatization, that is the domestication of leisure. In a society where four households in ten still have no car, over half of unskilled workers and the unwaged have no holiday away from home, and attendances at the cinema and professional sports have dwindled, the home has become more than ever the necessary site of most leisure activities. The role of the television set is, of course, the crux of this, with consequences we examine below.

Confronting the increase in demand for public information, advice, and leisure facilities is a radical restriction in provision, as cuts in public expenditure have eroded the ability of statutory agencies to meet either their own development plans or the needs of local communities. A key area is the provision of information and advice services. Complex changes in the range and nature of consumer goods and a major expansion in the numbers claiming means-tested social security benefits have put severe pressures on such services. Reviewing this trend, a recent report by the National Consumer Council (NCC), notes that, 'In our survey we did not encounter a single agency that had not recently experienced a substantial increase in its workload or number of enquiries . . . all agencies accept that they are only meeting the information needs of a small proportion of the public. There is evidence to suggest a massive unmet need for information and advice provision' (NCC, 1983: 7). After expansion in the 1970s grant aiding for consumer advice centres was withdrawn in 1980, and roughly half of them disappeared. Recent restrictions in the Urban Programme have severed the funding for law centres and similar agencies, many of which have closed or live on the edge of extinction (*Inter-City Network*, 1984).

Public libraries have sought in recent years to expand their role as centres for information flows to the community. However, this has coincided with increases in the cost of books above the general rate of inflation, with attempts to increase the use of computers and on-line data bases, and with expenditure constraints across the library field. A government review of these developments concluded soberly that 'all elements within a national information network must expect to be subject to financial constraints, sometimes with consequences which could be disastrous for services which are dependent on them' (DES, 1982: 33).

Expenditure by public libraries on books has substantially declined in real terms since 1979, an apparent increase in book-stocks being due to libraries retaining old stocks longer rather than to new purchases (House of Commons (HC) *Hansard* Written Answers (WA), 18 June 1984, *col. 138*). Yet increased borrowing figures indicate growing demand, not least for new services and remote information sources. Paradoxically, as the Department of Education and Science (DES) report starkly noted, in libraries, 'The advent of computer based systems means that information is increasingly accessible only for payment' (DES, 1982: 34).

Post offices have similarly attempted to serve as generic information centres in recent years, especially in smaller or rural communities. Here again, however, increased demand has met with a new economic calculus. A recent internal report notes that, 'with current pressure on costs and the need to be both competitive and technologically efficient . . . the Post Office can no longer afford to support an over large network in urban areas' (Post Office, 1984a: 9). Behind the sparkling new post shops and new-technology window displays in the main city-centre post offices is a picture of part-time offices in rural areas and reduced services in the suburbs. The number of offices declined from 23,000 in 1977/78 to 20,500 in 1983/84 (Post Office, 1984b).

Information and advice services complement, to a degree, the formal provision of the education service. Yet recent cuts in education expenditure are penalizing precisely those social groups whose need for other information services is high. Whereas education expenditure accounted for 6.25 per cent of national product in 1975, current plans project a fall to 4.5 per cent in 1986/87 (Hughes, 1984: 22). More particularly the uncertain futures of many unemployed manual workers and the rapid change in the market for skills have put new pressures on continuing and adult education. Yet funding for adult education is to fall from £91 million in 1983/84 to £74 million in 1984/85 (Lords *Hansard* WA 29 June 1984, *col. 1220*). In 1983 the government announced an 8.3 per cent cut in funding for the Workers' Educational Association (WEA), and a 14.3 per cent cut in funding for university extra-mural departments. Rate-capping and reduced central government grants to local authorities further constrict the funding of WEA programmes, with a consequent reduction in classes and increases in fees which exclude many less affluent students (WEA, 1984).

The constraints on local government funding, most dramatically through rate-capping but also through a more general restraint in rate support (now administered through the Block Grant System), have led to severe pressures on the ability of local authorities to continue the extension of a full range of leisure and information services. Lower-income groups are, of course, disproportionately dependent on local authority services of this kind, and are severely hit both by their disappearance and by increased charges (Boddy, 1984). Increasingly the lack of finance forces local authorities to follow the philosophy outlined by a report on local services for the Department of the Environment prepared by private consultants, which concluded 'we would argue that all services should be charged at full cost, unless there is good reason to the contrary' (Coopers and Lybrand Associates, 1981).

This argument was paralleled in a key report by the government Information Technology Advisory Panel (ITAP), which suggested that the commercialization of information services would be viable only if material currently freely available as public resources was restricted and made accessible only for payment:

> The way in which (government) information is issued can strongly influence the development of new services in the private sector. The provision of official statistics on viewdata, for example, could add significantly to the attractiveness of a viewdata service. Conversely the production by Government of a free publication on a particular subject could render unviable a commercial service which is charging for the same information (ITAP, 1983: 35).

There is then, across the range of information, advice, and leisure facilities, a reduction in public sector provision and an increased use of market mechanisms to restrict demand. The ability of consumers to buy into these services is thus crucial. However, complementary to this shift is a substantial widening of the range of disposable incomes, penalizing those groups with least ability to pay for services for which charges are rising, and for whom private alternatives are inaccessible.

For those in work, for example, income ranges are wider now than for many years (see Table 5.1). In fact the relative position of the low-paid is no better now than in the 1930s, and is indeed worse than a century ago. This trend is exacerbated by the regressive impact of changes in taxation and national insurance contributions. Between 1978/9 and 1981/2 the lowest-paid decile received only 2.4 per cent of all after-tax incomes, a fall of 0.5 per cent in three years, while the top decile increased their share from 23.4 per cent to 25.6 per cent (*Economic Trends*, July 1984). Movements in capital taxation have similarly extended the gap between higher and lower incomes (HC *Hansard* WA 17 May 1984, *col. 238–9*).

TABLE 5.1

Widening wage inequalities: full-time weekly earnings as percentages of the corresponding median (men aged 21 and over)

	Lowest decile	Highest decile
1977	68.1	157.7
1980	65.9	161.6
1984	63.0	170.8

Source: *Low Pay Review*, 20 (December 1984), p. 13.

Outside the labour market the dependency of large numbers on means-tested social security benefits has totally demolished Beveridge's plan for 'security against want without a means test'. The inadequacy and recent curtailment of contributory benefits, and increases in the numbers of long-term unemployed and of lone parents, have forced large sections of the population down through the welfare state safety net. Whereas in 1948 one person in 33 was dependent on national assistance, by 1983 one in eight of the population relied on its successor, supplementary benefits, not including the numbers, in excess of a million, who fail to claim. In 1981 roughly 10.5 million people were living on or below supplementary benefit levels, a figure which has certainly increased since that date.

The new electronic market place

The overall picture, then, is of a general withering of public information and leisure provision coupled with a tendency to increase the charges for remaining services, making access to them increasingly a function of ability to pay. This movement is occurring in parallel with an intensification of income inequalities in which the disposable spending power of a significant section of the population has been reduced. As a result the less well off are disadvantaged twice over. They are priced out of the market for the newly commercialized services and dependent on public institutions which are themselves increasingly impoverished and unable to fulfil either their clients' demands or needs.

The resulting inequalities in access and choice created by these developments are further reinforced by the organization of the new information and entertainment industries based around emerging technologies in the video, computing, cable and telecommunications sectors. These initiatives are being promoted almost exclusively as commercial operations and consequently access to the goods and services they provide is primarily through the price system. To take advantage of the opportunities they offer, consumers not only have to buy or rent the necessary equipment, they have to pay for each item they use, either individually, as with video cassettes or viewdata information pages, or in packages, as with subscriptions to premium cable channels. The costs involved are currently beyond the pockets of most low-income households, with the result that they are unable to enter the new electronic market place. This is the case even with video, the most widely dispersed of the new home-based information and entertainment services.

Although domestic video cassette machines (recorders) (VCRs) have been obtainable since 1971, the market did not really begin to take off until 1978, the first year that relatively cheap Japanese models became available. As a result of this influx, the number of households with a VCR rose from 35,000 in 1977 to 580,000 at the end of 1980. The big push however came in 1981, Royal Wedding year. In a re-run of the pattern followed by the first generation of television sets, when penetration soared in Coronation Year, Prince Charles and Lady Diana's wedding produced a marked increase in the demand for VCRs, and by the end of 1981 there were an estimated 1.3 million VCRs in the country (*Screen Digest*, 1981). Around two-thirds of those actually in use were hired from one of the major television rental chains for monthly payment. However, even without the cost of purchasing the equipment, buying into the 'video revolution' meant an effective doubling of the £14 the average household already spent on obtaining basic broadcasting services through a medium-sized colour television set (see Pilsworth, 1983). This put it beyond the reach of most families at the lower end of the class structure. According to a large survey conducted by Audits of Great Britain (AGB), at the end of 1981, the penetration rate of VCRs for professional and managerial groups was 13 per cent, twice the average level for the population as a whole, while the rate for semi-skilled and unskilled workers and the unemployed was only 3.5 per cent (Kirkham, 1982).

Since 1981, the VCR market has expanded substantially, though there is considerable dispute about the exact figure. Estimates based on the number of machines delivered to the trade put the figure for mid-1984 at 6.25 million units (De Jonquieres and Crisp, 1984) whereas a major household survey estimated that only 4.68 million machines were actually installed and in use.

The results of an unpublished survey of households in contrasted areas of the Midlands, conducted by the Leicester Centre for Mass Communication Research at the end of 1983, suggest that this lower figure is the more accurate. They also indicate that the recent expansion of VCR possession has been concentrated in the middle reaches of the class structure, among white-collar and skilled workers, where penetration rates approached 30 per cent. In contrast, the rate for households headed by unskilled or unemployed workers was only just over half this, 16.9 per cent. Inequalities in access to the new home information and entertainment facilities are even more marked in the case of micro computers, where the absence of rental arrangements obliges consumers to buy a machine.

Easy-to-operate home computers were first introduced into Britain at the end of the 1970s but were mainly confined to hobbyists and enthusiasts. The mass market did not really take off until Sir Clive Sinclair introduced the improved version of his basic ZX model in 1981, and the British Broadcasting Corporation (BBC) launched the two Acorn models to accompany its computer literacy course in January 1982. From that point on, ownership increased dramatically. At the end of 1981, only 200,000 households in the United Kingdom had a home computer. By the end of 1983, this figure had jumped to 2 million, and by the first few months of 1984 penetration was variously estimated at between 11 per cent and 14 per cent. Here again, though, this gross figure disguises a wide range of variation between the top and bottom of the income scale. Although a basic home computer system is relatively inexpensive and many retailers offer easy credit terms, it remains a luxury that many families cannot afford. The results of the Leicester Midlands survey, for example, revealed a clear linear relation between ownership and socio-economic status. Whereas 23 per cent of the professional and managerial households sampled possessed a computer, the corresponding figures for white-collar workers, skilled workers and unskilled and unemployed workers were 11.6 per cent, 6.7 per cent and 3.6 per cent respectively.

It could be argued that this stepped take-up is entirely characteristic of newly introduced consumer durables and that, with time, computers will follow the pattern established by previous innovations with penetration trickling steadily down the income scale. This argument ignores two important points, however. In the first place, the pattern of diffusion for goods such as television sets and washing machines was established under conditions of rising affluence and economic expansion. We are now in a very different situation characterized by high levels of structural unemployment and widening income differentials. Consequently, the new consumer commodities are very unlikely to reach the same high levels of penetration. Secondly, home computers differ from traditional television sets carrying standard broadcast transmissions in two important respects. The pace of technological innovation renders existing models inadequate or obsolete at a much faster rate, and the full benefits of ownership only accrue to users who are able to purchase the array of peripherals and programmes to operate the machine to maximum advantage. Keeping abreast of the home computer revolution therefore requires substantial additional expenditure at regular intervals. Consequently, the more affluent consumers enjoy a permanent and increasing advantage within the emerging computer market place. In addition, extra benefits accrue to households that can afford to buy into more than one of the current innovations in home information and entertainment facilities. Home computer users, for example, gain access to one hundred 'free' programmes and a network linking them to other users if they can afford the £60 annual subscription to British Telecom (BT)'s Micronet system and the £50 for a modem that links their computer into the telecommunications network. Similarly, VCR owners who live in an area receiving the new cable television services, and who can afford the £15 or so monthly subscription to the full range of channels (including the premium feature film service), substantially increase the range of programming they can record off-air for the price of a blank cassette. The monthly subscription to cable services rises to roughly double this figure to include a range of interactive services. Yet £30 a month is more than double the current cost of broadcast reception to a household (including rental or set purchase) and is nearly a fifth of the income for a couple on supplementary benefit. Recent surveys reported in the trade press suggest that, at least in the medium term, only a third of households could or would afford cable subscriptions at these levels.

A similar pattern of unequal take-up also characterizes the new television-based information services. The most basic of these are the teletext systems operated by the BBC and Independent Television (ITV) companies. As with home computers, the breakthrough for these services came in 1981. In March 1980, only 80,000 households had a television set adapted to receive teletext transmissions. By March 1983 this figure had almost doubled to 1.4 million (IBA, 1984: 46) and estimates for mid-1984 put the figure at 2.16 million, about 10 per cent of the country's households. Unlike the more sophisticated interactive services offered by BT's Prestel network, teletext systems only require consumers to buy or rent a suitably adapted set. The information services themselves are provided free of charge. Despite their relative economy, however, recent research shows that access to these services is still markedly skewed towards the top end of the class structure, with professional and managerial households being more than twice as likely to own a teletext set as the population as a whole (Young and Rubicam Ltd, 1984). This is likely to be a temporary phenomenon, however. Penetration among lower socio-economic groups is likely to increase considerably in future since many of the larger television sets available from the major rental companies now incorporate teletext facilities as a standard feature. Moreover, the fact that the information itself is provided free makes teletext unique among the new television-based information and entertainment industries. Indeed, it is more accurate to see it as an extension of public broadcasting services, rather than as part of the new configuration of commercial services, such as video, cable and direct broadcasting by satellite (DBS), where access is determined by ability to pay.

In contrast, the services currently provided over the telecommunications network are based firmly on the payment-for-use principle. Consequently, inequalities in access are already considerable and are unlikely to lessen significantly in future. Even the basic telephone is far from being a universal utility. According to BT's own estimates (supplied to the authors), over 4 million households in Britain are currently without a phone. The vast majority of these contain families on low incomes. This situation is unlikely to improve much in future for two reasons. Firstly, the prices of domestic rentals and local calls are almost certain to rise after the current controls agreed as part of the privatization package are relaxed or removed. As one survey of international telecommunications charges noted: 'British telecommunications pricing is clearly biased to favour services used by business. Telex charges are at bargain basement levels and so are long distance telephone calls ... but local calls are far costlier in Britain than elsewhere' (Vines, 1984). These differentials are the result of a re-gearing of tariffs in favour of business users instituted in the spring of 1982. This involved phasing out the established practice of subsidizing the losses on local calls out of the profits on long-distance and international calls, and cutting the cost of the services most heavily used by corporate subscribers. In 1980, for example, a three-minute transatlantic call had cost £2.26 (in 1983 prices). By 1983 the price had fallen to £1.63. BT's aim was to steal a march on its newly licensed rival, Mercury, which was specifically aiming at business customers, and to persuade the American multinationals operating in Europe to avoid the higher prices charged by many of the continental national telecommunications authorities (PTTs) by routing their transatlantic traffic through London.

Providing enhanced and expanded services for business users is one essential plank in BT's corporate strategy. The other is to encourage existing domestic subscribers to make more calls and to subscribe to the developing array of value-added services provided by the Prestel system. Installing first telephones in poorer households is not seen as a viable option, however, since, as the Marketing Director of Local Communications Services, Nick Lane, candidly admitted: 'When you add customers you tend to add marginal customers with less income to spend' (De Jonquieres and Crisp, 1984). Consequently, without a significant growth in community terminals installed in libraries and other public places, or subsidies to poorer users, the households currently without a telephone are likely to be excluded from the benefits of the new telecommunications-based information, shopping and banking services, for the foreseeable future. Nor are they equally available to every household with a telephone. Here, as elsewhere in the new electronic market place, choice is dependent on ability to pay.

When BT's Prestel service was launched in 1979 it was conceived of as a mass public utility which would have three million subscribers by 1983. In the event, take-up fell far short of this target and was heavily concentrated among business users. The main deterrent was cost. In addition to buying or renting the necessary reception equipment, Prestel users had to pay for calls to the central data store for the time they were connected to the computer and for each 'page' of information they consumed. An average user could expect to pay around £35 a month in 1980 (see Young and Grey, 1980), which, as the early enthusiasts admitted, was high enough to prevent the service from becoming a regular source of information in all but the most affluent homes (Winsbury, 1979). After a period of concentrating on building up the system's business custom, BT has recently renewed its efforts to attract domestic users to Prestel by offering additional services such as home banking and shopping, and access to software for home computers.

The most ambitious scheme to date is Homelink, a joint venture between BT and the Nottingham Building Society, with the collaboration of the Bank of Scotland, Thomas Cook the travel agent and a number of retailers. This is a nationwide service offering a range of home banking and shopping facilities as well as access to Prestel's basic data base without the need to purchase the normal equipment. Subscribers are given the necessary keyboards and adaptors to turn their television set into an interactive terminal free of charge when they join. Once on the system, they can take advantage of a range of special offers on goods and services, transfer funds at the touch of a button, and place up to three free small ads of their own at any one time. Moreover, the system is relatively cheap to use. At current prices, BT estimate that someone making one hundred transactions and taking full advantage of cheap call rates could expect to pay around £25 a year. However, these advantages are only open to the relatively affluent. The scheme's publicity promises that 'Once you've got HOMELINK, it's like free membership of an exclusive club.' In fact, membership is far from free – it is expensive. To qualify for entry to the system, subscribers either have to open an account with the Nottingham Building Society with a minimum deposit, initially set at £1,000 though later reduced, or take out a mortgage with them. This puts it well beyond the reach of low-income families.

As the recent Prestel experiment in Gateshead demonstrates very clearly, bringing the same services to the poorer sections of the population requires extensive public subsidies. This venture grew out of a study conducted by the University of Newcastle for the large retail chain, Tesco. It identified two main groups who were unable to travel into the city centre on a regular basis. The first group was made up of the elderly, the disabled and mothers with young children, and the second comprised the 25 per cent of the local population who were too poor to afford the bus fares. Their immobility meant that they could not take advantage of the greater choice and cheapness offered by the big city stores, or of the main information and advice centres located in the centre. To address this problem, the University, in collaboration with Gateshead Borough Council and Tesco, launched a service using terminals installed in local libraries and telephone links to the local Social Security headquarters, to provide convenient access to information services and the opportunity to order goods from Tesco for free delivery to the doorstep. In terms of meeting the needs of the poor, the elderly and the disabled, the scheme has been a considerable success, but it has only been possible because of the public subsidy provided by a £100,000 government grant. The system is now being extended to sheltered housing and individual homes using facilities supplied by Rediffusion Computers. Here again though, subsidy plays a key role, with Rediffusion loaning £80,000 worth of videotex equipment.

Conclusion
The picture that emerges from this brief review of current trends is of a

thriving electronic market place in which prevailing patterns of consumer detriment – the compounded disadvantages of low-income groups – are being replicated as new communications and information services come on stream. This trend is the result of widening income inequality, constrained provision in the public sector, and the considerable costs of access to services in the private sector.

Many of the new services require large-scale investment by the corporations which provide them, with what are sometimes uncertain long-term returns. The pressure for secure custom among high-income groups is intense. High entry costs to this market place, together with continuing high costs of consumption, provide an effective barrier of exclusion to large numbers of less affluent households.

There is still a great deal that is uncertain about these trends. Many questions remain to be explored, yet much commentary has been restricted to empirically shaky negative or positive futurology. The negative version tends to a technological demonology, aghast at the mechanistic environment being conjured by electronic innovation, or to an Orwellian paranoia about the growth of video and computer surveillance. Positive futurology tends equally to focus on the technology, but with an ecstatic enthusiasm for the gadgetry marvels or social revolution embryonic in the circuitry. Both visions pose important questions but in seriously blinkered ways.

We would argue that the important issues posed by the new communications technologies are best addressed by revisiting the basic questions about social inequality and patterns of social access and exclusion which are the traditional key concerns of social research. We know far too little about the impact and development of the trends we have preliminarily described in this chapter. The new communications market place is a social phenomenon, and a vital key to examining changing patterns of social and cultural inequality.

References

Boddy, M. (1984) 'Local Councils and the Financial Squeeze', in M. Boddy and C. Fudge (eds.), *Local Socialism?* London: Macmillan.

Coopers and Lybrand Associates (1981) *Service Provision and Pricing in Local Government.* London: Her Majesty's Stationery Office.

Department of Employment (1984) *Employment Gazette*, 92 (8) August.

DES (1982) *The Future Development of Libraries and Information Services.* Library Information Series, No. 12, (Department of Education and Science).

Financial Times (1984) 'Generation of Unemployment', 26 September: leader column.

Golding, P. and G. Murdock (1978) 'Theories of Communication and Theories of Society', *Communication Research*, 5 (3): 339–56.

Guardian (1984) 'Home is Where Computer Is', 18 June: 22.

Hughes, J. (1984) 'The Inequality of Impoverished Education', *Poverty*, 58: 19–24.

IBA (1984) *Annual Report and Accounts, 1983–84.* London: Independent Broadcasting Authority.

Inter-City Network (1984) No. 25 (November): 1–2.

ITAP (1983) *Making a Business of Information: A Survey of New Opportunities.* London: Her Majesty's Stationery Office (Information Technology Advisory Panel).

Jonquieres, Guy De and Jason Crisp (1984) 'Profits are the Priority', *Financial Times*, 19 October: 22.

Kirkham, Mike (1982) 'The Need for VCR Research', *Admap*, July: 404–6.

NCC (1983) *Information and Advice Services in the United Kingdom*. London: National Consumer Council).

OECD (1984) *The Employment Outlook*, Paris: Organization for Economic Cooperation and Development .

Pilsworth, Michael (1983) *Be Your Own Programme Controller*. Speech to Fourteenth Broadcasting Symposium, University of Manchester, March 1–3.

Post Office (1984a) *The Post Office Counters Network: A Strategy for the Future.* London: Post Office.

Post Office (1984b) *Report and Accounts, 1983/84*. London: Post Office.

Screen Digest (1981) 'World Video Status Report', November: 235.

Vines, Steve (1984) 'BT's Long Distance Bargains', *Observer*, 29 January: 28.

WEA (1984) *The WEA in 1984*. London: Workers' Educational Association.

Williams, R. (1983) *Towards 2000*. London: Chatto and Windus.

Winsbury, Rex (1979) *The Electronic Bookstall: Push Button Publishing on Videotex.* London: International Institute of Communications.

Young, I. and I. Grey (1980) *The Cultural Implications of Videotex Services in the UK*. London: Communications Studies and Planning Ltd.

Young and Rubicam Ltd (1984) *Time and Space*, September/October: 11.

III

ISSUES OF REGULATION AND PRIVACY

6

Regulation and deregulation: telecommunication politics in the United States[1]

Muriel G. Cantor and Joel M. Cantor

Although the United States government has been directly involved in creating telecommunications policy since the invention of the telegraph (Schiller, 1982), social researchers have shown little interest in how government policy has influenced media institutions. In fact, until very recently most researchers separated the study of 'telecommunications' from the mass media. However, under the Communications Act of 1934, the United States government regulates both broadcasting and common carriers such as telephone and cable television. Without 'telecommunications', that is, the telephone long lines and co-axial cable, national radio and television would never have been possible, and the interconnection of television and the 'newer' technologies is discernible to even the most uninformed. The focus in this chapter is on how the regulatory climate has changed in the last several decades and how these changes reflect the growth and adoption of technological innovations as well as the political culture and climate.

The history of US government regulations, communications law and related topics has been covered in detail but not until recently did the focus change to analysing the political climates in which telecommunications policies are formed and how these policies influence both the 'software' (e.g. information and entertainment) and the 'hardware' (e.g. cable, video-tape recorders, satellite dishes) available to the public. This change is due partially to the new technologies available for transmitting and receiving data, information and entertainment, the growing markets involved, both in the United States and throughout the world, and the realization that what is transmitted and how it is transmitted through wires, radio and television can influence the daily lives and cultures of those reached.

The model of communication in the United States most frequently presented by both industry and lawyers is that it is a free-enterprise system existing at the pleasure of the government, but essentially autonomous. The model takes at face value the formal autonomy granted business enterprises dealing with the manufacture and transmission of culture and presents the government as an outside interference which encroaches upon organizational and individual freedom. For more than fifty years (since 1927), commercial interests have been the most powerful influence on content, programming decisions, and technological developments. However, it is difficult to separate government and business interests. Rather than being antagonistic, they have been mutually supportive through the years although one or the other may be more powerful depending on the political and social climates prevailing at the time.

Both media and the means of transmitting media content are either considered organs of the state in which they exist or are relatively free and autonomous. In the United States freedom of speech is regarded as a legal right and the government at best is seen as having minimal if indirect influence on telecommunications (including broadcasting). However, the government has actually regulated broadcasting directly since the Radio Act was passed in 1927. Rules and constraints are imposed on broadcasting from which the press and other print media are free. As the Act has been interpreted and applied, it usually favours broadcasters over public interest groups, leading social scientists such as Herbert Gans (1972) to claim that little precedent exists for the US government to participate directly in cultural creation. In reality, although the broadcasting industry is largely a private enterprise, and as such is protected by law and tradition, the government does involve itself in both the creation of programmes and their transmission (Cantor, 1980). This involvement is difficult to measure because, never static, it has been dynamic and evolving. Government policies and involvement with broadcasting from its origins has continually changed in response to pressures from business and public service interests and other participants in the political process since 1927. It is, of course not possible to examine the process by which all laws were passed and rulings adopted, both major and minor, throughout the last six decades. Our emphasis will be on how the development and adoption of the newer technologies has changed the way the game of politics in broadcasting and related areas of telecommunications is now being played.

Background of telecommunication policy and regulation

The first Radio Acts of 1910 and 1912 dealt with radio as merely a device for point-to-point wireless communication useful for military and marine use. They were never intended to deal with broadcasting as we now know it and therefore were not adequate to keep order among the large number of stations that emerged during the early 1920s. Also, because of the way the 1912 Act was written, Herbert Hoover, then Secretary of Commerce, could not refuse any requests for licences. So many stations were trying to broadcast by 1924 that it became imperative for Hoover to avoid jamming and divide the spectrum by assigning stations to specific frequencies. However, the Supreme Court had to rule his action illegal because the 1912 statute had not included that specific right.

The government (perhaps with security interests also in mind) and private interests found it necessary to agree that new legislation was needed to impose order and regulate the assignment and use of broadcast frequencies. The 1927 Radio Act that resulted provided the legal foundation for the broadcast industry by creating a commission as the regulatory agency to handle broadcasting, establishing the basic system as it is in the United States. The system included national radio networks linked by telephone lines (owned by American Telephone and Telegraph (AT&T)), local stations on temporary renewable licences, and an overall regulatory commission, the Federal Radio Commission (FRC), later, after 1934, to be replaced by the Federal Communications Commission (FCC). Congress gave these agencies the power to uphold 'the public interest, convenience, and necessity' by allocating frequencies and licensing local stations.

Rapid technological change and innovation were the hallmark of the twentieth century and by 1933, only six years after the original act was passed, it was obvious to all (government and industry) that the broadcasting law was still not comprehensive enough to cover the new growing and changing electronic communications industry. A committee convened in 1933 at the request of President Roosevelt recommended that a new agency be established to regulate all interstate and foreign communication by radio and wire, including telegraph and telephone, a recommendation resulting in the Communications Act of 1934 and the FCC. The new agency has regulated all broadcasting and other telecommunications since that time.

The Communications Act of 1934, with amendments, thus remains the basic law covering all over-the-air television and radio, cable television and other common carriers (such as telephone). The major areas of jurisdiction vested in the FCC are issuance of licences to local broadcasters and regulation of the technologies. Section 326 of the Act specifically forbids the FCC to regulate programme content. The courts have interpreted that to mean that the FCC cannot censor material before it is broadcast. However, over the years, contrary to what is generally believed, the FCC has imposed controls over content, but in subtle ways.

Because the regulatory powers given the FCC are so broad, the various Commissions with changing memberships over the years have interpreted and applied those powers differentially. Thus the style and content of regulation changed over the years — at times with increased regulation and at other times (as now) decreased. This ebb and flow of control did not depend solely on how the FCC implemented the Communications Act but also on court decisions of cases challenging the regulatory process, especially decisions relating to free speech and the interpretation of the public interest clause in the law. In addition, Congress has influenced the process by holding hearings on relevant issues and through amending the law itself. Also the way anti-trust legislation (the Sherman and Clayton Acts) has been applied to the broadcast industry has affected both the content and the control of television programmes. An anti-monopoly clause was written into the original 1934 Act — how that clause has been interpreted also reflects how differential power is dispersed among various supporting and competing organizations involved in broadcasting and telecommunications.

In addition, the applicable laws and amendments were written and interpreted within the context of larger political processes. One can conceptualize the legislative and legal process as a struggle or a game in which various players have more advantage, power and skill over others. Many of the participants in this on-going game, of course, represent the business interests such as multi-national and national broadcasting owners and producers, distributors and manufacturers of various kinds of equipment. Other players represent the government — FCC, the Congress, the courts, the White House, and the other government agencies such as the State, Commerce and Defense Departments. Less powerful but still part of the game are citizen groups, often representing minority interests. Many who wrote about these struggles in the past stress controversies about content, such as violence on television. Although most often discussed in the social science literature (Rowland, 1983), such struggles are actually trivial in the game of public regulation and control over communication when compared to the struggles among business interests to acquire profitable technologies and use those technologies to advance their interests. However, even these kinds of conflicts are often waged in the guise of public interest or free speech whereas profit and competing advantage can be seen to be the sole motivating factors.

The 'industry' has changed, of course, since the 1934 law was passed, but not as fundamentally as reading the popular press might lead one to believe. The hold of the three commercial networks over what is essentially a protected industry has changed little over fifty years. For example, over 75 per cent of the audience still watch programmes being broadcast on the three networks during every hour of the broadcast day (*Forbes*, 1985). The FCC is still mandated by Congress to make and change regulations and the courts still rule on whether these regulations are legal under the constitution. Through the years the courts have selectively ruled to delete or change some regulations but for the most part FCC regulations have been upheld. Congress has amended the 1934 Act many times, but attempts at a comprehensive rewrite of the basic Communications Act have essentially failed. The FCC still remains beholden to Congress for its existence and power although this power has been differentially interpreted by various court decisions, by successive administrations and by different members of the FCC itself.

Regulation and radio

Immediately after its creation the FRC outlined its ideas on the requirements of providing programmes in 'the public interest'. In its 1929 *Great Lakes* opinion, the Commission held that broadcasters were expected to provide a balanced or 'well rounded' programme structure, including programmes of agricultural information, religion, education and discussion of public issues. In addition the FRC held that the broadcasting of programmes or materials that tended to injure the listening public − attacks on civic or religious groups, for example, or fraudulent medical advertising − would raise serious questions about the desirability of granting licence renewals to owners of offending stations. Several stations were taken off the air because of the objectionable character of material they broadcast. These rulings led the National Association of Broadcasters (NAB) in 1928 to establish its first voluntary code (Barnouw, 1978). Most of the objections to content by the FRC and later the FCC were over commercial advertisements, the over-use of phonograph records and the failure to provide balance in discussions of controversial public issues.

These early standards were further elaborated by the FCC in 1946 in a memorandum, *The Public Service Responsibility of Broadcast Licensees*. According to the 'Blue Book', as it came to be known, broadcasting stations were expected to balance their programming by including in their weekly schedules reasonable numbers of programmes on education, news, agricultural information and issues of public importance, as well as programmes serving the interests of local non-profit civic and religious groups and labour organizations and programmes intended to appeal to minority interests and tastes, such as classical music. In addition, the number of commercially sponsored programmes and the number of advertisements included in the stations' weekly schedules were to be limited.

These rules and the issues they address became the core areas of controversy as broadcasting itself changed over the decades. Broadcasters from the beginning were angered that the Commission's requirement for 'diversity' forced them to provide programmes that would not attract advertisers. They considered such rules an infringement of their First Amendment (free speech) rights but were more concerned over whether the FCC had the authority to establish limits on their profits, that is, on commercial time. The courts ruled that only prior constraints could be considered censorship and that the FCC did have the right to determine whether a station was programming (both commercials and regular programmes) in the public interest. Many have argued with some justification that, regardless of the rules and court decisions, commercial broadcasting, taken as a whole, still does not provide true diversity because network-affiliated stations schedule similar types of programmes opposite each other during the broadcast day.[2]

Although new technologies have become widely available during the last four decades, these two issues, programme diversity and commercial advertisements remain salient. For example, throughout the 1960s the Commission rewrote the rules to make it easier to exempt radio stations from providing a 'balanced' schedule. The rapidly increasing number of radio stations, combined with the growing importance of television, forced the FCC after 1950 to modify its requirements. Its solution in the major markets was to allow certain stations to develop highly specialized types of programming aimed at limited segments of the total audience, for example, all-news, jazz and classical music. Thus radio broadcasting changed from a national system of scheduling controlled by networks to local control; and when television in turn adopted the radio schedule during each time period almost intact, it also inherited the rules concerning programme diversity and commercial announcements.

Television and regulation
Not only did television assume radio's programming and its problems, but some others were added.[3] During the 1960s, some social action groups involved themselves in the regulatory process, questioning the power of the FCC to regulate in the 'public interest' without consulting the public itself. In addition, these action groups believed that broadcasting as a powerful force could generate community and international conflicts and perpetuate the inequalities and discriminatory relationships existing in American society. The impact and influence of citizen groups on broadcasting during that period has been documented and debated. Now, twenty years after the United Church of Christ successfully challenged the licence renewal for

WLBT-TV in Jackson, Mississippi, because of its overt racism, researchers who have been following citizens' pressure group action on broadcasting claim that their impact has become minimal (Montgomery, 1984; Hanks and Pickett, 1979). However, it should be pointed out that a cumulative effect cannot be denied because such groups are typically invited to contribute testimony in Congressional hearings when legislation involving broadcasting is under consideration. Such calls to participate may nevertheless be no more than courteous gestures 'for the record' because the results of two decades of activism have been somewhat disappointing. Just a few, very few, FCC decisions have favoured the demands of citizen groups, and many of the problems associated with limited access to the political process still remain.

There is general agreement that the 1960s and early 1970s generated more regulation, regulation different from earlier decisions. Because of the scarcity of channels, the Supreme Court consistently ruled that broadcasting differs from other media. Broadcasters, in contrast, believed that they should enjoy the same freedom and privileges as the press and magazines. Basically the controversy has been over how the First Amendment to the Constitution should be interpreted. The Supreme Court in 1969 (the famous *Red Lion* decision) declared that the scarcity of channels required broadcasters to present both sides of controversial issues and to provide a forum for ideas, upholding the Fairness Doctrine.[4] The press, on the other hand, has always been free from the requirement of presenting issues 'fairly' because there is no perceived scarcity of opportunities to present views through print.

During the same period, there was also concern over what citizen groups, programme suppliers and independent broadcasters perceived as the increasing power of the television networks. Because the networks controlled their affiliates (each network has approximately 200 station-affiliates and up to twelve network-owned stations in the largest market areas), these groups with justification have protested the centralized control of television content and lack of diverse content made available to the audience. By the early 1970s, the FCC adopted several regulations which seems to limit such power (Prime-time Access and Financial Interest), rules which the networks are trying to have rescinded. With the growth of cable, the networks believe they are at a competitive disadvantage in relation to the pay television channels which under law are not similarly regulated (Cantor and Cantor, 1984). However, a review of many other decisions shows that, compared to the local stations, the networks still enjoy favoured status under the law.

Present and future controversies

The above discussion has been presented to show that although compared to that of other countries US regulation over broadcasting has appeared minimal, the role of the government has nonetheless been intrusive and strong. It is true that from the middle 1970s on there has been a shift in policy toward deregulation, implemented primarily through the FCC. However, battles continue to be fought over the same issues of content and advertisements, and more recently the uses of new technology. Today as in the recent past, the most frequently offered solution to resolve the many-faceted debates over the extent of public control over broadcasting is to rewrite an updated version of the Communications Act of 1934.

While strict libertarians, the networks and the recent administrations all agree that broadcasting should be deregulated, citizen groups and some social scientists, fighting what at times seems to be a lost cause, continue to lobby for more (or at least continued) regulation. Congress has the power to regulate and could pass laws which could change the structure of the industry. But of the many laws introduced to that end, none passed. The most recent attempts to write a new Communications Act have tried to accelerate deregulation. Bills introduced during the Carter administration, for example the 'Communications Act of 1979' (US Congress, House, 1979), would have completely deregulated radio and eased rules for television, changing the basic telecommunication monopolies and conglomerates. For public interest and citizen groups, the most distressing proposal was to eliminate the Fairness Doctrine. After lobbying both from industry sources (afraid that independent television stations and pay television would proliferate) and public action groups, the bills were withdrawn. At the same time the public action groups considered it a victory just to maintain the status quo. However, the victory over deregulation was to be short-lived. When attempts to rewrite the communication law itself failed, government policy shifted to the FCC to change it from supporting regulation to advocating deregulation. (There was a general trend toward deregulation of all regulated industries during the Carter period.) However, deregulation for broadcasting turned out to be much more complicated than for industries such as trucking and airlines.

The 1934 Communications Act allows the FCC to rescind its regulations as well as write them; it therefore could, if it wished, carry the process of deregulation rather far without new legislation being required. The general commitment to deregulating the broadcasting industry within the Carter and Reagan administrations is supported by the belief that new means of transmission and distribution of programmes (especially cable and video-tape recordings, and the possibility of wide adoption of satellite transmission) have already made the regulations concerning diversity and advertisements obsolete (and perhaps the Fairness Doctrine as well). The political game of broadcasting is therefore occurring at two different levels, one economic and the other ideological. The first involves new and old business interests struggling over control of the new telecommunications technologies and access to American and foreign markets (Tunstall, 1984). The second involves a radical and fundamental change in philosophy which could remove the last vestiges of public control over broadcasting. This philosophic or ideological change involving issues of scarcity and access to the 'airways' has resulted in both Congress and the FCC moving toward deregulation. For example, in 1984, the FCC deregulated some aspects of both radio and television broadcasting by curtailing requirements for public interest programming and allowing increased air time for commercial messages (*Broadcasting*, 1984d).

Telecommunications and public policy

Because it has become increasingly difficult to separate broadcasting from telecommunications, the tendency to deregulate has serious consequences for all communication policy decisions, international, national and local. Elsewhere we suggested that to abolish the prerogative to regulate at the federal level through the FCC might diffuse the play deeper and wider, back into the hands of Congress and others at the supra- and sub-federal levels (Cantor and Cantor, 1984). We also predicted that the emergence of new technologies would result in new and changing coalitions and alignments of players depending on the issues in contention. A lesson now apparent is that no one had the foresight or wisdom to predict all of the economic and social consequences under way. It is possible that to open telecommunications to market competition was to invite chaos with the principal beneficiaries the partners of the more than one hundred law firms in the Washington area specializing in telecommunications policy.

Broadly speaking, all the players in the game of deciding and influencing telecommunications can be described on a continuum of power as major or minor, and on a continuum of time as permanent or transient. The recent steps toward deregulation have not changed those categories or the players that have been involved. If anything, the list of players has lengthened and they are now so motley and numerous that it would be difficult to compile a definitive list. In a recent compilation just one major and continuing player, the NAB, listed 78 court cases and 134 separate issues in its own disputes with the government (NAB, 1984). Players are organizations and individuals in both the public and private sectors.[5] The federal, state, county and municipal levels of government are represented, including their administrative, legislative and judicial branches. In the larger game, organizations such as the NAB must work hard to make their voices heard above the din raised by all the others trying to eliminate or modify regulatory control.

The most powerful and permanent players for telecommunications as well as for television are, of course, Congress and its creature, the FCC, which it monitors closely to see how well it administers the powers it granted and could take away, powers deriving from the Communications Act of 1934 (as amended) and the Communications Satellite Act of 1962. Another powerful and permanent player, lurking in the background, is the Department of Defense, user of most of the spectrum space allocated for governmental needs (Mosco, 1979b). The Department and other security-related agencies always stand ready to make their requirements known which are then usually handled as priorities by Congress and the FCC.

The major and permanent players at the international level are the FCC, Congress, the White House, and Offices within the Departments of Commerce, Defense and State. Major and permanent players at the national level are the FCC, Congress, at times the Department of Justice (if the issue of monopoly were involved), the federal Court system (including the Supreme Court when a constitutional issue is involved such as the First Amendment) and, more recently the White House itself.[6] A transient player might be the Federal Trade Commission which, under an activist Chairman, attempted to regulate the types of advertisements broadcast on children's television programmes. Another transient player is the Office of Management and Budget which, under guidance from White House advisors, might disrupt programmes by withholding funds appropriated by Congress. Major individual players are the incumbents of key legislative committees in the Senate and the House of Representatives. One such key player is the Chairman of the Telecommunications Subcommittee of the House Energy and Commerce Committee who can control the destiny of legislation by, for example, delaying hearings.[7]

The state level includes as major and permanent players the FCC, Congress (in its ability to enact preemptive statutes), the Governors' Offices, state legislative bodies and the regulatory agencies and commissions they appoint (some for cable), and the state judicial systems. County and municipal governments add still another layer of players. For example, cities with cable systems might have cable commissions to regulate them. These levels can also function as national players; for example, the National League of Cities (NLC) maintains a lobbying office in Washington. The complexity that can arise from mixing these levels of government is admittedly enormous even before all the minor and transient players are included.

We would like to illustrate such complexity by describing the battle that has been waged over legislation to deregulate the cable industry at the municipal level. It lasted four years. The cities were satisfied with the status quo because the income they received from cable operations offset declines in federal subsidies and tax revenues. The cable operators, burdened with the debt of their start-up costs wanted to reduce the percentage of income they paid the cities and to have the freedom to drop programmes which do not produce advertising revenue, such as public service channels. AT&T lobbied against the bill because they thought it would create a loop-hole which would allow cities to regulate the data-transmission services of telephone companies.[8] The opposing factions would have been close to a compromise if it were not for a Supreme Court Decision limiting the right of Oklahoma to delete advertisements for alcoholic beverages in signals originating out-of-state, a decision which emboldened the cable operators to insist on further concessions from the cities (*Broadcasting*, 1984c).

The power of the FCC to regulate cable had never been made explicit and court rulings were necessary to affirm its role. FCC's authority over cable began in 1963 when it extended its authority from issuing licences for microwave stations to regulating the microwave signals themselves. The following year, it extended its authority to all cable systems, whether or not microwave was used. The FCC saw its role at the time as guarding the revenues of local broadcasters from direct competition by cable systems carrying programmes and advertisements from stations in nearby cities. The FCC therefore limited cable to carrying just signals of local origin. (It is possible that the FCC was also protecting the interests of AT&T in microwave transmission.) The FCC was challenged in court but defended its ruling by citing its mandate from Congress to regulate 'interstate commerce by wire or radio'. The Supreme Court ruled in favour of the FCC in June 1968, holding that the Commission had the right to preserve local broadcast services and to ensure the equitable distribution of broadcast services throughout the regions.

Launching of the satellites and the burgeoning of investment in distant-signal transmission, for example, Home Box Office (HBO), forced the FCC to reconsider its strict protectionist stance towards local broadcasters. Comments and recommendations on rule changes were invited from the broadcast industry, the cable industry and television production companies who in effect were invited to write the very rules under which they were to be regulated.[9] The set of rules finally released in February 1972 allowed cable operators outside of local television markets the right to import all distant signals, a right also given to cable operators with fewer than 1000 subscribers. The FCC had given the multiple-system operators in the cable industry the freedom needed at the time to advance their interests (FCC, 1984).

Over the past decade, the larger cable system operators found many of the rules still confining and sought modification or relief. Some rules they had eliminated by challenging them in court. By July 1981, all remaining restrictions on importing out-of-region distant signals had been eliminated and cable operators could carry an unlimited number. However, one proviso remained: they could not drop any local station to make room for them – the 'must carry' rule. This regulation was the one regulation that the cable industry especially wanted to see eliminated (NCTA, 1981). As in the Japanese game of *go*, in Washington politics one can always try to encircle an opponent. If one thinks the FCC is not moving quickly enough to change a regulation, then (as shown) one can bring court challenges or one can find friendly Senators and Congressmen to rewrite the laws. The latter is usually the preferred strategy when an issue is particularly complicated, such as the overlapping regulatory authorities of the FCC, the states and the cities. Another example, perhaps too controversial for the FCC to resolve on its own because of the media giants and financial interests involved, is that of cross-ownership (whether cable systems should be owned by telephone companies or television broadcasters). The simplest thing to do in that case is to package the problem and turn it over to Congress where the special interests involved can fight it out.

The process of legislative relief began when the cable industry prevailed on Barry Goldwater, the Republican Senator from Arizona, to introduce S. 2172, the Cable Telecommunications Act of 1982. It would have strengthened the role of the FCC in regulating cable and, for the first time, established a national policy by transferring much of the authority from cities to the FCC. The NAB opposed the bill because it would give the FCC the authority to drop 'must carry' rules, that is, allow cable systems to drop local stations from their channels. Although the bill did pass the Senate Commerce Committee, it was never placed on the Senate calendar for a vote and it died when the session ended. The measure was reintroduced by Goldwater as S. 66 in January 1983 at the beginning of the next Senate two-year session. The Commerce Committee immediately scheduled hearings and passed the bill on to the full Senate which passed it by June. The US system of government requires that legislation also pass the House of Representatives before being sent to the President for signature, and a House version was introduced the following October by Representative Tim Wirth (Democrat from Colorado), Chairman of the Subcommittee on Telecommunications. Any differences between the final versions of the Senate and House bills would have to be ironed out by representatives from both houses in a 'mark-up' session.

The Senate, caught between the broadcasting and cable industries, neither abolished nor included the 'must carry' rule in its bill; rather, it added words to support the concept, but just in principle. S. 66 also restricts the grounds on which cities might refuse to renew existing franchises and places a ceiling of 5 per cent of gross revenues on the fees that cable operators have to pay to cities. Probably the provision in the bill of most interest to empire-builders in the industry is that all federal, state or local restrictions on cable–media cross-ownership were prohibited. The media giants had got what they wanted.

H.R. 4103, the House bill, passed its Subcommittee in record time (one month) but not without some changes. A requirement was inserted which for the first time established requirements for Equal Employment Opportunity for the cable industry. The cross-ownership controversy was renewed because the House version banned newspapers and television broadcasters from owning cable systems in the same locations. Both the Senate and House bills placed a ceiling of 5 per cent on city franchise fees. However, the final version of the House bill still did not satisfy all the parties involved and, for different reasons, it was attacked in turn by the NAB, the NLC (with the US Conference of Mayors), the National Cable Television Association (NCTA) and AT&T. Ideally, the cities simply wanted to keep things as they were. The cable industry wanted complete regulatory relief and freedom from sharing profits with anyone. AT&T did not think that the cable industry should go unregulated while telephone systems still were.

The struggle continued. It was not until June 1984 that all parties (under pressure from a now-impatient Tim Wirth who was threatening to shelve the legislation) agreed to a compromise which the House Energy and Commerce Committee could pass (*Broadcasting*, 1984a). However, before the bill could be submitted to the House Rules Committee to clear to the House floor, the cable owners again withdrew their support, warning that they would use their influence with friendly Congressmen on the Rules Committee to block its passage. Because the June Supreme Court decision on Oklahoma had thrown doubt on all forms of local regulation, they thought that stalling would force more concessions from the cities (*Broadcasting*, 1984b). The cities welcomed the opportunity to avoid further talks which could lead to further loss of local authority. Time was also on the side of the cities. Unless a compromise could be reached in the few weeks remaining before Congress adjourned both bills, the Senate one again, and the House version as well, would die.

The confusion was also worsening. The National Association of Realtors and other landlord and real estate interests had entered the battle by launching a vigorous attack on a provision which would have permitted the operators to wire the apartments of tenants without first obtaining the consent of the property owners. Freedom was the issue – whether tenants as consumers are subject to the control of their landlords. However, the real argument, as usual, was over profits – whether the cable operators should be forced to pay access fees to the apartments.

The possibility that the Senate bill might again die enraged Bob Packwood, Republican from Oregon, Chairman of the Commerce Committee, who wrote a letter to the NLC urging them to 'return to the negotiating table with the cable industry in a good faith effort to resolve your differences' with NCTA. 'Next year may be too late', he added. 'Our legislative schedule may prevent consideration of cable legislation, and in the meantime, the courts and the FCC may further define the limits of existing [municipal] regulations' (*Broadcasting*, 1984c).

Finally, all compromises that could be obtained were obtained, and in the very last minutes before Congress adjourned H.R. 4103 passed. (The provision allowing access to tenants' apartments was dropped to save the bill.) At this point, a reasonable person might presume that it was done with and all could go home. However, the battle was far from over. To demonstrate how cumbersome and frustrating the regulatory process is in the US, just in the matter of access to tenants' apartments, the NCTA simply announced that it would move its lobbying efforts from the federal level to the state and get the same law passed state by state (Young, 1984). The type of chaotic and unruly process that has been described could not and probably would not happen in the United Kingdom or in other countries. Regulation in the United States starts from antagonistic positions and the role of Congress and the FCC is to mediate toward negotiated settlements. Also, unlike in other countries, the process is litigious – if you disagree with the rulings you get, file law-suits challenging the right of the agency to do its job, and if you cannot think of anything else, claim that the First Amendment is involved. Or, taking another approach, charge your competitors with monopoly or restraint-of-trade practices so that the Department of Justice would have to investigate and perhaps file anti-trust actions. You can also bribe. Make substantial contributions to the campaign chests of those legislators who favour your interests. The US approach to soliciting campaign contributions, Political Action Committees (PACs), makes it both legal and proper. If you are a trade association, invite your favourite Senator to your annual meeting as a speaker and be sure to pay a handsome honorarium.

CABLEPAC, the PAC of the NCTA, does not waste its resources; members of the House Energy and Commerce Committee are included on its list of beneficiaries. Money fuels the regulatory process and, as a process, it will not change because it provides a livelihood for so many of the players. The staff of the FCC itself is beholden to the process for its jobs. Thus, there is an invitation toward collusion. If bills do die, one can hear a collective sigh of relief because the game can go on and jobs and earnings are assured. The only way to lose is to let one's attention wander and, heaven forbid, actually let a bill pass!

Conclusion
The theme of this chapter is that regulation has not disappeared but did change dramatically since the Communications Act was passed. Telecommunications industries, broadly defined, underwent decisive changes through technical advances too numerous and complicated to be listed here. What is important here is that it is impossible to separate telephone and computers from broadcasting, film-making and printing. A variety of new communication and information services are being introduced and planned. Television, film, radio, telephone and print are inseparably connected by the technology of data transmission and linked by computers. These changes do require different definitions of free speech and public interest. For example, the term 'mass communications' is probably no longer as meaningful as it once was. Audiences for television are becoming segmented, although not at the rate others predicted a few years ago. Social scientists interested in policy remain committed to examining questions relating to access and composition of the audience, even when the policy makers have clearly chosen the side of private interests and profits. From the above discussion, it is clear that Congress has encouraged the FCC to work towards its own demolition (unless, of course, there is another change in political climate). But deregulation does not mean that government will no longer be an active player because, through support or non-support, it will still help or hinder various commercial interests. Just as telecommunications and broadcasting have been converging, innovation and change have also generated splits within the telecommunications and broadcast industries. Some who examine the relationship between these industries and the FCC claim that it is too simplistic to view the FCC as simply 'captured' by the established industries (Mosco, 1979a; Krasnow et al., 1982). Just as it was the industries that pushed regulation in the 1920s to protect their growth, the very same industries (with some new players) now want deregulation to further their growth. The attempts to rewrite the Act during the Carter administration, as noted earlier, failed but the FCC through its rule-

making power was able to accomplish the intent of Congress without having to resort to direct legislative change. However, it can also be pointed out that while not overtly 'captured', decision-making by the FCC in the regulatory process is so interactive with major industrial interests that they usually can get what they want without having to apply pressure directly. The 1934 law was written originally to support the major industrial structures of the time (Radio Corporation of America (RCA), Westinghouse, General Electric and AT&T) and, as written, can remain in place to give industry the support and protection it wants. New players may be added and new technologies but the same political struggles continue through legislation, court decisions and regulation. Through law and tradition, the government supports private interests. The players may change and the list may lengthen but the game remains the same.

It is also evident that there never is nor could ever be a clear path toward developing an industrial policy on telecommunicaitons in the US which would be neutral and equitable in serving everyone's interests. In a society and economy based on competitive struggle, and with the telecommunications industry already falling into the hands of just a few giants, the role of government will be merely to serve and facilitate their interests. With this perspective, the current programme to 'deregulate' is merely a façade behind which protection for one set of special interests is shifted to protect still others. Thus, what appears to be disappearance of regulation is merely the group in control changing the rules to prevent others from regaining control. One prediction can be made with some degree of certainty: the stage is being set for a final centralization of the industry (as with broadcasting in its origins) into the hands of an ever-diminishing number of telecommunications giants, with no governmental procedure or entity in place to regulate them.

Notes

1. Where not otherwise cited, the historical material in this article (especially those applicable to radio) can be verified by examining Barnouw (1966, 1968 and 1978); Head (1976) and Summers and Summers (1966). In addition to using secondary sources, the authors used primary documents from the FCC, interviewed FCC and other government officials and have attended Congressional hearings and audited a number of public lectures since 1968.

2. The controversies surrounding commercial advertisements have been muted somewhat by recent Court and FCC decisions. For example, in a recent (June 1984) FCC television deregulation decision, all restrictions on advertising time were lifted on 24 September 1984. Also, the Supreme Court, ruling that the NAB code of ethics was a constraint of trade, eliminated all efforts by the industry to regulate itself.

3. Radio was not considered as 'harmful' as television. Almost from its beginnings, television entertainment programming was subject to scrutiny by Congress, citizen groups and the press. See Rowland (1983) for a review of the violence issue.

4. The Fairness Doctrine, first an FCC regulation and later added to the Communications Act by amendment, clearly states that broadcasters are 'to operate in the public interest and to afford reasonable opportunity for the discussion of conflicting views on issues of public importance' (FCC, 1971: 52). Although television has been mostly deregulated, this provision remains in the law.

5. A major newcomer to the game is the small consumer of telecommunications products and services who is behaving unpredictably. The consent decree ending the seven-year-old anti-trust suit against AT&T permitted it to retain its long-distance service while limiting its former operating companies and other independent telephone companies to just local service. The decree also opened the long-distance market to competitors such as MCI and Sprint which, to begin their operations, priced their services below AT&T's (whose rates are still subject to FCC control). To the dismay of AT&T, customers ignored their long-distance bills, paying just the local telephone companies. Customers are no longer as passive as they were when AT&T as sole-supplier could cut off service if bills were not paid. Observers estimate that losses in 1983 were 5 per cent of sales for AT&T and 10 to 12 per cent for the rest, making the loss to AT&T (according to documents filed with the FCC) as high as $3.5 billion and the total estimated loss for its rivals as high as $300 to $500 million (*Forbes*, 1984).

6. The White House has been involved directly and indirectly in telecommunication policy decisions. For example, Kennedy tried to reorganize the FCC in 1961; Nixon established a White House Office of Telecommunications Policy and an Office of Telecommunications in the Department of Commerce, later to merge into the National Telecommunications and Information Administration in the Department of Commerce in 1978. Reagan also intervened personally with the FCC on behalf of the movie industry during its controversy with the networks over syndication profits.

7. The actual name is Subcommittee on Telecommunications, Consumer Protection, and Finance.

8. The most detailed source is consecutive issues of *Broadcasting* which over the last few years has followed the cable–city battle closely. More convenient summaries can be found in the journal's section 'Where Things Stand', published quarterly in the first issues of January, April, July and October.

9. The short-lived White House Office of Telecommunications Policy took an active interest in the process, which in itself must have been intimidating to the FCC.

References

Barnouw, E. (1966) *A Tower in Babel*. New York: Oxford University Press.

Barnouw, E. (1968) *The Golden Web*. New York: Oxford University Press.

Barnouw, E. (1978) *The Sponsor: Notes on a Modern Potentate*. New York: Oxford University Press.

Broadcasting (1984a) 'Commerce Committee clears H.R. 4103', 2 July: 35–7.

Broadcasting (1984b) 'Back to the Drawing Board (again) on Cable Bill', 23 July: 40–1.

Broadcasting (1984c) 'NCTA – Cities Set to Try Again', 17 September: 31–2.

Broadcasting (1984d) 'Where Things Stand (TV Deregulation)', 1 October: 83.

Cantor, M.G. (1980) *Prime-Time Television*. Beverly Hills, Calif.: Sage.

Cantor, M.G. and J.M. Cantor (1984) 'United States: A System of Minimal Regulation', in R. Kuhn (ed.), *The Politics of Broadcasting: An International Survey*. London: Croom Helm.

FCC (1971) *The Communications Act of 1934 with Amendments and Index Thereto, Recapped to Janury 1969*. Washington, D.C.: Government Printing Office (Federal Communications Commission).

FCC (1984) *Information Bulletin: Cable Television* (June). Washington D.C: Government Printing Office (Federal Communications Commission).

Forbes (1984) 'Money Rolling Out', 9 September: 142 – 4.

Forbes (1985) 'Cover Story: Still the Strongest Game in Town', 25 March: 216 – 20.

Gans, H.J. (1972) 'The Politics of Culture in America: A Sociological Analysis', in D. McQuail (ed.), *The Sociology of Mass Communications*. Harmondsworth, Middx.: Penguin.

Hanks, W.E. and T.A. Pickett (1979) 'Influence of Community-Based Citizens Groups on Television Broadcasters in Five Eastern Cities: An Exploratory Study', in D.S. Dordick (ed.), *Proceedings of the Sixth Annual Telecommunications Policy Research Conference*. Lexington, Mass.: Lexington Books.

Head, S. (1976) *Broadcasting in America: A Survey of Television and Radio*, 3rd edition. Boston, Mass.: Houghton Mifflin.

Krasnow, E.G., L.D. Longley, and H.A. Terry (1982) *The Politics of Broadcast Regulation*, 3rd edition. New York: St Martin's Press.

Montgomery, K. (1984) 'The Political Struggle for Prime Time' (May). Unpublished paper. Los Angeles, Calif.: Theater Arts Department, University of California.

Mosco, V. (1979a) *Broadcasting in the United States: Innovative Challenge and Organizational Control*. Norwood, N.J.: Ablex.

Mosco, V. (1979b) 'Who Makes U.S. Government Policy in World Communications?', *Journal of Communications*, 29 (1): 158 – 64.

NAB (1984) *Broadcasting and Government: A Review of 1983 and a Preview of 1984*. Washington D.C.: National Association of Broadcasters.

NCTA (1981) *A Cable Primer*. Washington, D.C.: National Cable Television Association.

Rowland, W.D., Jr. (1983) *The Politics of TV Violence: Policy Uses of Communication Research*, Beverly Hills, Calif.: Sage.

Schiller, D. (1982) *Telematics and Government*. Norwood, N.J.: Ablex.

Summers, R.E. and H.B. Summers (1966) *Broadcasting and the Public*. Belmont, Calif.: Wadsworth.

Tunstall, J. (1984) 'Communication Technology and Deregulation: for Export'. Unpublished paper presented at the ESRC Workshops on New Communications Technologies, Bristol, 6 June.

US Congress, House (1979) 'Communications Act of 1979: H.R. 3333'. 96th Congress, First Session. Washington, D.C.: Government Printing Office.

Young, G. (1984) 'House Vote a Defeat for Cable', *Washington Post*, 13 October: E52.

7

Information law, policy and the public interest

James Michael

There is no coherent body of rules in the United Kingdom now recognized as 'information law', but the fundamental thesis of this chapter is that there should be, if only for purposes of analysis and debate. Legislation and the development of case-law on the subject is likely to proceed on the piecemeal basis that is particularly characteristic of common-law countries. The special relevance of new communications technology to information law is that it, like other past technological advances such as the automobile, presents society with relatively new forms of human activity which are likely to require regulation. Two fairly commonplace observations should perhaps be borne in mind in considering how the rules relating to the dissemination of information are developed: the first is that the law almost always lags behind changes in technology, usually seriously so; the second is that legal solutions to new problems tend to be modifications, often very inadequate, of the legal rules adopted for the previous generation of technology (as the law of copyright is still far from able to cope with the photocopier).

The law relating to communication technology is made particularly difficult by the nature of the activity being regulated. 'Information' itself is an abstraction, and the 'communication' of information encompasses a very broad range of human activity, from the whispered opinion (which may be a slander) to the international television broadcast (which is regulated not only by national rules but also by various international treaties). Quite apart from difficulties in establishing legal rules relating to information, there is a basic problem even in writing about communication: as succinctly as possible, it is that the medium of discourse is also its subject.

Despite these problems, it is suggested that consideration of the rules relating to information as a whole may assist in deciding what new rules should be devised about the use of new communication technology. Two propositions are suggested to represent the core of information law. The first is that the law relating to information does one of three things: it may prohibit certain communications, it may require others to be made, or it may remain neutral. This first proposition assumes a system of sanctions (and sometimes rewards) to

102

ensure that behaviour generally conforms to legal rules. The second proposition is that information law is a series of answers to the basic questions of who should know what, and when, and how.

To 'know' in this context simply means to acquire information, which may be true, false, distorted, or debatable. The dissemination of truth provokes little objection generally, although the truth of a communication may sometimes make it more objectionable, rather than less, as in the otherwise diverse areas of personal privacy, commercial confidentiality, and national security. The proposition that the dissemination of error should be tolerated, and that the 'market place of ideas' should require truth to compete with error, is still relatively recent and far from universally accepted. Even in liberal democracies most people would qualify the language attributed to Voltaire about defending to the death the right of those with whom he disagreed to speak. Toleration of offensive speech is difficult enough to achieve; to promote the dissemination of minority views (as in 'access' channels or subsidies to publishers) is even less likely to gain popular support.

Considering the roles of information law in terms of 'the public interest' is, in one sense, simple: few law-makers would argue that the purpose of law is to serve anything other than the public interest. Beyond that bare assertion is a kind of utilitarian calculus with a libertarian gloss: rules should promote the greatest good of the greatest number, with respect for the rights of minorities.

But the peculiar nature of information makes the application of such a calculus awkward. The provision of information to people is intimately related to other decisions about the public interest in a way in which the provision of other commodities, such as electricity, is not. It is also more difficult to calculate costs and benefits in the supply of information than for other commodities: people obviously die without food; it is not so obvious what the effects of ignorance are. While there may be degrees and kinds of ignorance which can be measured, the measurement is more complex than counting the housing stock or the number of households with running water.

Leaving aside, for the moment, the notion of a 'human right' to receive and impart information, it is not surprising that some countries might consider the supply of other commodities to have priority in the public interest. An irrigation network can be defended as being more immediately in the public interest than a network of television stations. Although Western Europe itself is not now faced with such stark choices, there are more subtle equivalents. Should, for example, the provision of fibre optic cable systems have an equal claim on public funds to the replacement of crumbling sewers?

Such arguments are particularly relevant to public service broadcasting, which may roughly equate the provision of information with the provision of other essential goods and services. The arguments are also relevant to the degree and direction of regulation in a market economy. The usual justification for such regulation is the existence of natural monopolies, or at least markets in which there is a tendency toward monopoly or oligopoly. As will be considered later, these arguments have rather less force when applied to new communication technology than they did in the earlier days of radio and television. Their continuing force is now based more on the economics than the technology of electronic communication.

There is not space here to consider thoroughly why receiving and imparting information is considered to be a human right (and even one to be preferred over other rights, in the view of the US Supreme Court). It is perhaps enough to suggest two approaches, with rather different consequences. One is that there is a 'natural' right to freedom of expression, with the most emphasis placed on keeping the restrictions on expression imposed by law to a justifiable minimum. Another is to consider that the widest possible dissemination of the widest possible range of information is essential to the functioning of a democracy. The first is generally satisfied if people can say almost anything without legal penalties. The second, if acted upon, requires intervention in the market place of the media of communication, if not of information itself. The second approach can also lead to paradoxical legal rules. An example is the generally accepted law of copyright, which restricts the right to reproduce information in certain forms. The purpose of such restriction is, ideally, to provide sufficient return through a temporary monopoly to encourage the production of literary and other work.

Despite the status of 'right' accorded to communication, it must be recognized that no society is completely pluralistic, and that all are organic to some degree. One extreme is a theocracy (which may be secular) in which all communication is carefully regulated to promote the dissemination of truth and repress that of error. Liberal and pluralistic societies also have their organic characteristics, however, some of which are both functional and cultural. Insisting on the use of a common language is functional in the sense that it is of obvious utility in communicating at all; but is also cultural in the sense that many people, however multilingual, would feel uneasy if the use of their mother tongue were diminished by the increasing use of another. Linguistic politics may come to replace the confessional politics with which they are associated in some countries.

Decisions about the rules of information law must at least be made with an awareness of organic values, of which language is only one. An immediate example of such values is the French subsidy to

Francophone direct broadcasting by satellite (DBS) for the express purpose of promoting French culture. Language apart, arguments about information law in the United Kingdom often invoke 'cultural' values. Falling cinema attendance is seen as a loss of communal experience as well as a decline in revenue to finance films. The splintering of broadcast television audiences by video, cable and satellite is criticized as a 'privatized culture' which destroys a sense of public culture.

It is possible to deride such arguments and urge diversity for its own sake. This approach, for economic reasons to be considered later, can lead to a false choice from a multiplicity of channels. As in other markets (detergents, for example) there can be imitation on essential qualities with fierce competition on marginal ones.

All of this may perhaps be thought to apply only to the regulation of electronic broadcasting. But the same complex of values also applies to other media for communicating information. Printing presses in the eighteenth and nineteenth centuries allowed the wide circulation of anonymous pamphlets (among the literate) which promoted reform and sometimes revolt. The statutory requirement that publications contain the name and address of the publisher was passed to check the spread of republicanism from France to England. Cassette recordings of the Ayatollah Khomeini played an important part in the Iranian revolution (which, not incidentally, invoked traditional cultural values).

New communication technology will require new rules, and the process of formulating these should include a continuing reassessment of what best serves the public interest. It is suggested that a classical liberal approach of striving for the minimum of state restrictions is no longer sufficient; even its necessity is questionable if promoting diversity of expression requires limiting expression by those in dominant (usually economic) positions. Respect for organic values in society must be a factor in determining questions of public interest, but it should be considered that economic and social restraints, even when not expressed in law, can restrain diversity of communication quite as much as legal restrictions.

Technology is important right across the range of communication, and to the rules about it, ranging from the 'leak' of a photocopied document to the structure and content of broadcast television. An illustration of how law and technology can converge at several points began in July 1984, when a British civil servant named Clive Ponting photocopied two memoranda and posted them to a Member of Parliament.

Broadcasting and secrecy: an illustration

Although the existing legal rules that make up information law are scattered across traditional legal categories, they occasionally come together in particular cases. One example was the ban by the Independent Broadcasting Authority (IBA) on transmission of the programme 'MI5's Official Secrets'. The IBA justified this on the ground that the programme involved a breach of section 2 of the Official Secrets Act. Criticism of the decision was based on two arguments. One was essentially a matter of criminal law. The commissioning authority, Channel 4, argued that there would be a good defence to any criminal charge, and referred to the recent acquittal of a senior civil servant, Clive Ponting, on charges under the Act. The second argument was directed at the very structure of the IBA: that the body charged with the dissemination of programmes should not also be the quasi-judicial body to decide what programmes should be allowed and what should be forbidden. The decision was quickly reversed, and the reversal may have been influenced by the dissemination of the information through the two alternative technologies of film and video cassettes.

The legal regulation of these technologies illustrates some of the inconsistencies in information law as it now is and as it is developing. The exhibition of films in the United Kingdom is regulated by the Obscene Publications Act (1959), but it is also regulated on a local basis under legislation which originally was for the purpose of protecting the public from the danger of fire from inflammable nitrate stock. Much, but not all, of this local regulation is effectively delegated to the British Board of Film Censors, which has no official legal powers regarding films. (One inconsistency is that the rules relating to importing films, as in importing books, are more stringent than those relating to their exhibition.)

Until the Video Recordings Act 1984, video recordings were subject to no other regulation than that which applied to printed matter (unless the recordings were publicly exhibited). The 1984 Act, when it comes fully into effect, will establish a statutory system of certification for video-tapes enforced by criminal sanctions. For once, the law responded quickly to a new technology, but perhaps a period of reflection might have resulted in better legislation. The result of the Act is that information which is essentially the same will be subject to one set of legal controls if it is distributed in the form of video recording, but will be subject to a different, and less stringent, form of regulation if it is distributed in the form of cine-films.

Using the basic formulation of questions, it would seem that the 'how' of communicating moving images, whether by video-tape or cine film, does not really justify a difference in legal rules. There is more of a difference in the 'how' between the availability of video-tapes in shops and the national broadcasting of the same programme, but the burden of justifying different legal rules should still be on those who would impose them.

The case of the Channel 4 programme also illustrates another characteristic of information which affects the law regulating its dissemination: nothing is ever completely secret from everyone, or completely known by everyone. The regulation of information is thus always a matter of degree, and frequently the degree is determined by the medium of communication. Another case involving Channel 4 illustrates the point. The trial of Clive Ponting was mostly open to the public. The press and public were free to attend, and free to repeat what was said in court, subject to those provisions of the Contempt of Court Act 1981 that a published report be 'fair, accurate and contemporaneous'.[1]

Channel 4 proposed to broadcast a nightly programme during the trial which would consist of sections of the day's transcript being read out by actors. On the first day of the trial the judge made an order under the Contempt of Court Act (1981) forbidding such broadcasts. The basis for his order was that the jurors' recollection of the testimony given by witnesses might be distorted if they were to hear the testimony repeated by actors on television. Channel 4 quickly recruited newsreaders instead of actors, and no action was taken after the programmes were broadcast.

Multiplying broadcasting
The fact that there are now four nationally broadcast television channels in the UK illustrates the importance of degrees of communication in determining how information is to be regulated. It also introduces economic influences into both the content of the rules and the process of their formulation. It is a commonplace observation that if the 'old' technology of the rotary printing press were introduced today it would probably be accepted that the users of such presses should be licensed (as printing was until the end of the seventeenth century). This would be justified not only by the dangers to society of the possible dissemination of 'dangerous' information, but also on the ground that the economics of newspaper publishing could only support a limited number of periodicals.

The licensing of radio and television broadcasting is still said to be required by the technical requirements of those media; there are only so many frequencies available, and regulation is necessary to prevent interference. This was only partly true in the past, and has been made even less so by new technology such as satellite and some forms of cable (which, in primitive form, was actually used in the UK for dissemination of audio and video signals at the very beginning of 'broadcasting' without wires). The economic justification for limiting the number of video or audio channels is that the viewers and listeners themselves, rather than the frequencies available, are considered to be a public asset. Their value is in their numbers, either in terms of the fee which they can be compelled to pay, or in terms of the advertising revenue which they represent.

Until relatively recently it has been accepted in this country that strict government limits on the channels for radio and television were necessary, even if the reasons were not alway explicit. That is no longer the case. Partly because of the economic character of the Conservative government and partly because of new communications technology the future of video and audio communication is likely to be a multiplication of channels. In place of the 'market place of ideas' of the nineteenth-century libertarians there is likely to be a technological 'market place of information'.

This multiplication will require money, and the most likely source will be from advertising. (Another source, fees from 'pay-view', would almost certainly depend on the new technology of interactive cable television, which is now unlikely to live up to its promises because of difficulty in raising capital.) If there is to be relatively unregulated advertising, legislators, both national and international, will have to re-examine the supposed value in the 'free flow of information' to decide whether that value extends equally to commercial speech. A persuasive legal opinion has been published which argues that the right to 'receive and impart information' in Article 10 of the European Convention on Human Rights protects commercial speech as much as other forms of communication (Lester and Pannick, 1984).

A common reaction in the UK to such proposals is (as in a series of press advertisements opposing the multiplication of channels) that multi-channel television, heavy with advertising, is not only bad in terms of the quality of programmes, but is also un-British.

A new European information order?
However un-British it may seem, new communication technology offers an increased potential for 'broadcasting' with a multiplicity of channels and a greater diversity of programmes, including advertising. By the ratification of the European Convention on Human Rights in 1951 and accession to the European Economic Community in 1972, the United Kingdom accepted basic rules which now make it more difficult to maintain a purely national regime for the regulation of communication. ('Broadcasting' is expressed in inverted commas because new communication technology makes it increasingly difficult to distinguish between programmes transmitted

to the public at large and 'private' communication such as that by telephone. As already suggested, the barriers to interactive services that would blur this distinction even further are more economic than technological.).

These basic rules are a mixture of ideology and economics. The ideology is a liberal one, as expressed in Article 10 of the Convention. The economics are those of the market (which itself is also an expression of an ideology). The communication of information is peculiarly protected both as a human right and as an economic commodity. (It is not unique, however, and may be compared to the free movement of labour.)

The commitment in international law by the United Kingdom both to the right to receive and impart information and to the free movement of goods and services is likely to bring into question the validity of legal restriction on communication. Thus far, the questioning (and it has not been limited to British law) has been primarily under the Human Rights Convention before the Commission and Court in Strasbourg. This case-law approach to permissible restrictions on communication is now being supplemented by a more civil-law approach.

In December 1984 the Committee of Ministers of the Council of Europe published a set of recommended principles to govern the communication of television and radio by satellite. The principles are relatively deferential to national authority in terms of determining the multiplicity of channels. It is in terms of programme standards that the principles are most interesting.

These standards are, inevitably, expressed in general terms, but they impose positive obligations as well as defining permissible limits. The five basic programme standards under the Second Principle deserve quotation in full.

a) news shall not be presented inaccurately or in a partial manner;
b) programmes shall not be indecent and in particular not contain pornography;
c) programmes shall not infringe the rights to respect for privacy and family life; they shall respect the views of others;
d) programmes shall not give undue prominence to violence or incite to race hatred;
e) programmes shall respect the sensitivity and the physical, mental, and moral personality of children and young persons especially when large numbers of them are likely to watch.

(Committee of Ministers of the Council of Europe, 1984)

These may be thought to be unexceptional, but they become more specific, and perhaps more debatable, in the accompanying commentary. For example, the ban on pornography is considered to be absolute (assuming an agreed definition), with such material permitted 'not even for programme systems accessible to restricted groups (e.g. "adult channels") for at the international level such systems would defy real control'.

The principle of respect for the views of others is not explained so explicitly, but raises even more fundamental questions about the notion of offensive information. 'The notion of "views" includes moral and religious convictions. Where a programme is addressed to the public in different countries, the service providers should make sure that the views of people in those countries are not disregarded and they should take them as much as possible into account when they decide which programmes are to be transmitted.'

Another principle also presents intriguing possibilities, although the explanation is largely in terms of sporting events. It is that 'All efforts shall be made to avoid that the acquisition by one service provider of exclusive rights for an event of high public interest will result in depriving a large part of the public of the opportunity to follow that event on television or radio.' If 'event' can be extended to include particular programmes, the principle might be a limit on censorship by economic power rather than by regulation. For example, it might be violated by actions such as the purchase by a Swedish citizen to the rights to 'Death of a Princess' in 1979, which he then announced would not be shown or distributed to avoid offence to Saudi Arabia. (On the other hand, such action might be in accordance with 'respect for the views of others'.)

A separate principle for the 'right to reply' would have particular implications for British broadcasting law. Until now, most of the argument over whether there should be such a right has focussed on the written press. The principle recommended by the Committee of Ministers makes it clear not only that the right of reply (which was the subject of an earlier recommendation in 1974) should also apply to broadcasting, but that trans-border transmissions should make the right available to non-nationals and non-residents. It is questionable whether the recently-established Broadcasting Complaints Commission is sufficient to establish such a right.

Although these are recommendations rather than law, they are close to being an advisory opinion on what international law is likely to require or allow. It is perhaps worth noting that there is no mention of restricting advertising in the Recommendations. On the other hand, requiring respect for the views of others raises a basic question about information law, whether national or international: should the communication of information be restricted simply because of disapproval by most people, and if so, why?

Data protection and privacy

'Data protection' is perhaps the clearest example of new legal rules which have resulted directly from new communications technology. It is, however, also a particular aspect of the law relating to personal privacy, which has existed in one form or another for about a century. Although a right to privacy is not yet recognized in the law of the United Kingdom, its extensive development in the United States derives directly from English law, and even from one particular case.

The story of how Queen Victoria's Consort was successful in preventing an exhibition of family etchings, and how that success provided a basis for a law review article by a Boston attorney irritated by publicity about his daughter's wedding, is a familiar one in the literature of privacy (Wallington, 1984). In *Prince Albert* v. *Strange* (1849) a set of etchings executed by the royal couple had come into the hands of a publisher who proposed to display them and to publish a descriptive catalogue. The Prince was successful in stopping both, and suppressing the catalogue was particularly important. Reproduction of the etchings probably would have been prohibited then under the law of copyright, and certainly would be now. The catalogue, however, contained only information about the etchings rather than the particular form of expression which they were. In order to restrict the communication of that information, as distinct from the unauthorized reproduction of the etchings themselves, the court resorted to a doctrine known as the law of confidence.

In the USA the doctrine provided a basis for the law review article which is generally regarded as the first clear articulation of the right to privacy in that country. The Boston attorney, Samuel Warren, was not pleased by newspaper coverage of his daughter's wedding, and was inspired to write an article in the *Harvard Law Review* with his partner, Louis Brandeis (Warren and Brandeis, 1890). Combining the law of confidence with other doctrines such as the law of defamation, they argued that there was a common-law right to privacy. The essence of this right is that the individual should be able to control information about himself.

This right to privacy rapidly expanded beyond the relatively narrow bases of confidence and defamation. The law of defamation is concerned with compensation for communication of information injurious to reputation which is false. Except for the offence of criminal libel, there is no general rule in English law against damage caused by the communication of true information.

US law went beyond these doctrines fairly quickly. One of the earliest developments was a New York State statute providing a right to compensation for the unauthorized commercial use of a person's likeness. Privacy law in the US developed initially as a tort, or civil wrong, providing a basis for compensation in suits between individuals. By 1960 the right to privacy was described in a leading California law review article as encompassing four distinct torts: intrusion, disclosure of embarrassing private facts, casting a 'false light' on individuals and appropriation of a name or likeness (Prosser, 1960).

Shortly thereafter the right to privacy was elevated by the Supreme Court to the status of a fundamental Constitutional right. Although it is not articulated as such in the Bill of Rights, a right to privacy was found by the Court in the 'penumbra' of other specific rights such as those against unreasonable searches and seizures. This right was held to be violated by a state statute regulating the sale of contraceptives, and the law was declared void (*Griswold* v. *Connecticut*, 1965). It was also used to invalidate a law imposing penalties for watching pornographic films at home (*Stanley* v. *Georgia*, 1969).

That decision provides an interesting contrast to the arguments which resulted in the Video Recordings Act 1984 in the UK. The US reasoning was that although the law might constitutionally regulate public showings, the Constitution requires greater justification for laws regulating activity within the privacy of the home. The Video Recordings Act establishes a special regulatory regime for video recordings which does not apply to cinematographic films. The basic reason for this is that with the spread of video machines it became far more likely that video recordings would be watched at home by children. Assuming the harmful effects on children of depictions of sex and violence, Parliament was persuaded that the law to affect the content of viewing at home should be more rather than less stringent than the law regulating showings in places open to the general public.

The politics of data protection in the UK
The Data Protection Act 1984 was the product of particular legislation in some European countries which felt that it was required by some aspects of new communications technology, which in turn led the British government to legislate in order to avoid hypothetical economic sanctions. It does not fit easily into the four common-law torts which the law of privacy developed into the US, although it does mesh more with the US notion of a constitutional right to privacy and the complementary statutory right of access to official information, in one respect at least.

The closest that data protection comes to the four torts is to those of intrusion and the disclosure of embarrassing private facts. In narrative terms, it begins with Article 8 of the European Convention on Human Rights, which says that

1. Everyone has the right to respect for his private and family life, his home and his correspondence. 2. There shall be no interference by a public authority with the exercise of this right except such as is in accordance with the law and is necessary in a democratic society in the interests of national security, public safety or the economic well-being of the country, for the prevention of disorder or crime, for the protection of health or morals, or for the protection of the rights and freedoms of others.

The Convention was drawn up soon after World War II by members of the Council of Europe (which is older, larger and less binding than, and not to be confused with, the European Community). In one sense the right to data protection as an aspect of the right to privacy was to prevent the recurrence of very real harm which had resulted from the accumulation of information about people by national authorities. The existence of detailed records on people in many European countries had made it easier for the Nazis to seek them out and exterminate them. But the right to privacy guaranteed by Article 8 does not obviously require legislation to regulate the collection of information about individuals. Such legislation was a direct result of the development of vastly more efficient data processing. Before the use of transistors and then microchips for computers the inefficiency of recording information on paper provided basic protection for privacy of a sort. Data processing equipment made it possible to collect and store much more information and, even more important, to retrieve and collate it.

The first national legislation was in Sweden, and it may well have developed from the Swedish constitutional principle of public access to government records. As in the United States, this legal right is subject to an exception if disclosure would infringe personal privacy. But that could not be used as a reason for denying an individual a right of access to records concerning himself, and Swedes therefore had a right of what is now called 'subject access' long before the Data Law of 1973.

It is useful to compare the broad outlines of the Swedish Act with the US Privacy Act of 1974. The Swedish Act was limited to automatically processed personal information, while the US Act included manual files. But the Swedish Act regulated such data processing in both the public and private sectors while the US Act covered only information collected by the federal government. Perhaps most important was the method of regulation. The Swedish Act established a Data Inspectorate to register all automatic processors of personal data and to exercise extensive powers on behalf of the data subjects. The US Act placed more reliance on self-help, establishing a right to inspect records and have them corrected, with appeals to the federal courts for enforcement.

During the 1970s national data protection laws proliferated in Europe, and talks were begun to develop a common standard. In part this was to reach a basic standard for protection in the spirit of the Convention on Human Rights, but it is unlikely that the Data Protection Convention would have been achieved so quickly if that had been the only reason. Equally, if not more important, was the possibility that national data protection laws might become, or be deliberately used as, non-tariff trade barriers to what are rather inelegantly known as trans-border data flows. In groups of countries committed in theory to the elimination of national trade barriers, such as the European Community and the European Free Trade Area, it is not unknown for national health and safety rules to have the coincidental effect of protecting national industries from foreign competition, and it was at least conceivable that data protection laws might have a similar effect on national data processing.

From this point of view, perhaps the most important part of the Convention was, and is, Article 12, which states that 'A Party shall not, for the sole purpose of the protection of privacy, prohibit or subject to special authorisation trans-border data flows of personal data going to the territory of another Party.' Although subject to some qualification, this Article establishes the basic rule that Parties to the Convention are members of a common information market. Only four cases seem to have been reported in which national data protection legislation had a commercial effect in limiting trans-border data flows of personal information, all of them involving limitations imposed by Sweden, but it was that argument which persuaded the British government to introduce the bill which became the Data Protection Act 1984.

But it was not as though proposals for such legislation were new in the UK. As the 1960s turned into the 1970s a number of private members' bills for the protection of privacy had been introduced, some of which were specifically concerned with data protection. A result of these bills was the appointment of the Younger Committee on Privacy, which reported in 1972. The Committee was hampered somewhat by limitation in its terms of reference to invasions of privacy from the private sector, and requests to be allowed to consider the public sector as well were refused by both Labour and Conservative Home Secretaries. The Committee recommended that basic rules be adopted for the automatic processing of personal data.

The UK took an active part in drafting the Convention, and its basic principles are remarkably similar to those proposed by Younger. The growing European pressure for legislation during the 1970s was reinforced in the UK by domestic influence. Two White Papers on computers and privacy were published in 1975 (Cmnd. 6353 and

6356), and the Lindop Committee on Data Protection was appointed in 1976. The Lindop Committee reported in 1978, proposing legislation to comply with a Council of Europe Convention, which then was available only in draft form (Cmnd. 7341).

The Labour government did little on data protection in the few months between publication of the Lindop Report and the general election of 1979, and the process which resulted in legislation was largely one of negotiation between Conservative ministers and various pressure groups. The coalition for legislation was an unlikely one, linking informally groups such as the National Council for Civil Liberties and the British Computer Society. Data processors were in the unusual position of an industry demanding that it be regulated, being persuaded that international trade would suffer if the UK did not sign and ratify the Convention.

Meanwhile, another aspect of British information law was being challenged under international law. Mr James Malone was arguing in Strasbourg that official telephone-tapping had violated his right to privacy under the Human Rights Convention.

Surveillance and privacy

The case of Mr Malone began in 1977 when he learned during his trial for receiving stolen property that his telephone conversations had been intercepted. (He was later acquitted.) It was unusual for him to discover this, because a peculiar aspect of telephone-tapping in the UK is that the direct evidence obtained by such interceptions is never used in court. He then brought a civil action which was unsuccessful. Having thus exhausted his domestic remedies, Malone applied to the European Commission of Human Rights which found in 1983 that there had been a violation of his rights, and referred the case to the European Court of Human Rights.

Malone had also argued that his right to privacy had been violated by the policy use of 'metering' information. This practice is particularly relevant to the social consequences of new communications technology. Metering is simply recording the numbers dialled and the duration of conversations, and does not record the substance of conversations. Using existing technology it is done by attaching a special device to a particular line at the telephone exchange, often at the request of a subscriber to check the accuracy of billing, but sometimes at the request of the police for other purposes. The use of such information by the police will become far more important with the introduction of System X exchanges, which will provide an automatic print-out of such information for every telephone.

The British government denied that the policy had used any

metering information about Malone's telephone, and the European Commission of Human Rights was unable to determine whether the facts presented the issue of whether any such use of metering information was an invasion of privacy. But a change in procedure before the Court allowed the metering issue to be considered. The rules of procedure which went into effect in 1983 allowed third parties to submit written observations on cases before the Court. The British Post Office Engineering Union (POEU), some of whose members are involved in telephone-tapping and which had advocated legislation to regulate it, was given permission to submit such observations.

This procedure is somewhat similar to third-party 'friend of the court' arguments before the US Supreme Court. In important constitutional cases such third-party interventions are often decisive, and they are often in the form of so-called 'Brandeis briefs' including sociological and psychological research.

In the *Malone* case the POEU submitted evidence that metering information was used by the police without even the administrative warrant from the Home Secretary required for telephone-tapping. Faced with this the British government admitted that it was the practice, argued that it was publicly known, and apologized if the Commission had been misled. In its August 1984 judgment the Court found that the UK had violated the right to privacy both by the system of telephone interceptions and by the policy use of metering information.

Information, values and research

Laws relating to the dissemination of information seem to be peculiarly linked to asserted, or perhaps even unarticulated, values, and difficult to explain on the basis of a utilitarian calculus. Some laws, such as those relating to pornography and espionage, may be justified on the basis of demonstrable harm caused by the communication of some kinds of information. But even those laws may be explained in terms of more basic aversion. The Williams Committee on Obscenity framed its recommendations (*Report of the Williams Committee*, 1979) in just those terms, and proposed that the regulation of certain public displays should be on the basis of how offended people were likely to be rather than the basis of demonstrable harm to those who saw such displays. Although espionage statutes are commonly framed in terms of the harm caused, or likely to be caused, by certain disclosures, some applications are more easily explained as punishment for a breach of trust, regardless of the consequences.

Section 2 of the Official Secrets Act 1911 is not just an espionage statute (its scope, and proposals for reform, will be discussed later), but the essential value expressed by the Official Secrets Act was articulated by the Court of Criminal Appeal in the case of *R*. v. *Fell* in 1963. It is an offence, said the Court, for a Crown servant to make an unauthorized disclosure 'whatever the document contains, whatever the motive for disclosure is, and whether or not the disclosure is prejudicial to the State'.

The peculiarities of the law of confidence can perhaps be explained by the special value which the courts place on enforcing obligations of confidentiality. It is enforced against those who were not party to the original promise, and there is no necessity to allege that damage will be caused by a threatened breach of confidence in order to obtain an injunction against such a breach. In brief, a promise to keep silence has been, and is, treated in law as a higher order of obligation deserving of special treatment. This is not to deny that some disclosures of information lead to demonstrable harm to identifiable interests. Much of the law relating to industrial and intellectual property (including patents, trademarks, and copyright as well as the law of confidence) is devoted to quantifying breaches of obligations in terms of commercial advantage. Many espionage prosecutions similarly turn on the advantage, real or potential, which the disclosures would give to a potential enemy. And convictions under the Obscene Publications Act depend on a finding that the material would have a tendency to 'deprave and corrupt'.

Yet there seems to be an added moral dimension to laws relating to who should know what, and when, and how. Obligations of confidentiality, whether owed to other people or to the state, are enforced even in the absence of damage caused by their breach. Moral disapproval seems to be at least as much part of the basis for laws relating to obscenity and pornography as is the harm caused by such communications. Perhaps the clearest articulation of such offended disapproval is in the relatively recently revived law of blasphemy, which bases criminality on the degree of offensiveness to Christians (which Lord Scarman thought should be extended to protect the feelings of adherents of other religions) (*R*. v. *Lemon and Gay News*, 1979).

There is a similar dimension to the related laws on access to government information and personal privacy. While it is possible to make a utilitarian argument for laws such as the US Freedom of Information Act and the Swedish *offentighetsprincip*, such arguments are both difficult to support with evidence and ultimately inconclusive. There may be evidence that public scrutiny of government is a disincentive for corruption and an incentive for efficiency usually in the form of breaches of law which might not have occurred had there been greater public knowledge. But it is at least possible to conceive of a benign secretive government which fairly benefits the population, and a transparent administration which is ineffective and unjust. One consequence of secrecy is that those in authority may appear better than they are, and of openness that they may appear worse. Opponents of such legislation in the UK often use just such arguments, and ask for proof that open government is necessarily better than a more secretive system. Such an argument can never be completely answered, and supporters of open government legislation must base at least a part of their case on the proposition that a greater degree of public knowledge is simply preferable to public ignorance.

Laws protecting personal privacy also depend in part on a simple preference for individuals to have rights to control information about themselves, and this is most sharply presented by the common assertion that only those who have something to hide want to protect information about themselves. Yet many people would object to public knowledge of information about themselves which it is difficult to consider as being shameful. In a survey commissioned by the Younger Committee on Privacy 33 per cent objected to publication of their address and 34 per cent to the publication of their telephone numbers (*Report of the Younger Committee*, 1972). To say that the objection of this significant minority to such publication is for the purpose of preventing other invasions of privacy by unwanted visitors or telephone calls is simply to ask other questions: why is there a desire for seclusion from such interruption? The Committee concluded that 'it is clear that the quest and need for privacy is a natural one, not restricted to man alone, but arising in the biological and social processes of all the higher forms of life'.

Sisella Bok (1983) perhaps came closer to explaining the reasons for desiring privacy in *Secrets*. From developmental psychology she argues that 'to realize that one has the power to remain silent is linked to the understanding that one can exert some control over events – that one need not be entirely transparent, entirely predictable, or . . . at the mercy of parents who have seemed all-seeing and all powerful'. This linking of privacy and autonomy is rather more subtle than the cliché which Bacon's dictum that 'knowledge is power' has become.

Knowledge (or information) is certainly not the only kind of power by which we may exert our will over others or over natural obstacles. It is not the only source of power in the legal philosophers' hypothetical island with two inhabitants, one of whom has a gun. And yet even there the knowledge of one or the other, or both, that the gun is not loaded would change the equation dramatically. Ignorance on the part of those who are subject to authority would seem to be an essential element in power relationships, but it may not be the only useful ignorance. Those who exercise power rarely explain it in simple terms of their will prevailing over that of others. Instead, it is usually expressed in terms of authority derived from some other source, whether it is supernatural, the will of the majority, or the inevitable process of history, and the source of that authority is usually believed.

From this discussion it is possible to postulate the following, which may seem to be stating the obvious: those who exercise power will seek the maximum ability to control information about how it is exercised, and they will also seek to limit the ability of those who are subject to that power to control information about themselves. Jeremy Bentham's Panopticon is an architectural expression of such power relations, in which the individual 'is seen, but he does not see; he is the object of information, never a subject in communication'. In the peripheric ring, 'one is totally seen, without ever seeing: in the central tower, one sees everything without being seen' (Bentham, 1791).

The thesis of this section is that the rules relating to the dissemination of information are not understandable or justifiable on utilitarian grounds alone. The implications for research are even more tentative, but one is that research to be used in deciding what those rules are to be should not be limited to the usual model of research into the effects of obscenity and pornography, that is, attempting to quantify the effects of certain kinds of communication on individuals. Equally important, although perhaps more difficult to design, would be research into the effects of ignorance of particular information in particular circumstances, which might well lead to the conclusion that in some circumstances an individual may maximize benefits as much by random as by informed choice when overloaded by information. If, as has been suggested, the rules relating to information are influenced as much by affect as by demonstrable consequences, perhaps there should be more research of the kind commissioned by the Younger Committee into the extent and intensity of feeling in the population about certain kinds of communication. Decisions about rules might then at least be informed as to the weight attached to some of the competing values which are always being balanced.

Conclusion

Although information is intangible (and so cannot be 'stolen' in English law) the rules relating to its communication are intimately bound up with the exercise of power in a society. The purpose of such rules, it is submitted, cannot be wholly explained in terms of verifiable harm or benefit, but is also expressed in terms of maintaining deeply-held values. One of these is the right to privacy; another is the right to know how authority is exercised.

The new communications technology requires new rules. In considering what information about individuals was publicly available the Law Commission quoted from its 1974 Working Paper on the law of confidence.

> The back files of a local newspaper may, *if properly and assiduously searched*, yield a good deal of information not generally known about a person who spent his early life in the area − his family and educational background, his business connections, his political beliefs and his personal and social problems (Law Commission, 1974).

When the Law Commission reported in 1981, it added the emphasis and said: 'It is important, however, to bear in mind that the ease with which such information may be retrieved will be greatly affected by increased computerisation.' The basic effect of the new communications technology is to make information available where it was not before. This is true not only of information about individuals which those in authority may collect by surveillance, but also of information which individuals may obtain about government. The now commonplace photocopier is an illustration, and was once described to me by someone photocopying a government document for unauthorized disclosure as 'technology's gift to democracy'. The function of the politics of information law is to see that the new rules relating to information will promote, rather than degrade, the complementary values of democracy and privacy. The contribution of social science research is not only to describe and analyse the effects of new technology, but also to investigate the depth and form of the values to be served by new rules, and to contribute to the process of defining the public interest (and interests) which express those values.

Note

1. The regulation of reporting of institutions such as courts seems to be based on an inverse relationship between the accuracy of the medium and its toleration: the less reliable the medium, the more likely it is to be allowed. The public are allowed into the Strangers' Gallery in the House of Commons, but not allowed to take notes (unless seated in the gallery below). Press and public may attend and take notes in (most) courtrooms, but they may not use pocket tape recorders (with a few rare cases in which permission has been given under the Contempt of Court Act 1981). Even when tape recording is permitted in court, the 1981 Act expressly forbids its use for broadcasting. And photography is still forbidden in most parliaments and many courts throughout the world. Where reporting by such devices is allowed, institutional control is often maintained. In a variation of the tendency of those who exercise power to control information about it, there is a tendency to exert greater control on more reliable media.

References

Bentham, Jeremy (1791) *Panopticon; or the Inspection-House: Containing the Idea of a new Principle of Construction*. London.
Bok, Sisella (1983) *Secrets*. Oxford: Oxford University Press.
Committee of Ministers of the Council of Europe (1984) 'Principles Governing

Television and Radio Via Satellite'. Recommendation No. R(84)22, published in *Transnational Data Report*, 3(2), March 1985.

Griswold v. *Connecticut* (1965) US Reports, Vol. 381: 479.

Law Commission (England and Wales) (1974) *Working Paper No. 58*. London: Her Majesty's Stationery Office.

Law Commission (England and Wales) (1981) *Breach of Confidence Report No. 110*. Cmnd. 8388. London: Her Majesty's Stationery Office.

Lester, A. and D. Pannick (1984) *Advertising and Freedom of Expression in Europe*. London: Marketing Commission of the International Chamber of Commerce.

Malone (1984) European Court of Human Rights, Judgement 4/1983/60/94.

Prince Albert v. *Strange* (1849) English Reports, Vol. 41:1171.

Prosser, D. (1960) *California Law Review*, 48:383.

R. v. *Lemon and Gay News* (1979) Appeal Cases: 617.

Report of the Williams Committee on Obscenity and Film Censorship (1979) Cmnd. 7772. London: Her Majesty's Stationery Office.

Report of the Younger Committee on Privacy (1972) Cmnd. 5012. London: Her Majesty's Stationery Office.

Stanley v. *Georgia* (1969) US Reports, Vol. 394:557.

Wallington, P. (ed.) (1984) *Civil Liberties 1984*. Oxford: Martin Robertson.

Warren, S. and L. Brandeis (1890) 'The Right to Privacy', *Harvard Law Review*, 4: 193.

IV

COMPARATIVE POLICY PERSPECTIVES

8

Policy perspectives for new media in Europe

Denis McQuail

What follows may be considered as an interim report from a research project concerned with policy-making for new electronic media in several Western European countries.[1] The project is concerned with reactions, at the level of public policy, to the similar range of challenges presented by the rapid development of new means and forms of (mainly audio-visual) media distribution. The challenge is posed most directly by the technology itself and whether it is perceived as a threat or an opportunity is very variable, both within and between national societies. Our primary interest has been in mapping and explaining this variety, as it shows itself in the formulation of policies and the making of plans. Response to the challenge is related, most significantly, to the past traditions and present media circumstances of each country, to the reigning political climate and to the balance of power between the various interests involved in any change. Our approach is to assume that chosen courses of action are the outcome of interaction between a number of actors in a given economic, cultural and political climate. The aim of this chapter is to present a comparative overview of the main issues underlying policy debates in Europe, the forces at work and the main directions so far indicated or taken. As will be apparent, much that happens is not very closely under the direction of any unified policy and part of the interest of the present situation lies in the mixture of conscious planning, free choice, accident and political and economic pressure which can affect the outcome.

Similarities and differences within Europe

Europe is far from responding as one to new media challenges, although certain elements are widely shared, even if they vary in the strength of their application. Amongst these elements are; forms and traditions of public broadcasting which have given rise to expectations about how media should be used in the public interest, however defined; lingustic distinctiveness, which puts nearly all European countries at a disadvantage, in world terms, compared to Anglo-American media; elements of private business and industry which want to profit from developments; continued consumer interest in, or demand for, media services additional to current television and radio broadcasting. Amongst the relevant factors which differentiate European countries are: size and self-sufficiency as a media producer; the kind and scope of the present broadcasting monopoly; the nature of the media policy-making tradition; the political complexion of the ruling administration; the relative strength of private business and industrial pressure for innovation; the current level of development of some of the new media (e.g. extent of the cable system); the degree of centralization of the state and the degree to which media policy is active and unified. Each of these variables plays some part in deciding the strength and direction of pressure towards media innovation, and the impression that there are more differentiating than unifying factors is not misleading. While each has a general and largely predictable tendency, there is often little consistency in the pattern of interassociation or the direction of effect in a given country.

This chapter is based on information about twelve countries – the four of Scandinavia; the three Benelux countries (Belgium –Netherlands– Luxembourg); four large European Economic Community (EEC) countries and Spain. This division is itself not unrelated to the question of media policy to the extent that the Scandinavian countries are all relatively small (in population) and have cultural/linguistic affinities with each other; the Benelux countries are similarly placed, although with rather more developed new media in the form of cable systems and a generally greater current supply of television content; and each of the four large EEC countries has some commercial or industrial ambitions in respect of both the home and the external market and thus both cultural and economic interests in expansion as well as protection. It is also relevant that the Scandinavian countries are still, by and large, the last stronghold of public service broadcasting monopolies without any commercial element (Finland excepted) and that each of the large EEC countries already has a mixture of private commercial and public service elements in its electronic media. Spain could be fitted more or less to the same pattern as other large European states but for its different political history, exclusion from the EEC and somewhat lower, and more recent, economic development. Luxembourg is a special case as the long-term home of commercial broadcasting in Europe and because of its minute size. The Netherlands is the largest (in population) of the European small countries and has features which help to locate it culturally with the Scandinavian group but industrially and commercially with its larger EEC neighbours. Some of this applies also to Belgium.

Other relevant lines of division could be drawn which cross these geopolitical boundaries. Two are of most interest to note, one having to do with political leaning, another with the degree of commercialization of the existing system. The countries with right-leaning or centre–right administrations include (mid-1984) the United Kingdom, (hereafter Britain), West Germany, the Netherlands, and those of the left, France, Italy, Spain and Sweden, with most others having coalitions difficult to characterize in such clear terms. While the first three, 'more conservative', countries are certainly active in seeking to develop new media, there is a good deal of movement elsewhere. The second dimension of variation mentioned separates out at least two countries, Britain and Italy (plus Luxembourg), as already far on the way to accepting a purely commercial sector of new media provision from three countries at the other extreme which have so far resisted any element of commercialism in the electronic media and have no plans as yet to admit it – Norway, Denmark and Sweden. In between lie countries with rather limited access for commerce. While Belgium belongs formally to the non-commercial group, the reality for most Belgians is somewhat different. Thus, for most of Europe, commercialization as such is a more central issue than for Britain, which has already a fully institutionalized private broadcasting sector. While concerns over the degree of public regulation are common to Britain and the continent of Europe, Britain does not face, as a matter of principle, the question of a break in an existing legal public monopoly. This at least represents the status quo before the latest 'communications revolution' and there will be reason to return to this particular principle of classification.

A third way of dividing countries which might seem relevant is according to the degree of formulation of an active or coherent policy for media development. However, this produces some odd and inconsistent results. Some countries with strong traditions of media policy-making, like Sweden, have as yet no clear or unified policy and some countries with no media policy, like Britain, are active in promoting specific changes. Three countries, France, Finland and the Netherlands have seemed active both in formulating policy and in putting it into effect. In Italy there is policy but no action. In Denmark and Norway there has so far been much deliberation but no action. Luxembourg pursues its own economic goals. In West Germany, much as in Britain, there are potentially major changes under way without coordinated policy. More sense could be made out of this if one distinguished between 'industrial' policy, which generally stimulates new activity, and 'cultural' policy, which generally has the reverse effect.

Issues posed by the potential of new media

So far, little has been said of the substance of the 'challenge' of new media, except that there is one. This matter can best be approached by way of the issues in the policy debate, but first it is worth drawing attention ot the centrality of television in the whole matter. An awareness of the versatility of the universal television receiver is relatively recent in origin. It opens the way to large-scale personal computer ownership, albeit mainly for game-playing. It becomes the cinema-at-home by way of the video cassette recorder (VCR). It invites new forms of supply by way of cable or direct broadcasting by satellite (DBS). It is a way of becoming linked to computer data bases and networks for new kinds of search or interactive communication. Television is, nevertheless, defined for most people as a ready source of entertainment and news and as such the many potential changes in communication functions, flows and relationships are likely to be secondary to matters to do with the supply of entertainment and information to large audiences. Public demand is still largely for a greater and more varied supply of what broadcast television is already offering, although the potential of new supply is much more than this. The point of these remarks is to underline the duality of what is happening or is in prospect — on the one hand the fulfilment of the dream of unlimited supply of television (still very restricted in some countries for many people), and on the other hand entirely new kinds of communication services and relationships, in which people interact and search according to their own taste and convenience. Most of the discussion, speculation and perhaps even (informed) public interest refers to the second aspect, but the reality of policy-forming and decision-making and of political infighting concerns the first. Over the expansion of television, more or less as we know it, there is most conflict, while the genuinely *new* media aspects tend to give rise to cautious acceptance, mild commercial interest and some consensual but vague social–cultural optimism. Potentially revolutionary changes in relation to telematics are being made by administrative act without wide discussion. In this respect, some aspects of the history of broadcasting are repeating themselves, As yet, there are few vested interests or firmly rooted claims, although options are being taken up as speculation or precaution.

These remarks about the centrality of television help to give shape to a discussion of the main issues, which do not differ very much from one country to another. The issues can be treated according to descending order of generality and the most general of all is whether or not to encourage the new media in an active way. Active discouragement is nowhere a very feasible option, but the take-off of new media usually requires positive or permissive acts such as, for example, to invest in cable or to remove existing restrictions. Apart from Britain, the countries which seem most inclined to positive acts in the immediate future are France, West Germany and the Netherlands. These are countries where governments are taking a lead and not necessarily those where strong pressure is building up from below for more new media.

Industrial or cultural policy motives
It is more useful to consider the choice between promoting an active industrial policy − of development for the sake of employment and future markets for hardware and software − or of following or extending an existing cultural policy. In the latter case, policy is dominated either by concerns about protecting or promoting the national language and cultural products or ensuring that the new electronic media continue to fulfil a number of social functions which have traditionally belonged to broadcasting − especially the securing of a wide distribution of information, education and culture. Opting for industrial policy is usually not in itself any more controversial − most people are in favour of more employment and of economic and technological progress − but there are problems about the means of achieving rapid development and about the possible effects on other media. There may, consequently, be an ultimate collision with the aims of cultural policy and it is this collision, actual or anticipated, which mainly shapes the substance of debate. A number of separate matters can be named in this connection. One is the risk of cross-border 'invasion' from satellites controlled by other countries and beaming content directly to cable antennas or, eventually, individual receivers. While smaller countries are most concerned about this, since the minority status of their languages may be further reinforced, larger countries like West Germany and France are also worried that the attractiveness of their larger markets could make them an especial target for new satellite senders. The reasons for objection are thus often as much commercial as cultural. In any case, it simply does become more difficult to operate a broadcasting cultural policy in the face of uncontrolled access from abroad and, at the same time, it becomes increasingly difficult to justify restrictions on such access.

A second matter of cultural concern relates to the potential damage to the newspaper through loss of readers and revenue, in those countries where the press is assigned various political and social functions and given special protection to help achieve these. This applies especially in Norway, Sweden and the Netherlands. Again an economic interest is involved, since the press is also run as a private business, with a need to retain sales and advertising income. Two other cultural policy issues are taken up below under other headings:

the share of new media which should be allocated to the public sector and the degree of protection which the latter should receive; and the question of commercialization in the sense of cultural 'dilution' and the increasing triviality of what is offered, as many more suppliers compete for a limited amount of audience attention.

The lines of conflict between advocates of industrial and of cultural policy are often quite clearly drawn, since the former are generally political parties of the right or business and industrial interests and the latter are parties of the left, many educational and cultural bodies, plus often the established press and broadcasting concerns. However, there is much that is unpredictable. A number of left-wing parties and trade unions are torn between potential economic advantage and cultural damage (or reduced opportunity) and there are objections amongst conservative politicians against too rapid or uncontrolled change. Behind such reluctance, there may be a mixture of motivation – moral, nationalistic, aesthetic, self-interested. In the case of at least one country – France – with an active policy-making and a left-wing administration, there seems to be a simultaneous pursuit of both industrial and cultural goals, and a mixture of goals, or of motives for seeking the same goal is far from uncommon.

On a further, but related, main choice – between public or private financial and institutional frameworks – there are a number of more specific and sharper issues on which actors have less room for manoeuvre. In general, the wish for development of new media goes with an industrial policy climate (the cultural reasons for positive encouragement of new media are somewhat restricted) and with a choice for private forms of finance. Apart from the inner logic of this association, there is simply a more or less universal agreement within Europe that there is no extra money to be expected either from general taxation or from licence revenue to pay for much new investment and running costs. It happens that commercial development of electronic media has been so held back in most countries that prospects for finance from this source seem quite promising, although not unlimited. In some cases there is pressure from already financed suppliers looking for access to national markets (e.g. Sky Channel) and in several countries there are groups, especially formed from publishers or cable operators, who are anxious to begin new media operations.

Commercialization

To admit private finance, or more of it, or in different ways are the options and they entail a number of problems, some pertaining to the theme of 'commercialism', some to the question of breaking an existing public monopoly. In those countries which have known a degree of serious competition for audiences between television or radio channels, especially where there is a financial and not only a political advantage at stake, there has for long been a fear of a decrease of quality in broadcasting, an increase in superficiality, a falling away from educational and cultural aims. Commercialism in this indirect or 'weak' sense has been said to have grown in France, West Germany, the Netherlands, Belgium and Italy, as well as in Britain. It is something which it is believed will spread to countries which have retained public monopolies and will accelerate in those countries which have decided to allow the exploitation of cable and satellite for subscription television, even where no advertising will be involved. This is a contentious issue mainly in the eyes of those bodies which are wedded to a strong social responsibility view of broadcasting, but this includes a number of major political parties. There is little sign that the general public in Europe has strong views on the matter and the notion of cultural dilution may well be taken as synonymous with more sport and entertainment, which are rather popular. Less subjective, however, is the high cost and limited supply of original entertainment material now being produced by broadcasting organizations and the relatively low price which most people seem likely to be willing to pay for additional supplies of what is supposed to be the same. There is an objective economic basis to this version of dilution through commercialism, which policy makers can at least appreciate.

The issue of 'direct' commercialism, in the form of the carrying of advertising, is less abstract and more polarizing, at the political level at least, especially in those countries (only Sweden, Norway, Denmark and Belgium) which so far allow no direct advertising on television or radio. Britain and Italy are unique in having a complete and independent television service financed entirely from advertising. Most countries simply accept some advertising at limited times, in order to defray some of the costs of the system. Here there is no particular problem of principle in financing more of the same media by admitting more advertising. That might well be the answer if the existing public (monopoly) services were to be allowed to develop the new media. This is rarely likely to be the case, for several reasons: the private sector presses hard for a share of the action; press interests are generally uneasy; the new media themselves are not necessarily very suitable as vehicles for the established forms of advertising. A further complication is that satellite services are already on offer which happen to carry (international) advertising and there is already quite widespread anxiety about the cultural and economic effects of this in some countries. Sky Channel, for instance, has managed to find a reception on cable systems, even if on a small scale, in a number of unlikely places, including Norway, Finland, Sweden and the Netherlands.

In this increasingly complex field of policy, one can distinguish a few basic patterns (options of policy). One is to concentrate new media growth outside the existing public sector, on the basis of indirect commercialization only — self-financing subscription services from a variety of sources (foreign public channels, new providers, local content, etc.). This is the most popular, or least controversial, option although it has long-term implications for the public (open broadcast) sector. It is likely to be the path in any country with an extensive or expanding cable network and could be expected were the monopoly to be broken in Denmark, Sweden or Norway. A second option is fully advertising-financed service, such as exist now in Britain, Italy or Luxembourg. The Independent Television (ITV) model has been eyed with interest by proponents of commercial television in the past (e.g. in West Germany) and more recently (e.g. in Spain), but has never been adopted and is unlikely to be so, partly because it is likely to be seen as over-elaborate, over-regulatory and costly. The model offered by Britain's Channel Four, which lacks several of these drawbacks, has been much admired but not, as yet, proposed elsewhere. Even so, something of this sort may well be the most feasible pattern for new cable and satellite services. A general reason for caution about fully commercial services on the American model is the considerable uncertainty about their commercial viability. So far, cable- and satellite-based provision in the USA has not generated much direct advertising revenue of its own. A third option (for a country) is to try to become a major supplier by way of publicly sponsored, but privately financed, satellite communication for nationalistic and/or commercial reasons. In general, the tendency to join what one cannot beat or to compete with what cannot exclude has been growing in Europe. Finally, there is the option of growth within the public sector, financed by more advertising time or by offering extra subscription services. Some of the reasons why this is not a very promising option were noted above, but it could happen on a small scale, possibly to balance more commercial developments elsewhere in the system.

One of the main issues raised by the possibility of more commercially financed new media provision is the potential effect on newspapers. This is a matter of particular difficulty where the press is subsidized, as in Sweden, Norway or the Netherlands, since subsidy schemes could well break down under new pressure. Its sensitivity as an issue depends on where the emphasis of the press protection policy lies (at national, regional or local level) and the level at which media commercialism might have an effect. An alternative solution to the problem of press protection is to allow it some share of the new media action. In this respect, Finland seems to lead the way, with much local newspaper involvement in new cable exploitation. In several countries, newspapers are also interested in the possibilities of video-text provision, with or without advertising. Where countries have an overall media policy, as in Denmark, Sweden or the Netherlands, there is usually an attempt to calculate the possible impact of new developments on newspapers and to delimit spheres of activity between the media.

The broadcasting monopoly issue

The main issue remaining for discussion has already been mentioned – the question of the continuation of public monopoly in broadcasting and the terms of its operation in relation to an enlarged private sector of electronic media. The forms of public control vary a good deal from country to country, but everywhere, apart from the special case of Luxembourg, which has a provate monopoly, virtually all broadcasting is subject to national or regional legislation as to the amount and kind of services which can be offered over the air or via cable. The general principle has been that cable services should carry national channels plus relays of foreign public channels and that what is offered should broadly conform to the standards of the national broadcast system. That principle is becoming increasingly difficult to hold to, as indicated by the relative success of commercial satellite services and their introduction into countries which otherwise forbid advertising. This, however, is only symptomatic of the widespread vulnerability of almost all public broadcasting which was once considered all-powerful in deciding what should be seen or heard. In fact this impression of power was widely mistaken and the true weakness of public broadcasting is being exposed. Its power rested entirely on organizational competence and financial resources delegated by governments in the interests of order and policy-making. The public opinion base on which public service broadcasting rested has generally been unreliable and mediated through politicians. Some of the forces which sustained public broadcasting in the past, including broad satisfaction with their services, the need for continued regulation of technical standards and the need to share available media and markets sensibly do still remain, but the whole position of public broadcasting has gradually been destabilized.

The relevant technological developments are mainly those which lead to a new supply of similar services outside the effective control of existing broadcasting monopoly regulation. This mainly means cable and satellite and where extensive cable systems have developed, for whatever reason, it seems very difficult to prevent some use of their capacity which ultimately undermines centralized legal control of television. Video is another new medium which has taken off almost entirely without regulation and has evaded restriction because the method of distribution (hire of cassettes) is not covered by existing laws. Public broadcasting seems only to have retained the initiative over the development of one of the new media – teletext, which is not yet seen as having major commercial possibilities. Thus, quite apart from the question of radio and television piracy, which has also been facilitated by technological developments, the existing monopolies are struggling to defend a declining share of the total electronic media industry on too many fronts. Moreover, they are doing so in an unfavourable political and economic climate, when there is no new public money for investment or expansion.

In a few countries, which have a rather total and restrictive monopoly, such as Denmark, Sweden and Norway, there is still some weight behind the demand for the end of the monopoly as a matter of principle. For the most part, however, the questions under discussion concern where to draw lines around the sphere of competence of the older public broadcasting service regime. Despite the threats of limitation and cutting back and the general uncertainty, in no West European country are there serious plans to abolish or fundamentally change the remit of any existing broadcasting authority. There are still vested political interests in having a strong, relatively centralized broadcasting institution sensitive to the needs of other major social institutions and able to set technical and content standards. Public broadcasting institutions were originally created from 'above', by governments and elites nearly everywhere, and their future still depends as much on what those above will want as on their performance in relation to new competition for the attention of audiences. One of the main strengths of public broadcasting is that it remains nearly everywhere the main source of national production of audio-visual content. As long as cultural policy exercises some pull, and it is far from expended, there will be strong pressure from above as well as from below to retain this national linguistic and cultural resource.

Positive aspects of cultural policy
The discussion to this point may have left the impression that new media policy is almost exclusively about television and, at that, its national or international flow; and also that cultural policy, where it offers a counterweight to industrial policy, is only restrictive or defensive. There are other aspects of the European policy-making scene. In general, the positive thrust of cultural policy is to be found in encouragement of decentralization, local and regional media services and interactive cable provision. These allow the new media to be applied to local social, educational and cultural needs and more access for minorities and more participation by citizens. On the whole, local radio has been less fully developed on the continent of Europe than in

Britain and the redrawing of the media landscape entailed in the coming of new media allows some attention to be given to this as an area of growth, partly to legitimate what has grown in an uncontrolled way. It is not easy to present a clear and simple picture, because much depends on whether or not there exists a fair degree of decentralization and of local/regional provision (as in France, Sweden, Italy, Norway and Finland) and widespread cable provision (as in Belgium, the Netherlands, Sweden and Finland). It also makes a difference if countries have active, government-sponsored media policies, since here the claims for local access and regionalism are at least likely to be expressed and taken some account of, if only to balance other more culturally negative (or commercially inspired) acts of policy. What emerges at least is that widespread lip service is paid to the need to secure some forms of access for local social or cultural groups (and cable tends, by definition, to be local). Secondly, there is a tendency to delegate the fulfilment or regulation of new projects of this kind to local or regional level, often implying an extension of the competence of the lower-level elected authorities. This kind of decentralization of control probably also brings with it a measure of deregulation, which both is convenient for central government, since control costs money, and also happens to be consistent with the spirit of more local access and participation. Perhaps only in France can one find a new media policy which strongly emphasizes decentralization, but the outcome will probably be no more decentralized than the current situation in some other countries. It is not being excessively cynical to present the positive tendencies of policy as, in general, more well-intentioned than producing much visible change. Aside from the economic aspects of the case, there are grounds for arguing that local and participant new media forms should not be imposed from above, but should come from the people themselves within a framework offered by the society.

In this context, one can also cite the experiments in local interactive cable provision such as are taking place in Milton Keynes, England, in several sites in West Germany, in Biarritz in France and in South Limburg in the Netherlands. While these are intended to encourage, *inter alia*, social, cultural and educational uses of new media, as part of an attempt to assess future potential, they were primarily 'economic' in motivation, if not commercial. It is very unlikely that the required investment would have been found from public sources for purely cultural and social aims. This leaves one with the conclusion that policy in Europe has not yet delivered, nor is likely to deliver, much that has a positive cultural impact, aside from questions of national and linguistic protectionism. Thus the loss which seems likely to be suffered by the existing public sector in its relative share of electronic media activity does not seem likely to be compensated by developments elsewhere – at regional and local level.

Telematics and video

The other distinctively new media, teletext, video-text and video, are easier to deal with briefly because policies, plans and expectations are either relatively unformed or not yet controversial. All of the countries dealt with have now introduced teletext on an experimental or established basis and mostly it has been left to existing public broadcasting authorities, because it technically is broadcasting. In the larger countries there has been a tendency towards regional differentiation of what is offered, which is likely to be extended as the service grows. There is also a policy of applying the service to social and cultural needs as well as the purely informational. The main emerging issues for policy have to do with potential commercial applications, competition with newspapers and access for providers other than the public broadcasting authorities. Video-text is also very widely installed in Europe, at least experimentally, and it has been introduced, even promoted actively everywhere for rather similar reasons – industrial or economic stimulation in various forms or simply 'keeping up' with the times and neighbouring states or tele-communications authorities (PTTs). Despite universal lack of success so far in generating new mass market, it is clear that policy favours video-text and it will be a permanent feature of the media landscape everywhere.

The third new medium, 'video', has, along with cable, produced the most dramatic and visible effects in media behaviour but has generated little policy-making. Because of its mode of distribution it falls outside the existing framework of supervision and has provoked little policy response, except in respect of copyright and content control. These are not unimportant, but the first represents a regulatory move in the interests of the industry itself and the second is likely to be somewhat marginal in its effects. In Scandinavia, where advertising has not been allowed on television, there has been some discussion as to whether such a ban should be applied to video as well, but nothing has been done and it no longer excites much interest. Another aspect of video – its capacity to introduce (by the back door) violence and pornography into the home via the television set – has been a matter of active discussion and specific laws to control this aspect of content have been introduced or are planned in several countries including Sweden, Finland, West Germany and Britain. However, video is likely to remain a largely unregulated medium, having become firmly established in the free market sector.

Overview

In order to summarize the situation it is possible, albeit risky, to name the main policy issue or issues for each country and then try to locate the policy tendency of each country according to some of the dimensions which have been discussed. The main issues for media policy seem currently as follows.

Norway and Demark: Whether to have a second television channel and what form it should take, which involves the question of the present broadcasting monopoly and that of increasing the supply of television content. Both countries have some interest in the protection of national language and culture from satellite 'invasion'.

Sweden: The maintenance of the present broadcasting monopoly financed by licence fees, which means that advertising on television is also an issue as is, indirectly, press subsidy policy.

Finland: Broadly, how best to advance an industrial/economic policy, on the basis of a mixed system of finance, and still protect Finnish culture.

West Germany: The introduction of a private, subscription-based, and advertising-financed media sector, based on cable – by what means and how quickly, with what technology.

France: Jointly the furthering of industrial and cultural policy goals, together with decentralization and devolution of power.

Netherlands: Extension of the television system outside the existing broadcasting monopoly and the relative share of public and private sectors in the new media sphere of activity. Consequences for the press are also at issue.

Belgium: The threat to cultural policy and economic interests posed by cable and satellite 'invasion', entailing a need for some domestic commercialization and plans for using the cable system.

Spain: Media modernization and decentralization in general plus the form and degree of privatization needed to pay for both.

Italy: Less an issue than a situation – of conflict between a centralized public service and state and a de facto *laissez faire* reality.

Luxembourg: How best to exploit commercial potential of satellite and cable development.

Britain: To promote all forms of information technology for national economic advantage on the basis of private investment and market demand.

These are very selective, somewhat subjective, renderings of what are often complexes of issues. One should recall that countries are at varying stages of policy-making – from early awareness to implementation – so that one cannot treat each country equally in terms of its issue agenda. The factors which help to identify key issues are also very variable, some being more enduring than others. The political complexion of government is one of the most important, but it is also subject to change with consequences for the climate of policy-making and often the actual agenda.

The same cautionary remarks apply to the attempt which follows to locate countries in terms of some of the choices discussed. For simplicity, only two dimensions are used, but they capture the most important sources of differentiation – one separating an emphasis on private rather than public structures of finance and control and the other separating an emphasis on industrial motives from an attention to cultural matters in the policy-making climate. It is especially difficult, even misleading, to give countries a single location, since several countries have divergent tendencies in their policy direction. The most extreme case is probably that of France, which appears to be seeking economic and cultural goals by means of both public and private initiatives. The difficulty is compounded by the possibility of placing countries according to their past, present or likely future position and a choice has been made for something labelled a 'tendency' of policy – usually a compound of present situation and desired or probable future. However, this can also be misleading, insofar as the 'past' still governs much of the reality of the present.

FIGURE 8.1

Electronic media policy tendency, by country, in relation to two dimensions: public versus private form and cultural versus industrial policy climate

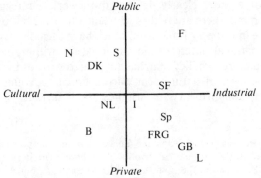

Key: B. Belgium; DK, Denmark; F, France; FRG, West Germany; GB, Britain; I, Italy; L, Luxembourg; N, Norway; NL, Netherlands; S, Sweden, SF, Finland; Sp, Spain.

Towards a European policy?

Little reference has been made to the existence of a European policy perspective as such, in the sense of a common view of, or plan for, the future. No such single policy perspective exists and it is almost bound to follow, rather than precede, separate national media policies, which are not yet everywhere in existence. Several of the lines of division within countries which make a common national policy difficult to achieve operate to a similar degree across countries, making for a divergence of outlook. Nevertheless, there appears to be a growing awareness of common problems and the need for reciprocal or cooperative action on some immediate practical matters, such as copyright, advertising and technical standards. Several countries are equally alarmed at the threat posed by satellites from 'offshore' or from the mainland (e.g. Luxembourg). Other people, especially in the public broadcasting sphere, are interested in the positive opportunities offered by satellites for Europe-wide channels or programmes. Following the Eurikon trials in 1982, a pan-European satellite TV service, 'Olympus', is expected to begin operation (mainly for informational content) in 1985. This is largely a European Broadcasting Union (EBU) initiative, strongly backed by the Netherlands Broadcasting Foundation (NOS) and a few other broadcasting authorities. The European Economic Community (EEC) has begun, with its 1984 Green Paper, to set rather general and permissive ground rules for intra-European broadcasting which involve advertising. Several other bodies at the European level are beginning to play a role, including the Council of Europe, the European Space Agency (ESA), Eutelsat and the Nordic Council. National telecommunications authorities are active in matters which have to do with cable and satellite networks. So while European policy as such does not exist, except in small fragments, there are some driving forces at work in the direction of a more clearly defined framework for regulation and cooperation and there are bodies with some limited, but overlapping, competence in respect of the issues which have been discussed. For the moment, national interest and sectionalism within nations have contributed more to policy than has any shared sense of European-ness and the prospect of a European Media Force, as counterweight to American media influence for instance, is still distant.

Note

1. The project was initiated within the framework of the European Consortium for Political Research (ECPR) and has involved the following investigators: M. Bakke, V. Petersen, K. Siune and B.S. Ostergaard from Denmark; C. Sorbets from France; H. Kleinsteuber from Germany; J. Tunstall and M. Palmer from the United Kingdom; G. Mazzoleni from Italy; K. Brants from the Netherlands; M. Flick, A Rolland, O. Vaagland and H. Ostbye from Norway; R. de Mateo and M. de Moragas i Spa from Spain; K.-E. Gustafsson from Sweden; M. Hirsch from Luxembourg; and H. Mäkinen from Finland.

Nevertheless, the views expressed in this chapter are those of the author, not those of the Euromedia Research Group nor of the individuals named. A first report of the work of the Group will appear in *New Media Politics*, Sage, forthcoming.

9

Europe and new communication technologies

Nicole Dewandre[1]

The advent of American deregulation in the telecommunications field has put pressure on Europe. The European countries react differently to it: the UK government has sold 51 per cent of British Telecom (BT); the French government has reorganized its telecommunications industry by merging Thomson and CIT-Alcatel and promoting new services (Teletel, memory cards); while the response of West Germany appears to be quite conservative.

The entire fields of information and communications are involved in such telecommunications initiatives. The ensuing debate about communications policy is dominated by two polar opposites:

the deregulation supporters, the 'market-oriented' people who believe that there is nothing better than the market to take care of communications;

the status-quo supporters who are 'sitting' on their monopoly because they believe that it is the only way to guarantee good service and public service.

This chapter attempts to establish the basis for a different line of questioning. It argues that, for a solution to policy questions to be reached, there must be a redistribution or clarification of the respective roles of the private and public sectors. This is so because, firstly, it is of strategic importance for a community that communications are provided efficiently, and, secondly, because the management of communications implies some choices that are to be made on a normative basis and cannot be made exclusively on efficiency criteria.

This approach identifies the conflicts that will arise in this area and hence prepares an agenda of choices to be made. In order to do this, the initial conditions (the trend) and market situation are described and a framework for analysis proposed.

The communication trend: the shift from product to function
Until recently, the function of communication was provided by the juxtaposition of simple networks which complemented direct communication: the telex, the telephone, radio and television broadcasting, and publishing.

What we are now witnessing is an integration of these networks towards a complex system of interaction (and interfaces). In effect, electronic switching, digitalization of continuous sources, multiplexing techniques, the development of higher performance transmission media (mono-mode fibre optics) are all technical advances which make possible: broad-band interactive communication; sharing of the same network by image data and voice, since all are converted into the form of binary digits; the multiplication of terminals capable of being 'hooked up' to the network (telephone, computer, word processor, telecopier, payment systems, cellular networks); the multiplication of value-added services that a network can provide.

The shift from the juxtaposition of simple networks to an integrated complex system[2] radically changes the attitude of the user. In the former case (juxtaposition of simple networks), he chooses for himself the best combination of products to satisfy his needs; while in the other situation he delivers to the network what he wants to transmit, in whatever form it may be, and it is left to those who manage the network to optimize its use as a function of data rates and destination. He no longer makes a choice of product/service; he is provided with the function.

On the production side, the integration of the network radically changes the context of the user's choices. Before, one had a national administration for the telephone and telex networks, a national or regional broadcasting institution, a telecommunications industry, an informatics industry and, finally, companies for cable TV distribution in some cases. Tomorrow, all these actors will have to play the same game, with the same set of rules, instead of playing in their respective fields.

The telecommunications and media situation – a growth market and a strategic sector

The telecommunications industry is considered by the European Economic Community (EEC) as a strategic sector, with regard both to its direct and indirect effects. The direct effect is measured by the contribution of the telecommunications industry to gross domestic product (GDP) (around 2 per cent in the EEC) and the investment required (0.7 per cent of GDP, over 16 billion ecus in 1981).[3] The scale of this industry is comparable to the most important sectors such as aerospace, electricity, electronics. Moreover, telecommunications represent a substantial part of electronic production of the member states (12 per cent in France, 17.7 per cent in Italy, 20 per cent in Belgium).

TABLE 9.1
An overview of European communications

| Country | Telecommunications | | Broadcasting |
	Carriers	Industry	
Belgium	RTT	Bell Telephone Manufacturing Systems (ITT subsidiary); ATEA (GTE subsidiary)	RTBF; BRT; BRF
West Germany	DBP	Siemens; Standard Elektrik Lorenz (ITT subsidiary); Detewe Philips	ARD; ZDF; WDR
Denmark	PTT, KTAS, FKT, JTAS		Radio Denmark
France	DGT	Alcatel & Thomson	TDF
UK	BT; Mercury	GEC; Plessey	BBC; IBA
Greece	OTE	ELVIL (under development)	ERT
Italy	P&T; ASST; Italcable; Telespazio	Italtel; Faci (ITT subsidiary; GTE (GTE subsidiary); Olivetti	Radio Italiana
Ireland	Bord	L.M. Ericsson (IRL) (subsidiary of L.M. Ericsson); Telecom Alcatel (subsidiary of CIT-Alcatel; Telection (subsidiary of AT&T)	RTE
Luxembourg	P&T		CLT
Netherlands	PTT	Philips	NOZEMA

Source: EEC.

Key: ARD, Arbeitsgemeinschaft der öffentlichen rechtlichen Rundfunksanstalten Deutschlands; ASST, Azienda di Stato per i Servizi Telefonici; AT&T, American Telephone and Telegraph; BBC, British Broadcasting Corporation; BRF, Belgische Rundfunk und Fernsehen; BRT, Belgische Radio en televisie; BT, British Telecom; CLT, Compagnie Luxembourgeoise de Télédiffusion, DBP, Deutsche Bundespost; DGT, Direction Générale des Télécommunications; ELVIL, Hellenic Electronics Industry; ERT, Elliniki Radiophonia Tikorassis; FKT, Fyn Kommunal Telefonselskab; GEC, General Electric Company (UK); IBA, Independent Broadcasting Authority; ITT, International Telephone and Telegraph; JTAS, Jydsk Telefon Atieselskab; KTAS, Kjobenhavns Telefon Aktieselskab; NOZEMA, Nederlandse Omroepzender Maatschappij; OTE, Hellenic Telecommunications Organization; P&T, Post and Telecommunications Administration; PTT, national telecommunications authority; RTBF, Radio-télévision belge pour la communauté française; RTE, Radio Telefis Eirann; RTT, Régie des Télégraphes et des Téléphones; SIP, Società Italiana per l'Esercizio Telefonico; TDF, Télédiffusion de France; WDR, Westdeutsche Rundfunk; ZDF, Zweites Deutsches Fernsehen.

The indirect effects are at least as important as the direct ones. The multiplier effect of telecommunications investment is very high and stands at the same level as the one for the construction industry: 1 million ecus invested today in the telecommunications infrastructure raises the global level of activity by 1.5 million ecus. Telecommunications effectively represent the prior condition for the establishment of new services in the economy.

The sector is, moreover, an expanding one owing largely to the potential of new technologies and there is much movement in the market place.[4] In this market place, the tension between extra-European links and intra-European links can clearly be seen. The strategic industrial system of communication is being totally restructured. The starting point of the system is, generally speaking, the juxtaposition of a telecommunications system and a broadcasting system. Each of these systems was highly fragmented into national segments. Thus one finds, in almost every country, a national administration to provide basic telecommunications services (telephone/telex), a national industry with a few national 'champions' and a broadcasting administration (see Table 9.1).

On the telecommunications side, the procurement policy of the administrations (who buy 70 per cent of the market) favoured the national industry. The result of this fact is a high fragmentation of the European market, with the duplication of R&D and the multiplication of systems (some nine public switching systems in Europe; three in the USA). Moreover, the investment level in Europe has been consistently lower than that in the USA, and is being overtaken by the one in Japan. Mackintosh International (1983) has evaluated the 'per capita expenditure on electronics', which is wider than just telecommunications, but is a good indicator given the interrelationships between the two sectors: in 1975, the EEC spent 90.5 ecus per capita on electronics, behind the USA (178.2 ecus) but ahead of Japan (72.3 ecus). In 1982, Japan came in second position (302.5 ecus) after the US (482.8 ecus) but ahead of the EEC (263 ecus). The rest of the world spent, in 1982, 85.4 ecus per capita on electronics.

The consequences of how this low investment level led to a lower penetration of basic services in Europe (see Table 9.2), lower revenues for the telecommunications industry and a weaker position.

This relatively weak position of European countries occurs at a moment when information technology (IT) markets are growing very fast and at a time when telecommunications are becoming more and more integrated with the informatics and telematics market, through the evolution of the switching systems, the integration of communication and micro-informatics and the customer premises equipment market.

TABLE 9.2

Main telephone lines per 100 inhabitants in the EEC, USA and Japan
(figures in parentheses denote rank order)

	1976	1981	1983
EEC	20.80 (3)	31.32 (3)	34.61 (3)
USA	37.89 (1)	40.69 (1)	41.81 (1)
Japan	28.57 (2)	34.18 (2)	35.29 (2)

Source: [PTT Consortium] (1983).

Table 9.3 shows this relatively weak position in terms of projected IT trade balance in the macro-sector of information technology. The significance of this trade deficit is related to the projected market sizes because the market size, in fact, measures the amount of lost opportunities.

TABLE 9.3

Market and trends balance in the IT industry
(billion ecus)

	Electronic components		Consumer electronics		Electronic data processing		Office equipment		Telecom-munications	
	1982	1992[a]	1982	1992[a]	1982	1992[a]	1872	1992[a]	1872	1992[a]
EEC markets	13.2	18	9.9	11	16.2	45	3.1	4	10	12
EEC trade	−1.6	−5	−3.4	−5	−1.4	−3	−0.4	−1	−1.4	2

Source: Mackintosh International (1983).
[a]projection

This relative weakness of Europe with respect to IT can also be interpreted in terms of the employment situation: the evidence provided by the interim report to the CEC (Mackintosh International, 1983) suggests that in absolute terms employment might decrease in Europe, while it would rise in the USA and Japan. The number of persons employed in the IT industry would be even larger, in absolute terms, in Japan than in the EEC by the year 1991 if a no-change strategy is followed in Europe.

The same report states that in relative terms (with regard to population) the European Community is already in the bottom position and this would worsen if nothing changes. When one realizes that the majority of jobs will be provided by IT in the next few decades, this situation is a rather alarming one for members of the EEC.

On the broadcasting side, the picture is also changing very fast. The economic weight of this broadcasting industry in the European

Community has been estimated to be 1.5 or 2 per cent of gross national product (GNP) and 1 per cent of employment (CEC, 1984). Three functions in this industry must be distinguished – managing the network, managing the diffusion of programmes and producing the programmes.

With regard to managing the network, the trend is to issue licences or to control the management of the network directly. Technologies are widening the possibilities of networks with the introduction of satellite and cable broadcasting.

With regard to the management of programme diffusion, regulations vary from member state to member state. The trend here is to open the market (as in Italy, France and the UK) and to allow associations to apply to an authority to get the authorization to broadcast.

The programme industry is in a bad shape. Europe does not today produce enough content for all the new channels to come. It is very expensive to produce for a national audience of a maximum of 15 million TV viewers (the UK audience), even more so since American productions can be obtained very cheaply on the market because they are already paid for. European producers try to collaborate in co-productions, mainly in French-speaking television (French, Belgian and Swiss). However, there is a very clear risk that Europeans will continue to get more and more American productions on their TV channels (see Table 9.4). It has been shown that 80 percent of programmes are sold

TABLE 9.4
Origin of films broadcast on television in 1981

Country of broadcast	Country of origin											
	France		Germany		Italy		UK		USA		Others	
	No.	%	No.	%	No.	%	No.	%	No.	%	No.	%
Belgium												
RTBF	160	48.8	15	4.3	24	6.8	12	3.4	107	30.0	17	4.9
BRT	11	6.25	7	3.98	4	2.28	24	13.64	104	59.10	26	14.77
France[1]			4	2.29	8	4.59	12	6.89	140	80.45	10	5.74
West Germany[2]	48	11.79			15	3.68	26	6.38	221	54.29	93	22.85
United Kingdom[3]	6	1.14	2	0.38	6	1.14			491	93.70	20	3.81

Films made in co-production are attributed to the first country of origin named.
Source: Working Group No. 3 from the Intergovernmental Conference for European Audiovisual Cooperation in 1983.
[1] TFI and FR3. For A2 there are no figures available on the country of origin.
[2] ARD and ZDF. The figures relating to ZDF include the first six months of 1982.
[3] Only BBC.
Key: A2, Antenne 2; FR3, France 3; TF1, Télévision française 1.
For other abbreviations see Table 9.1.

TABLE 9.5
Advertising data for Europe

Country	TV Channels	Maximum daily transmission time given to advertising (minutes)	Advertising income as % of total TV income (1981 figures)
Belgium	RTBF I and II	'Non-commercial' advertising started in January 1984	
	BRT I and II	None	
Denmark	Radio Denmark	None	
France[1]	TF1	24	61
	A2	24	53
	FR3	10	13
West Germany[2]	ZDF	20	40
	ARD I	20	30
	ARD II	(regional, no advertising)	
Greece	ERT 1	30	22
	ERT 2	45	25
Ireland	RTE 1	58	48
	RTE II	25	
Italy	RAI I	28	23.8
	RAI II	28	23.8
	RAI III	—	—
	Private radio stations	15% per hour (9 mins)	100
Luxembourg	RTL (French — covers the north of France and Belgium)	68	100
	RTL-Plus (German)	68	100
Netherlands[3]	Canal I	18	25[4]
	Canal II	18	(Transmission time increasing)
UK	BBC I and II	None	—
	ITV	90	100
	Channel 4	50	100

Source: CEC (1984).

[1] 1983.
[2] 1982.
[3] 1984.
[4] 1981.

Key: ITV, Independent Television; RAI, Radiotelevisione Italiana; RTL, Radio-télé Luxembourg; for other abbreviations see Tables 9.1 and 9.4.

and distributed by the USA (Riblier and Barbier, 1983). This is to be avoided both for economic and for cultural reasons. (Cultural exchanges are to be envisaged, cultural invasion is to be avoided.)

With regard to the financial constraints, these are met by licence fees, subscriptions (pay TV) in some cases, state subsidies, but mainly by advertising.

Advertising is the main way of covering costs and it is the object of regulation in most countries. It is felt that the consumer has to be protected against too much use of advertising. Hence, in most countries, there is a maximum transmission time given to advertising (see Table 9.5).

It is interesting to observe that RTL in Luxembourg covers all its budget with sixty-eight minutes of advertising each day, whereas ITV in Britain uses ninety minutes to do so. These differences illustrate how the main challenge to pan-European broadcasting in the future is the problem of harmonizing the regulation of the advertising market. In effect, if one channel is allowed more 'advertising minutes', it can lower the price for advertising and take market shares from the others which are allowed fewer minutes and have to ask higher prices to cover their budget. An absence of regulations would benefit the advertising industry since it would lower the price of the advertising minute. On the other hand, it would be unfavourable to the viewer, since he would have to watch more advertising in order for the broadcasting company to raise the same amount of money. Moreover, this would leave to a rich elite the ability to buy 'clean broadcasting'.

Within Europe there are also discussions about the problems of freedom of distribution and national sovereignty: satellite footprints do not recognize national frontiers. It is felt that these issues will be made obsolete by practice. Technical feasibility displaces political choice: today television viewers already receive foreign programmes. For example, in Belgium one can receive programmes from France, the Netherlands, the United Kingdom, Germany and soon Italy.

There is, of course, a significant difference between receiving a programme from abroad, made for the inhabitants of the country of origin, and receiving a programme from abroad especially directed towards people in another country. For example, a Belgian television viewer is not the target, in terms of advertising or information, of the French service, but he is the target of Luxembourg television. The latter case is much more problematic, since the regulations concerning the Belgian viewer do not have to be observed by foreign programming enterprises. This can be clearly seen in, amongst other things, the case of advertising, which is not allowed on Belgian television: companies use RTL (from Luxembourg) to promote their products on the Belgian market.

The analysis: towards the definition of a thematic field.
How to tackle the communications issue?

Having sketched the situation and problems as they are felt in Europe, one must try to order proposed ways for the future. To put the communications issue into perspective, we begin by recognizing that all economic transactions are supported by two 'institutions' necessary for the market mechanism to operate: namely money and a communications network. The communications network is necessary for the exchange of information, a prerequisite for the exchange of goods and services, while the social institution of money not only economizes on the information required to operate the market mechanism, but also allows these mechanisms to operate. However, both money and communications networks have a two-fold position in the economy: in forming the infrastructure of the market economy they may be considered *exogenous* to the market place; as economic activities of the banking and financial and telecommunications sectors, they may be considered to be *endogenous* to the market place.

The attitudes towards regulation are strongly affected by the dominant side of this duality that one chooses. Let us call exo-dominant the duality where the exogenous characteristic is taken to be dominant and endo-dominant the other one. The following example will make this clearer.

With regard to money, the exo-dominant duality would imply an international money market with fixed parities, or parities calculated in relation to the real state of the economy, whereas the endo-dominant duality would imply a floating system, where the parities are the result of supply and demand mechanisms.

This duality in the money situation and changes in its dominance have built up, over a long period of time, a very sophisticated apparatus of regulations and relationships on the international scene and in the national context, between the public and the private sector and between the financial and the industrial markets. These relationships are structured in two respective dialectical issues: the relationship between the public and the private sectors and the interface between the political and the economic spheres. It is the same type of 'equilibrium' (if one may say so in such an explosive monetary situation) that one must foresee and expect in the field of communications networks.

Experience shows that the public sector can mainly regulate, manage, produce, and subsidize. Each of these activities represents a different type of interaction between the public and the private sectors, and they are going, in the coming years, to be seriously affected. The public sector can open up new opportunities by backing these activities either more intensively or more indirectly.

Let us take, for example, two areas that affect the equilibrium conditions: the intensity of R&D in the telecommunications industry and the necessity of defining common standards. With respect to R&D resources, these are difficult to allocate in a competitive environment because of the uncertainties about their payback period and rates of return on investments. It can be observed that the way to finance R&D is either by public funds or by monopoly power on the market. The statutory conditions in which R&D-intensive industrial production can take place have still to be found in Europe.

With respect to common standards, agreement on these is absolutely necessary to create a market for communications equipment. A Belgian telephone cannot be hooked up into the French network, and so a Belgian telephone is of no use to the French population, or vice versa.

The standardization of the code of digitalization is also crucial to communication. A stream of bits does not mean anything in itself. One has to have the key to be able to understand it. In the analogue case, the electric signal representing an 'A' produces an 'A' when passing through the diaphragm, or when deflecting the electron beam. In the digital case, when the input signal is '11000001' the terminal equipment has to 'know' (needs to have been programmed) that it is an 'A' and, in order to be able to do this, it needs to 'know' that it has to consider a package of eight bits. In this sense, the importance of standards is increasing. The need to communicate does not create ipso facto the market, as is the case with the need to eat, for example. It can be said, in this spirit, that the communication market, in order to exist in an economic format (i.e. with goods to be produced and sold), needs to be defined by rules, by 'software'. This assigns a specific role to the public sector, and is a constraint on the equilibrium.

This points to the interface between the *political* and *economic* spheres given that the actual form of the economy is always one means, among others, of allocating goods and satisfying needs. However, needs and goods exist independently from the economy. There are some needs that society has decided collectively, that is on a political basis, should be satisfied. These are called 'rights' – the right to minimal subsistence, for example. The notion of right is extra-economical. It introduces a distortion in the mechanism of preference revelation. To manage a right, the state has to interfere in the production process or in the allocation process either by subsidizing (the right to education, the subsidization of schools), or by giving indemnity to the people (social security in Belgium, for example: a person chooses his doctor and is reimbursed afterwards up to a certain amount), or by producing the good or organizing the activity (the right to property, the courts to enforce civil law), or by associating a duty with the right (the right to be compensated in a car accident, when in the right, goes with the duty of taking out insurance).

With regard to these considerations, we need to identify whether communication should be considered as a need, a right or even as a duty. These terms require definition. By need is meant that access to the network would be provided to the people who want it badly enough to pay the price demanded by the producers, on the basis of the maximization of their objective function (profit or turnover), given the objective function of the users. By right is meant that access to the network must be provided to anyone, at a price that he or she can pay, without further conditions. In the case of a duty, each person would be forced to have a network connection to comply with the social rules. This would be the case if, without a network connection, one could no longer be paid or make purchases, for example.

To decide whether communication is a need, a right or a duty is a political decision and economic developments have to follow this decision.

On a territorial basis, the development of transnational communications networks may imply or intensify the 'conflict of authority' between the political sphere and the economic sphere. Communication techniques offer the technical means for creating a global market place in more and more products. The reference space within which an economic agent will maximize his objective function (utility, profit, etc.) is being extended, while his 'living environment' remains more or less the same (it remains rare for people to commute daily by plane, or for friends to meet by means of a video-phone). The enlargement of the economic reference space and the relative stability of the socio-political reference space pose problems of organization and of priority. They pose the fundamental question of the relationships between entities organized on political principles and the dimensions of economic transactions. What will be the significance of the new possibilities for separating the physical environment from the 'rational'? If the constraint of physical proximity is abolished, what becomes of the notion of 'society', or of 'belonging' to a society?

What sort of feedback would there be from the local units concerned to influence economic operations? Will we witness the emergence of new relations between economics and society (towards 'small is beautiful', or even towards a multiplicity of cloistered protectionist areas)? Is the possible erosion of old patterns of solidarity based on a national economy going to bring into question the legitimacy of some of our current mechanisms of socio-political regulation? One might, for example, consider on what basis and in what way the nation-state will undertake the distributive role which it fulfils today in education, social security or unemployment benefit, for example.

These two points of interface between the political sphere and the economic sphere (need/right/duty and territorial competence) are latent in Europe within itself and with regard to the United States; but they are crucial today to the southern hemisphere. Communication networks are at the intersection of several development strategies: from self-sufficient development to increased dependence. They represent a tool of critical importance for development.

Thus the way in which the equilibrium that is to be reached with regard to communication networks is multi-dimensional. Besides the need to master technological development and the necessity to gain or keep competitiveness in the production of these networks, a new definition of the communication function will be embodied in this equilibrium.

Conclusion: beyond the European syndrome

As this chapter has shown communication issues are of particular relevance for Europe. It is not only a question of industrial competitiveness and market share, but above all a question of existence and autonomy. The convergence of telecommunications and informatics has a demultiplying effect and causes a spectacular acceleration of technological change. We are witnessing the development of networks and the multiplication of services that these networks can render.

However, we do not know the sense that we want to give to these networks, nor their role. It is as if technological change were taking place in a vacuum. The fact that we are incapable of making sense of these technological developments is a dangerous symptom of losing ground. In this context, too often, in the attempt to keep Europe's competitive position Europeans lose their vision and look to their future across the Atlantic or in the direction of the rising sun.

The only chance of reversing this trend is through the construction of a European integrated community of 240 million people. It is only in this framework that it is possible to assign a specific role and sense to the development of technological change and communication networks. The real challenge that Europeans continue to face with respect to communications is to be able to organize it in order that they may exist as Europeans.

Notes

1. The author is a member of the Forecasting and Assessment for Science and Technology (FAST) team and wishes to thank particularly Riccardo Petrella, the Head of FAST, for his useful remarks, and expresses her gratitude to Professor Stanley Metcalfe, of the University of Manchester, for his helpful comments.

The FAST programme is run by the Commission of the European Communities (CEC). Its main aim is the multi-dimensional analysis of scientific and technological change so as to highlight its implications and consequences for the common research and development (R&D) policy and for other European Economic Community (EEC) policies.

The on-going research work (a summary of which is available on request from Programme FAST, Commission of the European Communities, 200 rue de la Loi, 1049 Brussels) is focussed on five major areas, one of which is communications:

Relationships between technology, employment and work

Transformation of services and technological change

Strategic industrial systems around communications

Strategic industrial systems around the food industry

Integrated development of renewable natural resources.

The funds for the programme are 8.5 million ecus (1 ecu (European currency unit) = US\$0.74) over four years. The team is composed of six researchers and eighteen man-years of visiting fellows. The team produces reports highlighting priorities for a European R&D policy.

2. We are not unaware of the existence of specialized networks, in particular packet-switching networks, but access to these networks is via the classical network and is user-transparent.

3. All figures cited in this section are derived from EEC data.

4. These moves include, among others, the ESPRIT launch initiated by the European Commission; the AT&T and Philips joint venture; the agreement between Compagnie Générale (CGE) and Thomson (two large enterprises in the French tele-communications industry); the AT&T and Olivetti agreement (concerning the personal computer); the Siemens and Philips agreement (for high-capacity random access memory); the privatization of British Telecom (the sale of 51 per cent of BT shares by the British government on 1 November 1984); and the agreement between (MCI) and the Belgian RTT (relating to long-distance calls to and from Belgium).

References

CEC (1984) *Television Without Frontiers*. Brussels: Commission of the European Communities. (COM(84) 300).

Mackintosh International (1983) *Interim Report to the Commission of the European Communities*. (Contract AH 83-367.) Luton, England: Mackintosh International.

[PTT Consortium] (1983) *Final Report to the CEC*. Brussels: PTT Consortium. (PTT Consortium consists of British Telconsult, Consultel SPA, Detecon, Nepostel and Sofrecom with the participation of RTT, P&T, Telecom Eireann Services International (TESI) and Luxconsult.)

Riblier, W. and J.P. Barbier (1983) *Nouvelles Technologies de l'Information et Création d'Emplois: L'Industrie Audio-Visuelle*. Brussels: Forecasting and Assessment for Science and Technology.

10

Broadcasting policy in Canada

Richard Collins

Canada and its communication order has long been a major site for the studies of scholars, broadcasters and policy makers. Latterly European broadcasters have begun to dub their fears of the future a fear of the 'Canadianization' of European broadcasting and have given space to the president of the Canadian Broadcasting Corporation (CBC) in the European Broadcasting Union *Review* (Juneau, 1984) to act as Cassandra.

Communication scholars have identified Canada as paradigmatic of a world condition of media imperialism (Schiller, 1969; Smith, 1980; Tunstall, 1977; and, for a critical assessment of the media imperialism thesis, Lee, 1980). More recently Canada's development towards a post-industrial or 'information' society (Bell, 1976) – an explicit policy goal of recent Canadian federal and provincial administration – has also attracted scholars' attention.

Communications have long been considered by Canadians as central to their national identity and existence. Canadian confederation, the inception of Canada as a unified nation-state, was conditional on the construction of a communications infrastructure – a coast-to-coast railway system connecting the eastern and western peripheries. This alignment of the railways was determined by military and economic judgements as to the threat posed to Canadian interests by the United States as well as by geography. In the twentieth century telephony, broadcasting and physical communications – airlines and roads especially – were developed to 'Canadianize' communications, all (with the exception of parts of the telephone system) under public sector initiatives. In addition, the national government consistently made communication issues a priority in an endeavour to Canadianize communications that were essentially dominated by the neighbour to the south, the USA, by funding public sector broadcasting, establishing regulatory bodies and enacting legislation to favour Canadian media production and use.

A statement in the introduction to the Department of Communications (DOC) 1979–80 annual report exemplifies the distinctive Canadian paranoia over loss of national cultural identity and fear of economic decline that will attend not keeping up with the information society Joneses.

150

In Canada as in many other countries, the production of information is becoming an increasingly important factor in the economy, but this shift to an information based economy will not be problem free. If Canadian industry does not participate in this expansion, the economic consequences could be serious indeed. The concern is far more than economic however. Canada's very survival as a nation is at stake. Data banks and information systems developed by foreign multinationals could dominate Canadian consumer and business markets. Extensive information on Canada and Canadians could be controlled by other nations. A deluge of foreign radio and television broadcasting could overwhelm the Canadian perspective and Canadian identity. In short, Canadian sovereignty could become a meaningless concept. (DOC, 1981: 6)

But Canada has never enjoyed communications sovereignty – the 49th Parallel has proved very permeable to the movement of printed works and cinema films and completely permeable to US radio and TV, though much national effort has been devoted to attempting to achieve communication sovereignty and many Canadians – whether Anglophone or Francophone – believe communications sovereignty is a necessary condition of a national culture, national identity and national survival. Several recent initiatives in the hardware sector have established Canada in a leading position in telecommunication switching, communication satellites and other product fields. Canada was the third country to launch a satellite (Alouette 1 in 1962) and the first to use a satellite for domestic communications in 1973. The present ANIK C3 series of launches in 1982, 1983 and 1984 were to implement the world's first direct broadcasting by satellite (DBS) service, and by the 1990s the Msat series are planned to fly which 'could reduce satellite dishes to the size of wrist watches' (cited in Melody, 1982: 3). Hyperbole aside, the commitment and progress are clear. Canadian policy is to prefer the 'sale of satellite hardware in international markets rather than produce programming content for domestic consumption' (Melody, 1982: 8).

Hardware rather than software has been the emphasis, and the absence of Canadian software – television programmes – that offers Canadian audiences the gratification equivalent to that yielded by US programmes has led to the absurd situation of substantial expenditure by Canadian consumers on domestic earth stations, which are purchased from the US in order to receive US satellite signals, and by the Canadian government on the satellite system delivering the CanCom TV services, the most popular of which are the US networks (the 3 + 1 system of CBS, NBC, ABC and PBS – Columbia Broadcasting System, National Broadcasting Company, American Broadcasting Company and Public Broadcasting Service).

The pattern of Canadian television viewing

The central dilemma that has underlain Canadian broadcasting policy since the inception of radio broadcasting in 1919 can be exemplified by the statistics below. Canadians predominantly consume American Television – whether from American or Canadian broadcasters. For a society that regards its existence as a nation-state as conditional on its communications, dependence on the United States, as the Canadian orthodoxy has it, is extremely dangerous.

Canadians watch an average of 23 hours of television a week (Juneau, 1984: 18), though Francophones watch more: 26 hours and 22 minutes per week (David, 1979). This time is divided between three sectors, the public sector, the commercial sector and the US broadcasters. In 1977 Canadians' access to television was as follows: 62.35 per cent of Anglophone Canada had access to four US channels and 45.61 per cent to four Canadian channels. In 1980 the Canadian TV audience divided between the three sectors thus: US stations 24.5 per cent, Canadian commercial sector 48.6 per cent, Canadian public sector 25.8 per cent, with a considerable Francophone audience consuming English-language television (Audley, 1983: 266).

These figures relate to the period prior to the introduction of Canadian satellite distribution of US television to all parts of Canada, and are based on viewing of US signals received off air or redistributed by cable: the US share of the Canadian audience is certainly higher now. The amount of US programming watched is even higher because very substantial parts of the schedules of Canadian broadcasters, particularly the commercial broadcasters, are of US origin.

In 1983 programmes of Canadian origin were divided as follows: Anglophone commercial sector around 13 per cent, public sector 35 per cent; Francophone commercial sector 31 per cent, public sector 34 per cent (Hoskins and McFadyen, 1984a: 15).

Most Canadians, most of the time, watch foreign, mostly US, television whether distributed by Canadian or US broadcasters. The reasons for this are very easy to see. They are not that Canadians cannot produce 'good' television ('The Kids of deGrassi Street', 'Fraggle Rock', 'Empire Inc.' and 'Wayne & Schuster' are all sold to the United Kingdom), nor that Canadians are unwilling to pay for non-US programming. The CBC's budget is about that of the British Broadcasting Corporation (BBC) on a population base half the size and Canadians subscribe about 40 per cent of the funds of US PBS stations receivable in Canada for the 'Principally British Service'. (This is true for PBS stations received in Francophone Canada – for example those transmitting from Vermont – as well as those serving Anglophones.) Rather it is that US has an enormous comparative economic advantage in producing audio-visual software.

Let us consider a particular example of a US programme seen in the UK and Canada. 'Dynasty' costs $850,000 per hour to produce; it will be sold into the UK market at approximately $20,000 and to Canada for substantially more: if it is bought by CBC Anglophone it will be for $20–30,000, if by CTV (the major commercial network) for $20–28,000, and if by Radio Canada, for $8–14,000 (*Variety* (1983): *TV World* (1982)). Even though the Canadian audience is substantially less than half the size of the British audience, Canadian broadcasters pay more than do the British for the US product, but however 'expensive' it is, the American product is cheaper than comparable home-produced programming. Canadian broadcasters pay more simply because they bid against each other for 'hot' US programming.

The disincentives against using Canadian software are evident. Hoskins and McFadyen (1982: 49) estimate that a mere 50 extra minutes of Canadian content in prime time would reduce the average price–cost margin to zero: that is broadcasters would go out of profit.

David McDonald, an ex-Canadian Minister of Communications, defined Canadian communication policy as distinguished by '"Technopia Canadensis" – a condition of intense focus on hardware and new technologies causing an inability to see long range effects' (1982).

The processes of cultural distribution and reproduction are conditional on a number of factors, including that which the Toronto School and particularly Harold Innis and Marshall McLuhan have emphasized: technology. World cultural patterns are shifting under the impact of technological change – this is one dimension of the putative shift identified by some commentators in developed countries towards a tertiary economy and an information society. Latterly, some Canadians have seen the new technologies and the new forms of market stratification they make possible as offering signs of hope that Canadian culture will be formed in a more diverse matrix than it has been in the past and that the market shaped by new technological forces will deliver what decades of state regulation have not. Lyman, for example, argues that 'Cultural content itself is also showing signs of global formulation through joint venture and other arrangements thus diminishing the overwhelming American presence of the past' (Lyman, 1983: 24).

Lyman's prognosis is far from being the experience of the present in Canada. Canadian cultural tastes remain substantially American. Hoskins and McFadyen (1984a: 4) cite an article in the *Edmonton Journal* of 22 May 1984 that reports the results of a Canadian government opinion poll of March 1983 which found that 81 per cent of Canadians polled opposed any control over American television signals allowed into Canada.

But Canadian elites remain sensitive to the point of paranoia about the American threat. Susan Crean, in her provocative book *Who's Afraid of Canadian Culture?* puts forward trenchantly the classic nationalist thesis and discusses 'The contradictory nature of whatever might be called our identity: bookstores, newsstands and movie houses where "Canadian" is a foreign word; Hockey Night in Canada with Boston playing Philadelphia in the US. . .' (Crean, 1976: 8). As already noted, this judgement has been appropriated and amplified by communication scholars and by other writers[1] constituting Canada as an exemplary site of communication imperialism.

The theoretical bedrock on which this set of judgements has been erected is the one created by Harold Adams Innis. In his *Empire and Communications* Innis (1972) set out what was to become the central thesis of the Toronto School − the determining role of communication technologies in the achievement and retention of social power.

Innis' prioritization of communication as the motor of social change and formation has been very influential; although to be sure the emphasis is not peculiarly his. But it is, I think, only in Canada that Innis could have formulated his central idea. It is perhaps too only in Canada, a society super-sensitized to the link between national unity and a communication system (without any distinction recognized between the distribution of *physical* and *symbolic* goods), that such an unlikely thesis expressed in gnomic formulations could become the dominant academic and political orthodoxy.

The orthodoxy of Canadian cultural sovereignty
Orthodoxy it is, as examination of the Applebert (Applebaum and Hébert, 1982) and successive broadcasting policy reports (DOC, 1983a, 1983b, 1984) shows. What, however, is new in the post-1982 wave of audio-visual cultural policy is a critique of the CBC/Radio Canada and the National Film Board (NFB) of Canada; an effort to reconstruct these institutional bearers of the national cultural and communications goals; and a new recognition that audio-visual policy is no longer solely a 'soft' or cultural issue but an economic one of primary importance for industrial policy: 'There is . . . a growing recognition that communications and information infrastructures tailored to a country's particular needs, and the software and cultural products to fuel them, are essential for development' (de Montigny Marchand, 1981: 13−14).

The Liberal party (the party of government for all but nine months of the last twenty-two years until the Conservative victory in 1984) established a Federal Cultural Policy Review Committee in 1980. The so-called Applebert committee (named after its joint chairmen Louis Applebaum and Jacques Hebert), reported in 1982 and opened fire on the CBC:[2]

This Committee fully endorses the criticism heard during our public hearing that CBC television is not sufficiently open to Canadian creative talent.... The CBC is that type of over-protected operation. It is not a monopolist, but the fact that it receives so much of its gross income from Parliament effectively shields it and its employees from having to respond to changed circumstances (Applebaum and Hébert, 1982: 276–7)

and applied more of the same criticism to the other sacred cow of the public sector, the NFB (see Applebaum and Hébert, 1982: 263-4).

The Applebert report's critique of the CBC and NFB, time-honoured public sector institutions considered to be bearers of the public interest and national purpose, and the tentative invocation of the market as a more effective instrument of public policy has been put into operation in the official policy papers (DOC, 1983a, 1983b, 1984). The Applebert report is essentially a document of transition, marking a shift from the traditional conception of Canadian media policy as a matter of struggling for the achievement of Canadian cultural goals through public sector institutions in what has been called (by Hershel Hardin, 1974) a 'Public Enterprise Economy' to the emerging new conception of communication policy as the leading edge of national industrial and economic policy. In this connection state intervention and public sector institutions are to assist Canadian entrepreneurs in seizing a commanding comparative advantage over foreign competitors for Canada in the international race to adapt to and lead the way in new technologies.[3]

There was dissent from CBC/Radio Canada's regime before the Applebert report, but dissent tended to be from those, like Lévesque (1978) and the Parti Québécois (PQ), who put themselves outside the mainstream of Canadian discourse and who did not challenge the role of the state but rather argued for a different state. Such dissent tended to constitute controversy over CBC and public sector communications politically rather than in terms of culture or economy. Political dissent such as that of Lévesque and the PQ from the regime of truth offered by CBC/Radio Canada is echoed by the federal government, in turn, using its policy initiatives to consolidate further its prescriptions for the political parameters within which the state broadcaster may operate.

In 1977 the then Prime Minister Pierre Trudeau commissioned the CRTC (the Canadian Radio, Television and Telecommunications Commission – the regulatory body) to investigate CBC/Radio Canada as to the adequacy of its fulfillment of the provisions of the 1968 Broadcasting Act and its injunction to contribute to national unity (CRTC, 1977: v). The CRTC firmly and properly rebutted the Liberals' initiative, but there is undoubtedly a sense in which (as numerous commentators including David (1974), Desaulniers (1984) and Raboy (1984) have pointed out) television – but not exclusively or even particularly Radio Canada – has acted as an enormous stimulant to Québécois self-consciousness and assertiveness.

But Raboy argues that the establishment of CBC/Radio Canada as a public sector institution under federal authority caused public sector broadcasting to serve one definition of Canada, one conception of the Canadian public: 'The Canadian experience shows how, by identifying and confusing an ideological notion like 'the nation' with a political project guided by the state, public television becomes a legitimation force for alignments of power, which have nothing to do with the democratic sense of public' (Raboy, 1984: 32). Raboy argues that the assertion of 'Canadian-ness' in public broadcasting against the 'external contradiction' of the United States meant that the public broadcasting system tended to subordinate the regional differences, provincial interests and most importantly the different cultural and historical experience of Francophone Canadians to those of the Anglophone majority.

Responding to the provisions of the 1968 Broadcasting Act (Canada, Parliament, 1967–8: Section 3g iv) tends to compel CBC/Radio Canada to follow the federal government's definitions of Canadian interest and identity which in turn tend to be those of the most populous region: Central Canada. In a country of diverse regional economic interests, cultural patterns and histories and two official languages, the comfortable complementarity enjoyed by European broadcasters, in which the categories 'state', 'nation', and 'public' tend to congruence, are not available to Canadians.

Federal policy and the new technologies
The 1983–4 policies of the federal government attempted both to rework the old contradictions that have shaped Canadian broadcasting and respond to the new circumstances that technical change has created. Thus the old themes of consolidating federal definitions of Canadian identity and protecting the threatened national identity from assimilation by American values remain constant hopes. To those, though, is added a recognition that communications sovereignty has been substantially lost in broadcasting and that neither can Canadians be prevented from consuming American television nor can Canadian television ever be more than a minority alternative to the dominant US force, and a new view that the old public sector standard bearers are ill equipped either to act as the cutting edge of Canada's new information software industries or to give Canadian audiences programming that speaks to their interest and experiences. There is therefore a shift towards a more market-oriented production system with a very substantial presence of inde-

pendent producers and with CBC/Radio Canada revalued and reconstructed more as a distribution channel than as a production agency.

The federal government's hope is that the ossified public sector institutions can be asset stripped: using the expertise of the NFB in training and that of CBC in distribution to foster independent productions and act as surrogate mother to the hoped-for infants of the private sector. Substantial federal funds are to be committed to stimulating the audio-visual production sector, and (interestingly and correctly) to supporting Canadian distributors. The CFDC (Canadian Film Development Corporation – renamed Telefilm Canada) development programme budget is to rise from $1.4 million to $2.6 million per annum. It is hoped that these measures will not just constitute Canada as a leading member of the 'information society' but, because it is judged that the audio-visual industries are labour-intensive, that they will reduce unemployment (see DOC, 1984: 22).

It is ironic that the transition in Canadian public policy, in the last days of the Liberal government, has come as a consequence of a 'trans-border data flow' and the decision of the Canadian government to orient its public sector warhorses to the market and audience needs and desires, and to concentrate resources so that internationally competitive programming can be produced. The pre-echo of this policy, the co-production by CBC, Radio Canada and the NFB of 'Empire Inc.', shows what can be achieved. The irony, of course, is that this success was a public sector initiative.

It is overwhelmingly clear that the criteria for audio-visual policy in Canada are now economic and not cultural. The achievements in which the *National Film and Video Policy* (DOC, 1984) takes pride are 'Porky's' (the 16th largest grossing feature film ever) and 'Atlantic City', a film whose representation of Canada was limited to an insulting one-liner about Saskatchewan. It is unlikely that the achievement of 'Empire Inc.' and the potentiality of other public sector series will be developed. They make up what is likely to be the swan song of the long movement in Canadian broadcasting history which put Canadian cultural goals in the foreground. It is ironic indeed that the sloughing off of their old skins by the public sector institutions came too late to give them a leading role in the new order.

The first indications of Marcel Masse's policies as the Communications Minister of the Mulroney government – including an $85 million cut in CBC's budget – suggest that Conservative policies to achieve national cultural goals will follow the liberal shift towards market rather than administered regimes. It is hard to dissent from the Canadian government's impatience with the state sector – a persistent motif of reports on Canadian broadcasting from Massey (in

1951) to Applebert has been the criticism of CBC's management (and Applebert was no kinder to the NFB). 'Empire Inc.' and the collaboration between the NFB and CBC/Radio Canada's English- and French-service divisions came too little and too late. However, academics may enjoin caution if government responds to a protected situation in which existing state and commercial broadcasters have been unable to achieve the desired cultural and economic goals by seeking success through the fostering of newer and smaller players in an environment of augmenting competition (in particular from satellite-delivered signals from the United States).

Broadcasting in Canada has always existed in spite of market forces. The state, through its licensing policies, has created an extremely profitable uncompetitive regime for commercial broadcasters in Canada and in establishing major public sector presences – notably CBC/Radio Canada – has institutionalized organizations that are imperfectly responsive to audience demand. The mix of public and private sector regimes under the tutelage of the state is by no means unusual (the UK, Australia, Japan and a number of Latin American countries follow similar models), through the presence of explicit political goals for broadcasting in Canada (see in particular section three of the 1968 Broadcasting Act) is fairly unusual, albeit not unprecedented. The constitutions of West German broadcasting entities – Zweites Deutsches Fernsehen (ZDF), and West- and Süddeutsche Rundfunk (WDR and SDR) for example – prescribe certain political goals. What is most distinctive about Canada, though, is the repetoire of measures promulgated by government in order to essay the achievement of national cultural goals in the face of competition from foreign signals.

These sentiments remain the basis of policy though the means of 'preserving and strengthening the cultural, social, political and economic fabric of Canada' have been changed. There has been loss of faith in the public sector administered regime and a significant shift towards a market regime promulgated in the policies of the last days of the Liberal government and consolidated by the Canadian electorate's overwhelming choice of the Conservatives in the 1984 election. The administered regime, which operates through the CRTC which requires as a condition of licence a proportion of Canadian content in TV transmissions (60 per cent overall and 50 per cent within prime time though there are exceptions and the definition of 'Canadian' is broad); through the provisions of Bill C-58 (Canada, Parliament, 1976) whereby the profitability of broadcasters is protected (though disadvantaging Canadian advertisers choosing US broadcasters as a vehicle for advertising), through the simultaneous substitution and random deletion rules for cable operators (again to augment the attractiveness of Canadian signals as a vehicle for advertising) and most of all through the extensive support for the public sector broadcasters, has been recognized to have failed to deliver the desired cultural and economic benefits.

The degree to which the market principle will penetrate Canadian audio-visual policy remains to be seen. There is clearly a limit beyond which commitment to market allocations is incompatible with a Canadian broadcasting system. Were it not for the state, broadcasting in Canada would not exist. But there is a good deal of evidence to suggest that the absence of market pressures has produced a broadcasting order that does not serve Canadians particularly well. The commercial sector enjoys very high profits as a consequence of the policies of Canadianization, though few benefits to the Canadian public are delivered in terms either of programming distinctively different from that of American broadcasting or in distribution to the tax payer of a portion of monopoly rents accruing to the broadcaster (e.g. through charging a fee for the licensed use of spectrum capacity or an adveritsing levy). The public sector is insulated from the pressures of consumer demand and therefore does not often enough find programme formats that combine both the 'Canadian-ness' that the public sector is there to supply and the gratification that audiences demand. That the capacity to produce such popular programming exists is undoubted; 'Empire Inc.' and 'Duplessis' offer English and French examples. That the production of excellent Canadian entertainment exploring the experience and concerns of contemporary Canada, offering audiences gratification comparable to those of the successful American melodramas, is not always enough is evidenced by the sad failure of 'Vanderberg'. To produce a Canadian audio-visual culture is not simply a supply-side question.

When these developments are placed in a comparative context, the UK for example, has enjoyed better fortunes. This has been due largely to its being able to control its own communication destiny and contrive a system which, whilst unequal in its distribution of benefits and now probably overextended, has more successfully than most national broadcasting regimes combined the gratification of popular taste with the production of programming of aesthetic quality that engages with the needs and experience of the audience. In the UK the health of broadcasting is declining; both the British Broadcasting Corporation (BBC) and Channel 4 are under a good deal of financial pressure leading them both to fall victims to the Canadian disease: programming American material in order to raise their audience shares. British policy makers have been able to create a broadcasting order with these characteristics (for which very strong but, I believe, not necessarily decisive public interest arguments can be made) because no serious external competition has been offered. This ability to make broadcasting history more or less in the terms of its own choosing has been conditional on factors denied to Canada and which the new distribution technologies will soon deny to the UK.

Turning to the rest of Europe, the new distribution technologies, at least new to Europe, of broad-band cable and communication satellites are leading to a loss of the communications sovereignty that has, until now, been enjoyed by the larger European states.

Information goods with a physical mass – books, newspapers, cinematographic films – have been relatively easy to control, though the United States has enjoyed a comparative advantage since the 1920s in the production of audio-visual software, film and television programmes, but European countries have been able partially to protect their film production industries by licensing distribution outlets or imposing import quotas.

In Europe, information goods without mass have remained substantially national monopolies in spite of the impossibility of national governments controlling reception of foreign signals. The propagation characteristics of Herzian waves at the frequencies used for television, and international agreement in radio spectrum allocation and regulation, has meant that the large European countries have been able to exercise communication sovereignty in electronic communications.[4]

The North Sea radio pirates that were successfully suppressed in the late 1960s by the joint action of governments through the Council of Europe are returning. (The *New York Times* (1984) estimates that there are 104 on- and off-shore pirate radio stations in the UK.) Essentially all these changes are ones that stem from the introduction of the 'new' technologies of satellites and cable, though it has to be said that cable at least is a venerable technology that, as a distributor of entertainment in the UK, goes back as far as the Electrophone, and that Holland, Belgium and Switzerland already have a 60 per cent penetration of cable, a level close to that experienced in Canada where 70 per cent of homes are cabled.

The two major factors that separate markets for the electronic delivery of information goods, distance and language, explain the differences in impact of US programming on the UK, on Anglophone and on Francophone Canada. Distance has insulated the UK from loss of electronic communication sovereignty to the US. Language has produced a distinct lag in the Francophone Canadian response to US programming, though the same tendencies to prefer US products are visible in Francophone Canada as they are in Anglophone Canada.

The communication sovereignty enjoyed by the UK has enabled it to limit television distribution capacity and match increases – new channels – to the ability of audiences to pay for the UK production necessary to fill distribution capacity. This matching of television production capacity to distribution capacity has permitted the successful maintenance of an 86 per cent British quota in the UK, while Canada cannot successfully maintain a 50 per cent Canadian quota.

However, the increase in distribution capacity envisaged by the proposed introduction of cable and DBS services will destroy this comfortable UK television symbiosis. Even if a mid-Atlantic US satellite with a footprint embracing the UK is not launched the colossal rise in distribution capacity following the introduction of cable and/or DBS will inevitably fragment audiences, reduce revenues per hour of programming and force UK broadcaster into the same dependence on US programming as that experienced by Canadians.[5] Quota restrictions will not stem this flow. Canadian content quotas exist but cannot be enforced because of the production/distribution mismatch. Unless non-US programming is simultaneously scheduled so audiences cannot avoid it (as are documentaries and current affairs on UK television, even a 90 per cent quota in a ten-channel system will not prevent audiences from choosing 100 per cent non-UK programming, as they will tend to do. ('Dynasty', budgeted at $850,000 per hour, will continue to tend to be more attractive than UK programmes budgeted at an average cost of $30,000 per hour.)

What Juneau (1984) warns of may yet come to pass in Europe, though it may be that scholars will wish to stand the media imperialism and Innis theses on their heads. What if national identity and survival are not conditional on cultural and communication sovereignty? What if the Canadian case so beloved of communication scholars as an example of the cultural imperialism thesis exemplifies not that thesis but the reverse: that nations can survive in robust health with no serious loss of unity and coherence, even when their media are, as Tunstall (1977) put it, American?

Notes

1. See, for example, Wilden (1980) where he argues that Canadian identity is always constructed in terms of what it is not: not British, not French, not American, and that a synonym for Canada is 'Notland'.

2. Since the publication of the Applebert report the federal government has produced three major policy reports and proposals (DOC, 1983a, 1983b, 1984).

3. The Applebert report is extremely vulnerable to criticisms both from culturalists (see Gathercole (1983) and Crean (1983) and economists (see *Canadian Public Policy* (1983), especially D. McQueen's article) but it marks a decisive shift in Canadian policy orientation and in 'making official' a critique of 'motherhood status' institutions.

4. National sensitivity to these issues is demonstrated by such examples as France's Minister of the Telecommunications criticizing Luxembourg's 'coca-cola satellites attacking our artistic and cultural integrity' (*Financial Times*, 1984) and Eric Jurgens, the Chairman of the Nederlands Omroep Stichting NOS, saying that 'Dutch language and culture are coming under increasing pressure' (Jurgens, 1982: 2–3).

5. Though the UK's role is not wholly that of victim; Sky Channel (owned by Rupert Murdoch's international communications conglomerate) now feeds more than 2 million European cable homes and is one of a number of British communications enterprises (not the least of which is British Telecom) attacking European markets in order to benefit from the break-up of the old European communication order (*Variety*, 1984).

References

Applebaum, L. and J. Hébert (1982) *Report of the Federal Cultural Policy Review Committee*. Ottawa: Department of Communications.

Audley, P. (1983) *Canada's Cultural Industries*. Toronto: J. Lorimer.

Bell, D. (1976) *The Coming of the Post-Industrial Society*. Harmondsworth, Middx.: Penguin (first published 1973).

Canada, Parliament (1967–8) *Broadcasting Act 1968*. Ottawa: Minister of Supply and Services.

Canada, Parliament (1976) (Bill C-58) *Income Tax Act 1976*. Ottawa: Minister of Supply and Services.

Canadian Public Policy (1983) (Montreal), 9.

Crean, S. (1976) *Who's Afraid of Canadian Culture?* Don Mills, Toronto: General Publishing Company.

Crean, Susan (1983) in *Canadian Forum* (Toronto), April.

CRTC (1977) *Report of the Committee of Inquiry into the National Broadcasting Service*. Ottawa: Canadian Radio, Television and Telecommunications Commission.

David, R. (1974) 'The Role of the French Network', *Circuit Fermé*, 10 (6).

David, R. (1979) *Radio Canada et la Culture Québécoise*. Montréal: Radio Canada.

Desaulniers, J.P. (1984) *Télévision et Nationalisme: de la Culture à la Communication*, paper presented at the International Television Studies Conference, London.

DOC (1981) *Annual Report 1979–80*. Ottawa: Department of Communications.

DOC (1983a) *Towards a New National Broadcasting Policy*. Ottawa: Department of Communications.

DOC (1983b) *Building for the Future: Towards a Distinctive CBC*. Ottawa: Department of Communications.

DOC (1984) *The National Film and Video Policy*. Ottawa: Department of Communications.

Financial Times (1984) (London), 31 May: 3.

Gathercole, Sandra (1983) in *Canadian Forum* (Toronto), February.

Hardin, Herschel (1974) *A Nation Unaware*. North Vancouver: J. Douglas.

Hoskins, C. and S. McFadyen (1982) 'Market Structure and TV Programming: Performance in Canada and the UK. A Comparative Study', *Canadian Public Policy* (Montreal), 8 (3) (Summer).

Hoskins, C. and S. McFadyen (1984a) 'International Competition in Television Broadcasting', paper presented at the International Business International Meeting, Singapore.

Hoskins, C. and McFadyen (1984b) 'National Policy Towards TV in Canada', paper presented at the International Television Studies Conference, London.

Innis, H. (1972) *Empire and Communications*. Toronto: University of Toronto Press.

Juneau, P. (1984) 'Audience Fragmentation and Cultural Erosion', *European Broadcasting Review Programmes, Administration, Law*, 35

Jurgens, E. (1982) Interview in *Broadcasting News from the Netherlands 1982/1*. Hilversum: NOS.

Lee, C. (1980) *Media Imperialism Reconsidered.* Beverly Hills, Calif. and London: Sage.

Lévesque, R. (1978) *My Québec.* Toronto: Methuen.

Lyman, P. (1983) *Canada's Video Revolution.* Toronto: J. Lorimer.

McDonald, D. (1982) 'Pay-Triation: Fulfilling a Canadian Promise', in R.B. Woodrow and K.B. Woodside (eds.), *The Introduction of Pay TV in Canada.* Montreal: Institute for Research on Public Policy.

Melody, W. (1982) 'Direct Broadcast Satellites: the Canadian Experience', paper presented at the Symposium on Satellite Communication, National Media Systems and International Communication Policy, Hans Bredow Institute, University of Hamburg.

de Montigny Marchand (1981) 'The Impact of Information Technology on International Relations', *Intermedia* (London), 9 (6).

New York Times (1984), 20 September: A17.

Raboy, M. (1984) 'Public Television. The National Question and the Presentation of the Canadian State', paper presented at the International Television Studies Conference, London.

Schiller, H. (1969) *Mass Communication and American Empire.* New York: Augustus M. Kelley.

Smith, A. (1980) *The Geopolitics of Information.* New York: Oxford University Press.

Tunstall, J. (1977) *The Media are American.* London: Constable.

TV World (1982) (London), July : 46.

Variety (1983) (New York), 5 October: 56, 57, 70, 71.

Variety (1984) (New York), 20 November: 40.

Wilden, A. (1980) *The Imaginary Canadian.* Vancouver: Pulp Press.

11

The Japanese approach to the development of new residential communications services[1]

Jill Hartley

Introduction

Of the many new or potential services made possible through continuing advances in communications technology, those capturing the greatest attention in Japan and most other industrialized countries are services for the general public such as multi-channel cable TV, satellite broadcasting and various home based 'tele-services'. The prospective introduction of household-oriented communications services raises several serious policy issues relevant to the entire communications field. The adequacy of existing networks and the question of how new infrastructural investment is to proceed is fundamental. Also crucial is how the regulatory regimes for both broadcasting and telecommunications are to be modified now that technical developments in distribution systems and service variety are undermining the traditional arguments for monopolistic supply. Finally, any significant developments in the communications and electronics industry are likely to be important considerations for industrial policy given the perceived 'strategic' position of this sector in the modern economy.

This chapter focuses on the major developments and government policies being pursued in Japan in the fields of cable TV, satellite broadcasting and the 'wired society' and its infrastructure. As such it provides an impression of the overall communications scene as well as points of reference to assist the reader in drawing comparisons with other countries discussed in this book.

We turn first to the context in which government policy is being formed and the role of the ministries in communications policy origination and implementation. We then consider the reasons for the government's recent legislation to overturn the domestic monopoly of Nippon Telegraph and Telephone (NTT) in the provision of public telecommunications services; NTT's extensive modernization programme and its pilot system are then discussed as infrastructural developments for a 'wired society'. This is followed by an account of the government's own 'wired society' trials. Finally, we consider the response in Japan to the utilization of cable and satellite distribution systems for broadcast television services.

Before proceeding it is useful to explore the five major features of Japanese communications policy identified in this chapter. Firstly, the extent of government involvement is considerable and contrasts particularly with the generally non-interventionist stance of the UK, North America and most smaller European countries. Whilst the degree of financial support is not necessarily more substantial than in Germany or France, it is the nature of government involvement which is the most interesting, operating as it does through two of its powerful ministries and their unique relationships with industry.

Secondly, although a number of governments, notably the German, French and Dutch, are supporting telecommunications trials, in Japan similar experiments of the 'wired community' type appear to have become an established feature of policy for communications development and plans for the next round are on a greater scale than is to be found elsewhere.

Thirdly, with respect to the emphasis placed on infrastructure and services, telecommunications elements are receiving the greatest attention in Japan and there is much in common with the planned, national approach towards telecommunications provision found in France and Germany. Broadcasting developments, notably cable TV, maintain a relatively lower profile but direct broadcasting by satellite (DBS)[2] is an exception with Japan's first service receiving government support.

Fourthly, on regulatory matters Japan parts company from the 'interventionist' countries and follows the liberalization example set out by the USA and the UK, both of which are without obvious national telecommunications strategies. Thus Japan pursues an ideological mix of policies combining deregulation and the promotion of private enterprise with a continuation of government oversight and intervention not readily found in either Western Europe or North America.

Finally, the dominant concern of most governments with new communications technologies is almost certainly to promote the competitiveness of their respective national communications and electronics industries, and this appears to be the principal objective of the Japanese government also. Although Japan appears to have an obvious advantage due to its relative strength in the electronics sector, in some respects its policy is the traditional one of following the 'working textbook' (Yamauchi, 1983) provided by countries more advanced in certain technologies and applications. However, in other fields of development and application Japan's position is at the frontier which necessitates a home-grown policy response. The status of Japan's communications experiments can be interpreted as representing both the importance of an innovative policy for Japan and the problems of devising such policies in the face of pronounced uncertainty.

Government objectives
The approach of the Japanese government towards the emergent communications technologies is predominantly an industrial policy. While expressions such as 'information society' thwart attempts at definition, the fact that between 30 and 50 per cent of the workforce in the advanced industrial countries is employed either handling or generating information, or in the manufacture of the hardware used for information-related activities, underlines the significance of the 'information sector' for the economy as a whole. Indeed the future strength of any national industry may well be determined by the competitive position of its firms in this sector.

Japanese success on world markets in this sector is considerable, accounting for approximately two thirds of the markets for both large computer memory chips and telephone sets, and a share in excess of 80 per cent of the video cassette recorder market. Its technological achievements in selected fields are also impressive, for example fibre optics, very-large-scale integration (VLSI) and high-definition television (HDTV). However, despite these strengths there is concern in government and industrial circles that Japan is less advanced than other countries, especially the USA, in terms of the extent to which it has developed an information service economy. This point is illustrated by Masuda (1983) who describes the American transition from a manufacturing to an information-based economy as occurring in the late 1950s, more than a decade earlier than in Japan. He also identifies the database service industry as the key to progress in information-related activities and observes that Japan's data base industry is only one tenth the size of the American one, and that most users in Japan depend heavily on US services.

This concern extends to the supply and application of new communications technologies. As information handling and telecommunications represents a major cost for many large corporations, if a competitive edge is to be maintained Japanese companies need to have the benefits of the same advanced services as their foreign counterparts. Further, a growing domestic market is seen as important not only in its own right but also as a testing ground for Japanese firms prior to launching their communications products and services onto the world market.

There is some evidence of lags in the communications field. From the outset Japan has had to devise methods of overcoming the problem its language creates for electronic information systems. There are up to 3,000 Chinese characters (Kanji) in common use and 100 other phonetic characters (Katakana and Hiragana). Conventional keyboard technology is highly inappropriate and instead documents and letters were handwritten. This accounts for the significantly greater use of facsimile communications in Japan compared with other countries.[3] Since the early 1970s, when Japanese word processors became available, office automation in Japan has been spreading, but systems are not as fast or as straightforward as those for the Latin alphabet. Communications systems such as teletext[4] also have to be adapted for the Japanese language and visual displays need to be more sophisticated too. It is not surprising, therefore, that in the application of computerized information networks for the business sector, for example, Japan could be as much as five years behind the United States; nor that on the consumer side the Japanese public videotex system, CAPTAIN,[5] only began commercial operation in September 1984 whilst Britain's Prestel system, admittedly a first in the field, has been commercial since September 1979.

Several responses have been forthcoming which affect consumer-oriented communications. The telecommunications ministry has been pursuing the development and application of a number of technologies which have been put on the agenda by advances in other countries. Secondly, and particularly striking, has been the sudden reform of the regulatory regime governing telecommunications network and service provision. Thirdly, concerns about whether the new communications systems will be accepted by the Japanese public have been heightened. A recent opinion survey conducted for the Prime Minister's Office (1983) revealed that more than 60 per cent of the respondents claimed that they had not even heard of major new information services.[6] One line of response has been the establishment of a number of committees by individual government ministries and NTT over the past couple of years to conduct research into the likely social impacts of the new media, for example the Acceptance of New Media Committee (reporting to the Ministry for International Trade and Industry (MITI)) and the Information Network System (INS) − New Media Utilization Committee. And fourthly, on a practical level considerable emphasis is being placed on a new round of government experiments using high-speed networks to investigate not only the technical feasibility of new systems but also, crucially, the design of new services and public attitudes towards them.

The role of the ministries

The government ministries most involved in initiating and implementing policy for the so-called 'new-media' field are the Ministry of Posts and Telecommunications (MPT) and, probably more familiar to those outside Japan, the influential Ministry for International Trade and Industry (MITI).

As the ministry responsible for the provision of telecommunications services, the MPT oversees the activities of the national common carrier, NTT, and has considerable licensing and regulatory powers. The granting of licences to broadcasting stations and cable TV operators, for example, is the responsibility of this ministry.

In addition it is pursuing a range of new media programmes (including trials) in which it is following general trends set by other countries such as videotex (CAPTAIN), teletext, electronic mail and DBS. It also promotes the establishment of technical standards for new equipment and services. The MPT is, therefore, able to influence the nature of communications developments throughout Japan. Its support for the national common carrier's telecommunications modernization programme has helped to determine the telecommunications emphasis in new infrastructural investment and probably explains the ministry's relative disinterest in commercial broad band cable TV although it has run trials in this field.

Further, in response to concerns about the direction and pace of development of an 'information society' in Japan, the ministry has launched a major initiative in the form of its 'Teletopia' programme of experimental wired communities.

MITI, as its name implies, manages international trade policy and actively promotes Japanese industry.[7] Its interest in the new media originates with its involvement in the computer and electronics industry where it is administering an impressive series of research programmes. These include the fifth-generation computer project and the next-generation base technologies programme (assigning an important role to semiconductor-related research) both of which are to span ten years and spend roughly equivalent sums of government money of the order of £270 million (Dore 1983).

In comparison with other countries the most significant feature of these programmes, and others, is the ease with which a collaborative research effort is secured between private sector companies and government laboratories. Cooperation of this nature is characteristic of the method of industrial policy implementation in Japan and extends to the new media trials sponsored by both MITI and the MPT. In general MITI alerts industry to its plans by issuing its 'administrative guidance' to large corporations. Although this guidance is not legally enforcible compliance is usually forthcoming. Indeed many companies employ ex-MITI officials to facilitate their liaison with the ministry.

As the technologies of computing and telecommunications have converged MITI has increasingly interpreted its responsibilities as including telecommunications aspects, previously the exclusive administrative domain of MPT. A degree of rivalry has developed between the two ministries and MITI's series of major experiments known as 'New Media Communities' to be launched virtually in parallel with Teletopia is evidence of this.

Regulatory reform in telecommunications

Developments in communications technology have been producing a reappraisal of state-regulated monopoly regimes both because of the increased feasibility of some types of network competition and the emergence of enhanced services whose supply is not governed by large-scale economies.

In the USA the regulatory framework for telecommunications has been undergoing a transformation at least since the late 1960s and in the UK a similar transformation has been brought about but in the space of only five years. Japan, like the UK, is instituting radical changes over a short period of time. In April 1985 three telecommunications laws were enacted which will fundamentally reorganize and liberalize its telecommunications regime. The motive behind the liberalization is clearly one of encouraging Japanese firms to be innovative and to diversify into the telecommunications business through providing increased opportunities and competitive pressure. MITI was a strong advocate of the reform, perceiving the current regime as a constraint on new developments.

The major impending changes are the denationalization of the public telecommunications monopoly NTT and the removal of its exclusive right to supply domestic public telecommunications services (including voice telephony). Kokusai Denshin Denwa (KDD), the international telecommunications services company, will also lose its monopoly.

NTT is to be converted into a single joint-stock corporation with two thirds of its equity to be sold by the Japanese government during the five years following enactment. Diet approval will no longer be necessary for activities such as investment plans but the approval of the Minister is likely to be required. Thus despite the move towards privatization it remains to be seen how independent of government the new company will be allowed to be.

Of greater significance is the opening up of the public telecommunications service market for competitive provision as defined by the second major tranche of legislation, the Telecommunications Enterprise Act (the third law coordinates the others with earlier legislation). Companies will be permitted to install their own facilities, including satellite communications systems, to offer services or to lease circuits from NTT and other companies owning networks. The principle of equal treatment for foreign enterprises was also agreed although the issue was highly controversial and there is some foreign scepticism about what will ensue in practice. The Japanese government has been under considerable pressure from the American government to open up the VANs[8] market for US companies and it is probable that this concession was seen as a necessary tactic in preserving Japanese–US trade relations. However, opening up the infant VANs market for strong foreign competitors seems a precarious strategy to follow, and is contrary to the standard Japanese approach of initially protecting its young industries. International Business Machines (IBM) and American Telephone and Telegraph (AT&T) are among the foreign companies intending to offer VANs under the liberalized regime in Japan.

The prospect of terrestrial network, satellite communications and value-added services competition also raises serious issues about the nature of the development of Japan's telecommunications infrastructure. NTT's telecommunications modernization programme to install a nationwide integrated services digital network (ISDN) will have been under way for several years by the enactment of this legislation. Rather than being Japan's sole ISDN as originally planned, it may become one of several networks competing for the most lucrative business communications traffic. Four industrial groups have already announced their interest in the common carrier communication business at the national level: Daini Denden, a consortium of electronics manufacturers established for this purpose;[9] Keidanren, Japan's foremost business federation; Japan National Railways (JNR); and Japan Highways Public Corporation.

Under these conditions it is not clear how able or willing NTT will be to deliver its investment programme (which is described below). Further, the US experience of post-deregulation pressure to increase local subscriber rates substantially does not offer an encouraging picture for the residential take-up of the new communications services which are intended to be supplied on the Japanese ISDN.

The information network system
The INS is the Japanese version of the ISDN concept (which is being pursued in some form in most industrialized countries), that is, the support of voice and non-voice services on the same network using digital transmission as a common denominator for all services.

This ambitious plan of NTT[10] provides a technical unity, at least on the theoretical level, for the plethora of information services presumed to be inevitable ingredients of an imminent 'information society' such as communicating home computers, videotex services for information, teleshopping, telebanking, security and even telemedicine. The INS is to be implemented through a process of the digitalization, expansion and integration of NTT's separate telephone, telex, telegraph, facsimile and data networks into a unified optical fibre system by the end of the century. The total investment required for the construction of the INS is estimated at ¥20,000–30,000 billion (£60–90 billion) (Wilkinson, 1984).

Optical fibre cables, communications satellites, existing microwave links and co-axial cables will all be utilized for the INS. NTT's first optical trunk line has been constructed between Sapporo (in the northern island of Hokkaido) and Fukuoka (in southern Kyushu). This 2,800 km trunk will constitute the backbone of the INS linking also (from north to south) Sendai, Tokyo, Nagoya and Hiroshima. Japan's first domestic communications satellite, the CS-2a, which was launched in February 1983, is too limited in capacity to be of practical use for the INS. However, NTT plans to utilize larger-capacity satellites in the future.

The major interface with the INS for the user is to be the home or business telecommunications centre.[11] Both of these units are to be built around five basic types of communication hardware: telephone; fascimile; data terminals; videotex; and video terminals with the facility to use more than one service simultaneously. Additional equipment to provide functions like telemetering (i.e. remote reading of gas, water and electric meters) and telecontrol (i.e. monitoring of appliances) is also envisaged.

The role that video communications will have in the INS has yet to be determined. Although teleconferencing will be made available for business customers it would not be economically feasible to install residential subscriber networks with a video capability. The problem is familiar, so too is the issue it raises – what relationships are Japan's broad band cable TV systems to have with the national common carrier? The MPT appears not to expect to resolve this issue until the turn of the century.

INS – an experimental Model System
One of the initial steps taken towards the implementation of the INS was the decision to test its technologies, services and its wider social impact on lifestyles and patterns of work through an Experimental Model System which would link homes and businesses with various electronic services. Experience of its operation, which commenced in September 1984 and will end in March 1987, is intended to guide the direction and pace of INS development as a whole. Following the end of the experiment, the INS will be expanded to ten major cities and by 1990 cities with a population of approximately 100,000 and higher are expected to be covered.

The system covers two thirds of Mitaka City, a suburb 20 km west of Tokyo. Also included is the Kasumigaseki section of metropolitan Tokyo in which are located the head offices of a number of companies with branches in Mitaka. Participants are either information providers (IPs), or users, whom NTT call 'monitors'. The IPs cover a wide variety of fields, e.g. banking, retailing, publishing, travel and security. Only 650 of the 2,000 monitors will be connected at one time and each monitor will have two or three different terminals which include digital telephones, video terminals including a viewphone; sketchphones which transmit handwritten graphics as well as voice; the videotex service CAPTAIN; and the video response system, VRS. The VRS is an information retrieval system similar to CAPTAIN but it uses moving picture information and sound instead of static frames. Equipment and information will be provided free to monitors who will only have to pay transmission costs.

Although many companies are interested in using the system, most of the applications made to NTT suggested quite conventional services such as home shopping, banking and local information services. Some companies are expected to experiment with 'teleworking' schemes where employees work from home or from satellite offices instead of commuting into Tokyo. The Mitaka Local Government was also approached by NTT and has devised various services utilizing the network. For example the public will be able to watch pre-recorded videos of the local parliament's debates through the VRS.

Acceptance prospects

As the telephone market approaches saturation in numerical terms the new information services represent the most important growth area for the telecommunications carrier business. Services for residential subscribers are an especially important area as their lines tend to have low average usage rates and are costly to maintain. However the feasibility of digital subscriber routes is perhaps the most problematic. A critical factor will be the price at which consumer terminals of various kinds are made available, as this outlay will represent one of the 'entry fees' to the INS.[12] Also crucial will be the tariff level and structure adopted for residential services. If competition in business communications traffic as a result of the new legislation forces NTT to raise tariffs for residential subscribers the appeal of new home-based services is likely to be diminished.

Evidence of resistance to certain aspects of the INS has already emerged. Teleshopping is perceived by small retailers as a threat to their livelihood in a similar way to the supermarket some years ago. Some school students who already spend up to three hours each evening at cramming schools, 'Juku', fear that two-way video services into their homes will increase the pressure on them to study. Some Juku already employ telex to communicate with students at home. A recent survey conducted by the Taiyo Kobe Bank revealed that more than 60 per cent of the housewives polled registered their opposition to the idea of their husbands 'teleworking' from home (FINTECH,

1984). This is probably not only because the typical Japanese house is quite small but also, and more importantly, because of a feared drastic disruption of traditional roles and lifestyle which teleworking could entail.

But attitudes towards the information society are by no means consistently negative. Nearly 60 per cent of respondents in the Prime Minister's Office survey (1983) thought a principal advantage of the information society would be increased convenience. Another particularly interesting feature of the same survey was that a home nurse/home medical consultation system was the most desired of the suggested services (63 per cent wanted such a service) with home security and telecontrol as the runner-up (52 per cent). The main reason for the appeal of 'telemedicine' is concern about medical care for the elderly. Although Japan's elderly form a smaller proportion of the population than in most industrialized countries, this proportion is growing faster. Also, whereas traditionally the elderly would be cared for in the family home in which two or three generations would live together, this system is changing and increasingly the elderly are unable or unwilling to live with their children.

New media trials
An 'experimental community' approach to new media applications appears to have become a well-entrenched feature in Japan of which several cable TV experiments and the INS Model System are examples. In addition various ministries are devising plans to take advantage of the opportunities presented by the new media. For example, the Land Agency has a project entitled 'Settled Living Information Sphere Plan'. Inevitably, the most impressive plans to date are the rival experimental projects of MPT and MITI, Teletopia and New Media Communities respectively which, together, will comprise 17 community systems. At this stage it is rather difficult to distinguish between them, and the ultimate objective appears to be to generate sufficient interest in the new systems to create centres of growth.

Teletopia
Most ministries are cooperating with this MPT scheme and NTT is also closely involved. In comparison with the INS Model System, Teletopia will be a larger-scale venture (ten areas are to be selected in 1985). The objective of Teletopia is to experiment with the concept of a 'highly communicating society', and to investigate its implications and benefits for the business sector and the community in general. The Teletopia infrastructure will be provided by the MPT and NTT whilst responsibility for applications rests with private sector companies, the

Ministry of Home Affairs and local governments. Existing cable TV systems will be utilized in Teletopia areas in order to avoid the duplication of high bandwidth cables for picture transmission and to provide a means of investigating future cable TV–INS relationships. Cable operators are being asked to invest in Teletopia and can obtain low interest rate loans from the government to assist them in doing so.

New media communities (NMCs)
This concept was the result of the deliberations of the Information Industry Committee which reports to MITI's Industrial Structure Council. Seven regions have been allocated for NMC systems which are planned to operate on a trial basis from 1985–8. Each system will differ to some extent in order to meet the varying social and regional communications needs of, for example, agricultural and industrial areas. System specifications were to be determined during 1984 and although in some cases unidirectional cable may be deemed sufficient the core technology is likely to be interactive cable TV. The NMCs are to be financed by local governments and industry with users being expected to bear running costs. MITI is financing the study for technical specifications at a cost of ¥100 million and will closely monitor the operation of the trial systems. Commercial systems are planned to be operational by the 1990s.

What this suggests is that Teletopia, NMCs and the INS Model System all embrace communications needs of the local economy and community in a comprehensive manner by drawing together industry, institutions, local people and local government to participate in the design and operation of the experiments. Financial participation by the private sector is also secured and the projects are to be run, at least partially, on a commercial basis. In the case of the INS Model System and Teletopia projects the telecommunications infrastructure will be provided by NTT, or NTT in conjunction with MPT, leaving private companies with the financial obligations arising only from the operation of the services they wish to offer. In this way experimentation with new media services by the private sector is encouraged and promoted through government initiatives. Competing parallel approaches may explore a wider range of technical possibilities, and inter-ministry rivalry is probably producing experimentation on a greater scale than would otherwise be forthcoming.

Cable television
Cable TV developed in Japan as a solution to poor quality reception, particularly in mountainous and semi-urban areas, and at the end of

the financial year 1982 cable systems served approximately 10 per cent of TV households, i.e. 3.7 million households (MPT, 1983). The majority of these, essentially community antenna systems, rebroadcast exclusively. A small but notable exception is the Japan Cable Television system, JCTV, which supplies English language programmes for 22,000 subscribers in major hotels and apartment buildings in the Kanto region.

Cable TV probably appeared on the government's agenda in response to North American developments. Both MPT and MITI have been financing cable TV trials since the late 1970s but there has not been explicit encouragement for widespread cable TV investment. Latterly, trials involving cable TV have shifted their emphasis from two-way video communication between homes and a TV studio to a wider range of telecommunications applications. Two current experiments are the Hi-Ovis project,[13] which is sponsored by MITI at Higashi-Ikoma in the Nara Prefecture, and the network in Tsukuba science city, a new town development outside Tokyo, which is financed by MPT and the Ministry of Construction.

Despite the combination of cable TV and telecommunications services in the ministries' trials, the role of new broad band cable TV systems in Japan is seen as largely confined to television entertainment – unlike in the UK, for example, where the government hoped advanced information services would be piped into homes 'on the back' of entertainment revenues. In Japan it is the telecommunications networks that are expected to deliver these services and cable TV's prospects are overshadowed by telecommunications plans, especially the INS. Indeed, it is possible that the INS, advancing more rapidly than cable TV, might incorporate the young networks in the future.

However, both current policy towards cable and recent developments make its prospects look somewhat brighter. Cable TV applicants no longer require the consent of the local broadcasting stations before the MPT will issue them with a licence to operate. In addition, although commercial bi-directional cable TV systems, which would be capable of providing interactive services such as 'pay per view' and teleshopping, have not been permitted in Japan legislatory reform is anticipated in the near future.

The new broad band cable operators are being awarded three-year renewable licences as are the conventional broadcasting stations. None of these have been refused a renewal and this practice is expected to be extended to cable TV. So far only two applications have been approved: the first licence was granted to the International Cable Network (ICN) to operate in Machida City, and the second to Tokyu TV for the adjacent areas of Yokohama and Shibuya. Not surprisingly it is organizations with appropriate infrastructural assets that have seen the opportunities offered by cable TV. The Odakyu Electric Railway Company is the major shareholder in ICN and is interested in expanding outside Machida possibly using railway lines as routes for optical fibres. Tokyu TV is backed by a railway company too.

In Europe the prospect of cable TV competing with the existing broadcasting services has created a debate about the future of broadcasting itself. This has not been the case in Japan where broadcasting reform is unnecessary for the development of fully-fledged cable TV services and the broadcasting environment is more liberal. There are already five commercial networks of affiliated stations in addition to the two national channels of the public broadcasting corporation, Nippon Hoso Kyokai (NHK). Thus, in most areas seven channels are already available for the viewer. It is difficult to gauge what the demand is for further channels, but as Japan starts from a higher base than say the UK and West Germany, one might expect the demand to be lower than in these countries.

Programme supply for multi-channel cable systems is a serious concern. A company such as ICN would not have the resources to compete directly in programme quality with the broadcasting stations and therefore must attempt to offer a different product to the viewer. Current restrictions on two-way services leave as possibilities only retransmission of out-of-area stations, satellite transmissions and locally originated programming. Experience in America and trials in the UK have shown community programmes to be expensive and unpopular. Will a different response be forthcoming in the Japanese cultural environment? The popularity of the Tokyo stations' programmes among viewers in other regions and the lack of a strong local emphasis on stations outside Tokyo suggests not.

A third problem for the new broad band cable operators is that there is no scope as yet to share programme overheads. In the USA the viability of cable TV has depended upon networking arrangements particularly utilizing satellite distribution to so-called 'super-stations'. In Japan, this perspective appears to be lacking. Nevertheless, there are prospects that the forthcoming reform will 'open' Japan's skies for telecommunications and broadcasting alike, with potential benefits for cable TV development.

Direct broadcasting by satellite
Space technology is one of the fields in which Japan is pursuing the American and (combined) European lead and is aiming to become self sufficient in satellite and launching technology. It is within this context that DBS should probably be viewed in Japan. Although the

public broadcasting corporation (NHK) has provided the bulk of the funding for the current project (about two thirds), financial support has also been received from the MPT through its concern for national broadcasting provision and from the government Science and Technology Agency (STA) and the National Space Development Agency (NASDA) because of its relevance to the Japanese space effort. Future DBS satellites are likely to receive less support from these other sources.

The nature of Japan's DBS development and the issues it raises provides a contrast with the European situation. Proposed European services aim to increase the number of channels for existing viewers and because of the countries' geographical proximity to each other shared systems and the cultural implications of signal overspill are prominent concerns. In Britain, where there were plans to commence DBS in 1986, there has been debate[14] over whether it would compete with cable TV and hamper the latter's development or promote cable by providing much-needed material.

Japan's current satellite broadcasting plans are essentially to extend national coverage to the 400,000 households in mountainous regions and outlying islands which are unable to receive conventional terrestrial broadcasts. The inclusion of these areas into the broadcasting system, particularly the islands of Okinawa, has political importance in Japan. There is a similarity here with Canada's broadcast policy objective of equal access to broadcast services by Canadians. Following an experiment from 1978 to 1982 Japan launched its first operational DBS satellite, the BS-2, in January 1984. Its two channels were allocated to NHK which intended more or less to duplicate its terrestrial service from May 1984. However technical faults with the satellite left only one functioning channel and the status of the service has reverted to that of a trial. At the end of 1985 a back-up satellite should come on stream enabling the service to operate as initially planned. Cable TV operators, therefore, are presented with a somewhat neutral DBS factor neither competing with, nor complementing, their own service.

This situation may alter in the future. Japan was allocated eight channels by the World Administrative Radio Conference (WARC) in 1977, only two of which have been reserved for NHK, and the BS-3, due for launch in 1989, will have one spare channel for a commercial service. NHK is intending to use the BS-3 to experiment with its HDTV system as well as continuing its two-channel service.

Conclusion
The overriding concern of communications policy in Japan is the promotion of the electronics and information industries. Two basic

approaches can be identified. Japan can be seen as following a 'textbook' provided by other countries in terms of reform in telecommunications regulation and an agenda for technological development even though, in many cases, it may be too soon to tell whether a particular technology will prove to be commercially successful. However, where Japan is situated at the technological frontier it is responding by experimenting with communications applications on a large scale as well as pursuing its own high-technology research programmes.

Notes

1. Some of the information drawn on for this chapter was acquired through interviews conducted by the author and Luke Georghiou during a recent visit to Japan. The author would like to thank her colleagues at the Policy Research in Engineering Science and Technology (PREST) programme for their comments, particularly Claire Shearman and Kenji Tanaka.

2. DBS can be defined as the direct (household) reception of satellite broadcasts which are of sufficient power to enable receiving dishes no larger than one metre in diameter to pick up the signals.

3. Facsimile terminals create reproductions of documents fed into the calling terminal. In the UK in early 1983 the population of facsimile machines was approximately 16,000 (Frost and Sullivan, 1974) compared with about 400,000 in use in Japan (interview with Ministry of Posts and Telecommunications (MPT)). While the growth of machines (from a small base) is rapid in Britain at about 10 per cent a year, in Japan the growth rate is several times faster.

4. A system for communications between word processors.

5. Character and Pattern Telephone Access Information Network. This interactive videotex system enables the access of information held in computer banks and its display on a television screen via the telephone network.

6. Cable TV, CAPTAIN (videotex), teletext, Information Network System (INS) and HDTV.

7. For more information about Japanese industrial policy and trade the reader is referred to Chalmers Johnson, (1982) *MITI and the Japanese Miracle*, Palo Alto, Calif.: Stanford University Press and Jon Woronoff (1983) *World Trade War*, Tokyo: Lotus Press. For more general reading see, for example, Endymion Wilkinson, (1983) *Japan versus Europe. A History of Misunderstanding*, Harmondsworth, Middx.: Penguin Books.

8. Any service which adds value to and contains substantial elements additional to the basic telecommunications network service may be covered by the term 'value-added network services', e.g. the storage of messages and the modification of the format, code or content of the message or protocol relating to it.

9. The group of approximately 30 firms includes Kyoto Ceramic Co. Ltd, Secom Co. Ltd, Ushio Electric Incorporated and Sony Corporation.

10. For more details see NTT (1984) and Kitahara (1983).

11. There will also be public terminals and a mobile communications service.

12. The newly introduced videotex terminals retail at approximately £3,000 including printer (Johnstone, 1984).

13. The results of the project are reported in VISDA (1983).

14. See, for example, J. Evans, J. Hartley, J. Simnett, J.S. Metcalfe and M. Gibbons (1983) *The Development of Cable Networks in the UK*, London: The Technical Change Centre.

References

Dore, Ronald (1983) *A Case Study of Technology Forecasting in Japan. The Next Generation Base Technologies Development Programme*. London: The Technical Change Centre.

FINTECH (1984) *Telecom Markets*. Financial Times Business Information, No. 20, 6 November 1984.

Frost and Sullivan (1984) *Electronic Mail and Facsimile Services in Europe*. London: Frost and Sullivan.

Johnstone, Bob (1984) 'The Japanese Connection', *New Scientist*, 27 September 1984: 24.

Kitahara, Yasusada (1983) 'INS – Telecommunications towards the Advanced Information Society', *Proceedings of the NTT International Symposium – Our Tasks and Approach for the Development of an Advanced Information Society*. Tokyo: Nippon Telegraph and Telephone Public Corporation.

Masuda, Yuji (1983) 'An Anatomy of Technological Competition', *Economic Eye*, March 1983: 8–11.

MPT (General Planning Division) (1983) *Report on Present State of Communications in Japan, Fiscal 1983*. Tokyo: The Japan Times Ltd (Ministry of Posts and Telecommunications).

NTT (Engineering Bureau) (1984) *INS: Tomorrow's Integrated Technology*. Tokyo: The Telecommunications Association (Nippon Telephone and Telegraph).

Prime Minister's Office (Japan) (1983) *Opinion Survey on New Information Services*. Tokyo (August).

VISDA (1983) *Hi-Ovis Project, Final Report, Phase 1 Experiment (July 1978–March 1983)*. Tokyo: Visual Information System Development Association.

Wilkinson, Max (1984) 'Japan's Telecommunications. Softly, Softly Comes the Revolution', *Financial Times*, 26 July.

Yamauchi, Ichizo (1983) 'Long-Range Strategic Planning in Japanese R and D', *Futures*, October 1983: 328–41.

Postscript:
the emerging agenda

The preceding chapters provide a cumulative picture of the interrelatedness of policy and research issues which derive from the convergence of telecommunication and computer technologies and the application of their systems and services. There is a core concern in all these contributions, including those that are devoted to exploring more purely academic questions about the development of more useful explanatory models for dealing with phenomena as potentially transformational as these. The focus of this shared concern is on how our generalized notions of the public good are or are not being served by public policies that deal with technological innovation in national and global media systems.

There is also an allied concern about the absence of open and wide-ranging public and scholarly debate about the political decisions being taken on the issues arising from the development and application of new communication hardware and software. For example, there should be an examination of public expenditure on technological innovation in defence strategies, of the redefinition of cultural industries such as broadcasting in terms of market-place practices rather than public service precepts, and of the cultivation of multinational investment in domestic hardware industries at the cost of colonization. The remaining pages of this book develop some of the issues which are germane to these debates and which point to an agenda of urgent concerns for policy-makers and scholars alike.

At one level of consequences, the application of sophisticated technologies to communication systems is clearly evident. Among the richest nations, domestic consumers, small businesses and large corporations use cable, satellite, computer and telecommunications services to meet their information and entertainment needs. Equally evident is the exclusion of the majority of less rich nations from this pattern of conspicuous consumption. For them, the prospect remains one of standing on the outside looking in at this international division of labour and goods, contemplating a deepening divide between the 'information rich' and 'information poor'.

At other levels, the consequences of technological innovation are more obscure. These are the levels of social and cultural change whose interactive processes and symbolic or material representations tend to manifest themselves more slowly and more subtly in society than do consumer preferences for new products such as video-cassette recorders or the unanticipated uses to which they are put such as time-shifting or advertisement-skipping. This at least is not new. As de Sola Pool (1983) has indicated, the ways in which the telegraph and telephone were actually used turned out to be rather different from those that were forecast for them.

This current wave of transformation is unprecedented, however. The scale and complexity of the technologies, restricted opportunities for entry into the market and rapid rates of product obsolescence, have produced a rolling agenda of policy and research issues relating to the public interest. The questions which they raise are in turn related to basic social values and political beliefs about the nature of liberal-democratic societies and the maintenance of plurality of opinion, equity of access, cultural diversity and personal freedoms (for example, freedom to speak and freedom from surveillance). Allied to these precepts is a consensus that communication and information systems function at least in part to serve some notion of the public good. This notion revolves around how we understand consumer 'rights', media 'freedoms' and governmental 'duties' and, in this instance, around how our political, economic and cultural institutions are responding to the challenges of technological innovation.

The search for answers to questions about institutional change and their interaction with shifts in perceptions and practices related to the public good provides one fruitful line of enquiry for comparative research across national and disciplinary boundaries. This task is complicated, however, by the typically pragmatic nature of much communications policy-making and by the fragmentation of responsibility for it. The division of administrative control over telecommunication, broadcasting and 'cultural' policies (however defined) varies from one national context to another, but rarely presents the communications policy-watcher or researcher with a coherent picture of a co-ordinated strategy at the national and international levels.

Perhaps because of the opaque and informal ways in which such policies are made, or perhaps because they are touched by the magic and mystery conjured up by popular myths about technology as something incomprehensible and apart, there has been little open debate about many of the public interest and social policy issues raised in this book. The interest of governments in these dimensions has lagged behind desires to use the leverage of new technology for economic growth and improved trade balances. The extent to which such priorities have come to dominate industrial strategies, and the extent to which their promised economic benefits have failed to materialize, demonstrates the pull technological determinism exerts among the nations of the North.

At this stage there is little evidence of these wider concerns in a climate of intensified international competition and in the aftermath of deregulatory policies in, for example, the United States and Japan. The subsequent acceleration of overseas investment by electronics multinationals in Europe and elsewhere has had profound consequences for the structure and viability of interdependent and client economies.

There is nothing new about ranking a nation as a world power by means of its economic takeovers. The current high-technology variant is merely the latest form of nineteenth-century territorial expansionism. The present contest between a few world players is one which involves extraterrestrial as well as extraterritorial domination and in which telecommunication and satellite systems are the carriers of national and corporate aspirations. There is little to suggest that this form of empire-building will exhibit a greater concern for the transmutation of national cultures or for the subordination of domestic economies than did its predecessors.

Similarly, there is one unknown variable in all this which neither past nor present empire-builders can predict: this is the rate of technological breakthrough and application still to come. What is clear is that so long as the race to be first with the newest continues (whatever the subsequent rates of take-up for nth-generation innovations), specific public interest questions will continue to arise. Existing consultative bodies at the international level – such as the Organisation for Economic Cooperation and Development and the International Telegraph and Telecommunications Union – will have to prove their continuing utility by meeting the challenges made to current legal and political frameworks by these complex new technologies.

There is a further, related area of policy concern which is also ripe for wider public debate. This is the area of cultural policy. The proliferation of electronic-media delivery systems, unmatched by any comparable increase in the range of content which they proffer, has given issues of cultural content a new relevance for governments facing up to the implications of cable and satellite penetration for the first time. Here the clash of cultures paradoxically becomes more evident as they are co-mingled. This raises questions about how any national public good is served by the images and messages of a global, 'show-and-tell' media system that uses the television screen. In an era of internationalized cultural production, which policies can or should sovereign states employ to defend and preserve national interests and identities?

There are no easy answers to any of the questions raised above. To take just one, if an historical perspective is applied to the problem of equal access to new communication networks by different societies and socio-economic groups, then equity in technological terms appears to be no more achievable than any other form of redistributive justice attempted so far. Equal access to the services provided by digital, fibre-optic or artificial intelligence systems becomes as relative a question as have earlier attempts to define or realign levels of poverty or affluence. Absolute levels of demand for communications have yet to be determined: little consideration has been given to how they should or could be met.

The business of finding answers to such vexed questions is integral not only to the political process but also to the work of social science. Lawyers, economists, sociologists and political scientists among others offer a range of perspectives and skills which can both inform and feed a more open debate centred on how national and global media systems serve different societies and audiences. Scholars can widen the arena of discourse by identifying the urgent questions about the social and political costs involved as well as the intended (if not always achieved) economic benefits of technological innovation.

This suggestion that social scientists have a role to play in policy-making about new media hardware and software is more novel in some quarters than in others. Historically, technical experts have been at the centre of the industrial and public development of new communications. The involvement of economists and social psychologists is more recent and is more evident in some societies than in others. It follows that some governments are farther down the road of assessing the unintended costs as well as the intended benefits of technological transformation.

What this brief discussion of the emerging policy and research agenda makes clear is that continuing innovation in the delivery systems of information services and cultural goods presents communications scholars with considerable challenges. At some levels of investigation there are correspondences between the order of these unknowns and those that inspired and haunted the first circumnavigators of the globe in 1521–2. As with Magellan's crew who were convinced that the earth was flat and that every day brought them closer to falling off the edge, so for many who seek to explore the wider shores of new communication technologies, a similar sense of adventure mixed with apprehension applies.

Marjorie Ferguson

Abbreviations

ABC	American Broadcasting Company
AGB	Audits of Great Britain
ARD	Arbeitsgemeinschaft der Öffentlichen Rechtlichen Rundfunksanstalten (West German syndicate of public broadcasting institutes)
ASST	Azienda di Stato per i Servizi Telefonici (Italy)
AT&T	American Telephone and Telegraph
A2	Antenne 2 (France)
BBC	British Broadcasting Corporation
Benelux	Belgium – Netherlands – Luxembourg
BRF	Belgische Rundfunk und Fernsehen
BRT	Belgische Radio en televisie
BT	British Telecom
CADCAM	computer-aided design – computer-aided manufacture
CADMAT	Computer-Aided Design, Manufacture and Test (UK government programme)
CAPTAIN	Character and Pattern Telephone Access Information Network (Japanese interactive videotex system)
CBC	Canadian Broadcasting Corporation
CBS	Columbia Broadcasting System (US)
CEC	Commission of the European Communities
CFDC	Canadian Film Development Corporation
CGE	Compagnie Générale d'Electricité (France)
CLT	Compagnie Luxembourgeoise de Télédiffusion
CNET/INA	Centre National d'Etude des Télécommunications/Institut National de la Communication Audiovisuelle (France)
CRTC	Canadian Radio, Television and Telecommunications Commission
CTV	Canadian Television
DBP	Deutsche Bundespost
DBS	direct broadcasting by satellite
DES	Department of Education and Science (UK)
DGT	Direction Générale des Télécommunications (France)
DIY	do-it-yourself
DOC	Department of Communications (Canada)
DTI	Department of Trade and Industry (UK)
EBU	European Broadcasting Union
ecu	European currency unit
ECRP	European Consortium for Political Research
EEC	European Economic Community
ELVIL	Hellenic Electronics Industry
ERT	Elliniki Radiophonia Tikorassis
ESA	European Space Agency
ESRC	Economic and Social Research Council (UK)

FAST	Forecasting and Assessment for Science and Technology (CEC programme for analysis of scientific and technological change)
FCC	Federal Communications Commission (USA)
FKT	Fyns Kommune Telefoner (Fyn borough telephones)
FRC	Federal Radio Commission (USA)
FR3	France 3
GATT	General Agreement on Trade and Tariffs
GDP	gross domestic product
GEC	General Electric Company (UK)
GNP	gross national product
HBO	Home Box Office (US cable company)
HC	House of Commons (UK Parliament)
HDTV	high-definition television
HMSO	Her Majesty's Stationery Office (UK)
IBA	Independent Broadcasting Authority (UK)
IBM	International Business Machines
ICN	International Cable Network (Japan)
IKBS	intelligent knowledge-based system
INS	information network system
IP	information provider
ISDN	integrated services digital network
IT	information technology
ITAP	Information Technology Advisory Panel (UK)
ITT	International Telephone and Telegraph
ITU	International Telecommunications Union
ITV	Independent Television (UK)
JCTV	Japan Cable Television
JNR	Japan National Railways
JTAS	Jyllands Telefon Aktie Selskab (Jutland telephone company)
KDD	Kokusai Denshin Denwa (Japan's international telecommunications services company)
KTAS	København Telefon Aktie Selskab (Copenhagen telephone company)
MAP	Microelectronics Application Project (UK government project)
MCI	originally Microwave Communications Inc. (USA)
MITI	Ministry for International Trade and Industry (Japan)
MPT	Ministry of Posts and Telecommunications (Japan)
NAB	National Association of Broadcasters (USA)
NASDA	National Space Development Agency (Japan)
NBC	National Broadcasting Company (USA)
NBER	National Bureau of Economic Research (USA)
NCC	National Consumer Council (UK)
NCTA	National Cable Television Association (USA)
NEDO	National Economic Development Office (UK)
NFB	National Film Board (Canada)
NHK	Nippon Hoso Kyokai (public broadcasting corporation)
NLC	National League of Cities (USA)
NMC	New Media Community (Japan)
NOS	Nederlands Omroep Stichting (broadcasting foundation)
NOZEMA	Nederlandse Omroepzender Maatschappij

NTT	Nippon Telegraph and Telephone
OECD	Organization for Economic Co-operation and Development
OTE	Hellenic Telecommunications Organization (Greece)
PAC	Political Action Committee (USA)
PBS	Public Broadcasting Service (USA)
PCM	pulse code modulation
POEU	Post Office Engineering Union (UK)
PQ	Parti Québécois
PREST	Policy Research in Engineering Science and Technology (University of Manchester)
PTT	national telecommunications authority
P&T	posts and telecommunications administration
RAI	Radiotelevisione Italiana
RCA	Radio Corporation of America
RTBF	Radio-télévision belge pour la communauté française
RTE	Radio Telefis Eireann
RTL	Radio-télé Luxembourg
RTT	Régie des Télégraphes et des Téléphones (Belgium)
R&D	research and development
SDR	Süddeutsche Rundfunk
SFI	Support for Innovation (UK government programme)
SIP	Società Italiana per l'Esercizio Telefonico (Italy)
STA	Science and Technology Agency (Japan)
TDF	Télédiffusion de France
TF1	Télévision française 1
TV	television
UK	United Kingdom
US(A)	United States (of America)
VAN	value-added network
VCR	video cassette recorder/machine
VDU	visual display unit
VLSI	very-large-scale integration
VRS	video response system
WA	Written Answers (record of UK Parliament)
WARC	World Administrative Radio Conference
WDR	Westdeutsche Rundfunk
WEA	Workers' Educational Association (UK)
ZDF	Zweites Deutsches Fernsehen

Index

Notes on contributors

Joel Cantor has degrees in psychology from the University of Minnesota and anthropology from American University in Washington, D.C. While on the staff of the National Institute of Mental Health he assisted the development 'of public health campaigns using print and film media. Most recently, because of his interest in problems of cross-cultural communication, he has been collaborating with M.G. Cantor on studying problems and issues involved in the international distribution of television.

Muriel Cantor is Professor of Sociology at American University in Washington, D.C. and has investigated the legal, political, economic and social contexts of American television entertainment since 1967. Her publications include the *Hollywood TV Producer* (1971), *Prime-Time Television* (1980), and *The Soap Opera* (1983) (with Suzanne Pengier). She is presently studying (with Joel M. Cantor) the syndication of American television entertainment programmes outside the US borders and is editing (with Sandra Ball-Rokeach) a collection of sociological studies on mass communications.

Richard Collins lectures in the Faculty of Communication at the Polytechnic of Central London and was a Centennial Visiting Scholar at Temple University, Philadelphia. He is an editor of *Media, Culture and Society* and secretary of the London Conference for Canadian Studies. He is the author of *Television News* (1976) and (with Vincent Porter) *WDR and the Arbeiterfilm* (1981).

Nicole Dewandre is an economist who has worked at the Commission of the European Communities since 1983 in the FAST (Forecasting and Assessment for Science and Technology) team. She has degrees in economics and civil engineering from the Université Catholique de Louvain, Belgium, and a Master of Science in operations research from the University of California, Berkeley. Before joining the Commission, she specialized in picosecond optoelectronics at the Laboratory for Laser Energetics at the University of Rochester, New York, and at the Laboratoire d'Optique Appliquée of the Ecole Polytechnique in Palaiseau, France.

Marjorie Ferguson is a Canadian teaching courses in sociology, educational policy and the media at the London School of Economics and Political Science where she is a lecturer in the Department of Social Science and Administration. She is the author of *Forever Feminine: Women's Magazines and the Cult of Femininity* (1983) and is currently engaged in comparative communications policy research.

Jonathan Gershuny is Professor of Sociology at the University of Bath. After undergraduate and postgraduate work at the Universities of Loughborough, Strathclyde and Sussex, he worked at the Science Policy Research Unit at Sussex University from 1974 to 1984, on such topics as the relation between the formal and informal economies, time budget analysis, and changing occupational structures. His publications include the books *After Industrial Society* (1977), *The New Service Economy* (with Ian Miles, 1983), and *The Social Division of Labour* (1983).

Peter Golding is Research Fellow at the Centre for Mass Communication Research, University of Leicester. He is the author of *The Mass Media* (1974), *Making The News* (with Philip Elliott, 1979), and *Images of Welfare* (with Sue Middleton, 1982). He is currently working on a programme of research investigating various aspects of communications processes and the development of social policy.

Jill Hartley has a background in industrial economics with a particular interest in the economics of technical change. She has worked in the field of industrial policy at the European Commission in Brussels and is currently with the Department of Science and Technology Policy at the University of Manchester where she is undertaking research into the economic and technological aspects of the development of information technology and the consumer acceptance of new communications technologies.

Denis McQuail is currently Professor of Mass Communications at the University of Amsterdam and, prior to that, taught in the Sociology Department of Southampton University. His main research interests have been in political communication, audience research and media evaluation for policy. His publications include: *Television and the Political Image* (with J. Trenaman, 1961); *Television in Politics* (with J. Blumler, 1968); *Towards a Sociology of Mass Communications* (1969); *Analysis of Newspaper Content* (1977); *Mass Communications Theory* (1983).

Stan Metcalfe is Professor of Economics at the University of Manchester, where he is a director of the Policy Research in Engineering Science and Technology (PREST) programme. He is the author of numerous publications and his research interests include information technology, space industry, competition and technological innovation and science policy.

James Michael has degrees from North Western University and the Georgetown Law Center in Washington, D.C. He has lived in London since 1972 and has an LL.M from the London School of Economics; he is currently a senior lecturer in law at the Polytechnic of Central London and is the author of *The Politics of Secrecy* (1982).

Ian Miles is Senior Fellow at the Science Policy Research Unit, University of Sussex, where he has worked since 1972. Originally trained as a social psychologist, he has researched a variety of topics including social forecasting, the impacts of unemployment, and the implications of information technology for work and non-work. His major publications include the authored books *The Poverty of Prediction* (1975); *The New Service Economy* (with J.I. Gershuny, 1983); *Worlds Apart* (with Sam Cole, 1984); and *Social Indicators for Human Development* (forthcoming). He has also co-edited *Problems and Progress in Social Forecasting* (1975); *Demystifying Social Statistics* (1979) and *The Poverty of Prediction* (1982).

Graham Murdock is Research Fellow at the Centre for Mass Communication Research, University of Leicester. He is author of *Organising the Imaginary* (forthcoming), and co-author of *Demonstrations and Communication* (1970), and *Televising 'Terrorism'* (1983). He has been Visiting Professor at the Universities of California and Brussels. His current work is concerned with the changing organization of the information and entertainment industries and with the social and cultural impact of new communications systems.